Multiple Criteria Decision Making

Series Editor

Constantin Zopounidis, School of Production Engineering and Management, Technical University of Crete, Chania, Greece

This book series focuses on the publication of monographs and edited volumes of wide interest for researchers and practitioners interested in the theory of multicriteria analysis and its applications in management and engineering. The book series publishes novel works related to the foundations and the methodological aspects of multicriteria analysis, its applications in different areas in management and engineering, as well as its connections with other quantitative and analytic disciplines. In recent years, multicriteria analysis has been widely used for decision making purposes by institutions and enterprises. Research is also very active in the field, with numerous publications in a wide range of publication outlets and different domains such as operations management, environmental and energy planning, finance and economics, marketing, engineering, and healthcare.

More information about this series at http://www.springer.com/series/13834

Gökhan Silahtaroğlu • Hasan Dinçer •
Serhat Yüksel

Data Science and Multiple Criteria Decision Making Approaches in Finance

Applications and Methods

Springer

Gökhan Silahtaroğlu
Kavacık South Campus
Istanbul Medipol University
Istanbul, Turkey

Hasan Dinçer
School of Business
Istanbul Medipol University
Istanbul, Turkey

Serhat Yüksel
Business and Management
Istanbul Medipol University
Istanbul, Turkey

ISSN 2366-0023 ISSN 2366-0031 (electronic)
Multiple Criteria Decision Making
ISBN 978-3-030-74175-4 ISBN 978-3-030-74176-1 (eBook)
https://doi.org/10.1007/978-3-030-74176-1

This Springer imprint is published by the registered company Springer Nature Switzerland AG.
The registered company address is: Gewerbestrasse 11, 6330 Cham, Switzerland

Preface

This book aims to evaluate different financial issues to reach sustainable economic development. In this context, assessments were made on 6 different important issues. In this way, it is aimed to identify the most important issues related to financial issues. In this process, both data science and fuzzy multi-criteria decision-making methods were considered. In this context, decision trees, artificial neural networks, text mining, and methods such as AHP, ANP, DEMATEL, MOORA, TOPSIS, and VIKOR were used. The most important contribution of the study is the use of these methods, which are frequently preferred in the literature, in the same book.

This book aims to integrate data science applications, such as web mining, text mining, and machine learning, with different significant majors like business, health, economics, finance, and engineering. Within this framework, different perspectives can be taken into consideration in this study. For example, machine learning approach can be used to analyze financial performance or big data methodology can be considered to evaluate the efficiency of the stock exchanges. Therefore, it can be said that this study offers a novelty by focusing on various significant majors at the same time. As a result, it is believed that this study makes a significant contribution to the literature.

In this book, detailed analyses are made on 6 different issues related to financial issues. In this context, financially important issues such as profitability in the banking sector, the factors affecting economic development, the role of the statements of the politicians on the financial system, and the factors affecting the exchange rate risk are examined. As a result of detailed analyses, development suggestions were made for each topic. Thanks to these suggestions, it will be possible to reach a more effective financial system and sustainable economic growth. Therefore, this book is intended to make an important contribution to the literature.

Istanbul, Turkey

Gökhan Silahtaroğlu
Hasan Dinçer
Serhat Yüksel

Preface

Acknowledgments

The authors would like to acknowledge the help and patience of their families in this book process. Without their support, this book would not have become a reality.

Second, the authors wish to acknowledge the valuable contributions of the reviewers regarding the improvement of quality, coherence, and content presentation of chapters.

In addition, the authors would also like to acknowledge the valuable help of Mr. Serkan Eti for his significant support about machine learning system.

Gökhan Silahtaroğlu
Hasan Dinçer
Serhat Yüksel

Introduction

In this book, analyses related to financial issues have been made. In this context, assessments were made on 6 different important issues. In this way, it is aimed to identify the most important issues related to financial issues. In this process, both data science and fuzzy multi-criteria decision-making methods were considered. In this context, decision trees, artificial neural networks, text mining, and methods such as AHP, ANP, DEMATEL, MOORA, TOPSIS, and VIKOR were used. The most important contribution of the study is the use of these methods, which are frequently preferred in the literature, in the same book.

In the study, firstly, the factors causing crises in developing and developed countries have been tried to be determined. In this framework, decision tree and fuzzy DEMATEL approaches are taken into consideration. In addition, the second chapter is related to identifying the influencing factors of economic growth for both developing and developed economies. For this purpose, decision tree approach and fuzzy TOPSIS methodology are considered at the same time.

On the other side, the third chapter aims to estimate the factors affecting the profitability of the Turkish banking sector. For this purpose, 34 different variables were firstly determined by literature review. In the first stage of the analysis, decision trees method is applied to select the most important variables. After that, fuzzy ANP approach is used to weight these variables. Similarly, the fourth chapter tries to understand the role of the politicians on the macroeconomic situation of the countries. For this purpose, the tweets of Donald Trump are taken into consideration. Text mining approach is used to evaluate these tweets and mostly used words are identified. After that, these keywords are ranked with the help of fuzzy VIKOR approach according to their impacts on macroeconomic performance.

In addition to them, the fifth chapter tries to understand the main influence of the politicians' disclosure on the stock exchange index. In this context, a machine learning model is built in order to understand the hidden patterns behind the daily changes (rises and falls) of Dow Jones index. Moreover, in the final chapter, it is aimed to determine the factors affecting the exchange rate risk of companies. In this context, firstly, articles in the ScienceDirect database that contain exchange rate risk in their titles, abstracts, and keywords are provided. Single, double, and triple words were identified in 152 different studies that were published after 2018, which met the relevant criteria. As a result of the analysis of these words, 4 different criteria that could affect the exchange rate risk were determined. The relevant criteria were then weighted with fuzzy AHP.

This book aims to integrate data science applications, such as web mining, text mining, and machine learning, with different significant majors like business, health, economics, finance, and engineering. Within this framework, different perspectives can be taken into consideration in this study. For example, machine learning approach can be used to analyze financial performance or big data methodology can be considered to evaluate the efficiency of the stock exchanges. Therefore, it can be said that this study offers a novelty by focusing on various significant majors at the same time. As a result, it is believed that this study makes a significant contribution to the literature.

Target audience and potential users of this book are defined below.

- Researchers
- Academicians
- Policy makers
- Government officials
- Upright students in the concerned fields
- Members of chambers of commerce and industry
- Top managers of the companies

Istanbul, Turkey

Gökhan Silahtaroğlu
Hasan Dinçer
Serhat Yüksel

Contents

About the Authors

Gökhan Silahtaroğlu is a professor of data science. He is Head of the Department of Management Information Systems at Istanbul Medipol University, Faculty of Economics and Administrative Sciences, Istanbul, Turkey. Dr. Silahtaroğlu received PhD in management sciences and quantitative methods from İstanbul University in 2005. His PhD thesis is entitled "Clustering in data mining and an application on students assessment." His working areas are data analysis, data mining, artificial intelligence, and machine learning. He has three different books related to text mining and system analysis. In addition to them, he has lots of articles related to data science, text mining, web mining, and machine learning.

Hasan Dinçer is a professor of finance at Istanbul Medipol University, Faculty of Economics and Administrative Sciences, Istanbul, Turkey. Dr. Dincer has BAs in financial markets and investment management at Marmara University. He received his PhD in finance and banking with his thesis entitled "The Effect of Changes on the Competitive Strategies of New Service Development in the Banking Sector." He has work experience in the finance sector as a portfolio specialist, and his major academic studies focus on financial instruments, performance evaluation, and economics. He is the executive editor of the *International Journal of Finance and Banking Studies* (IJFBS) and the founder member of the Society for the Study of Business and Finance (SSBF). His research interests lie in banking, finance, and financial crisis. He has more than 200 scientific articles, and lots of them are indexed in SSCI, Scopus, and Econlit. Also, he is the editor of many books that were published by Springer and IGI Global.

Serhat Yüksel is an associate professor of finance in İstanbul Medipol University. Before this position, he worked as a senior internal auditor for seven years in Finansbank, Istanbul, Turkey, and 1 year in Konya Food and Agriculture University as an assistant professor. Dr. Yüksel has a BS in business administration (in English) from Yeditepe University (2006) with full scholarship. He got his master's degree in economics from Boğaziçi University (2008). He also has a PhD in banking from Marmara University (2015). His research interests lie in banking, finance, and financial crisis. He has more than 200 scientific articles, and lots of them are indexed in SSCI, Scopus, and Econlit. Also, he is the editor of many books that were published by Springer and IGI Global.

Chapter 1
Introduction to Data Science and Machine Learning Algorithms

Abstract Data science has gained importance since available data and hardware facilities have been ubiquitous. Algorithms to process a huge amount of data and extract information were developed decades ago. However, due to the lack of high-capacity computers, it was not possible to use them on real-life data and problems. Today, from finance to medicine data science plays an important role to solve problems. Suffice it to say, machine learning algorithms are the core of this new phenomenon besides data itself. Artificial neural networks, deep learning, Support Vector Machines, Decision Tree Learning Models, and related algorithms have been used successfully and yielded very important results recently. On the other hand, text data have also gained importance being the fuel of machine learning in data science. Especially the emergence of social media and communication technology contributed to the popularity of texts in data science. In this chapter, concise introductions have been given about the most popular and also successful machine learning algorithms. This chapter will be helpful for those readers who do not have enough information about machine learning and its algorithms.

Keywords Data science · Artificial neural networks · Deep learning · Decision trees · Text mining · Support Vector Machines

1.1 Artificial Neural Networks

Neural networks are a set of algorithms designed to recognize patterns, inspired from the human brain and biological neural networks (Glorot & Bengio, 2010). They interpret raw input by labelling or clustering them by a kind of machine perception. Data patterns that they perceive are numerical data stored in vectors such as pictures, sounds, text or time series, and these data need to be converted into a certain data structure to make sense.

Artificial neural networks help us cluster and classify data in a meaningful way that directly solves real-life problems or help us solve those problems. You can think of them as a clustering and classification layer of the data you store and manage.

G. Silahtaroğlu et al., *Data Science and Multiple Criteria Decision Making Approaches in Finance*, Multiple Criteria Decision Making,
https://doi.org/10.1007/978-3-030-74176-1_1

They help to group unlabelled data by similarities between sample inputs and classify the data when there is a labelled data set to work on. Neural networks can also extract features to feed other algorithms for clustering and classification; so, you can think of deep neural networks as components of larger machine learning applications that include algorithms for reinforcing learning, classification, and regression.

What kind of problems does deep learning solve, and more importantly, can it solve our problem? To know the answer, we need to ask some questions: What outputs do I care about? Are these outputs the labels that can be applied to the data available: For example, spam, clean user or fraud, unsatisfied customer or happy customer. Are there any data to extract these labels? So, can I find data that has been tagged before, or should I create a tagged dataset?

1.1.1 A Few Concrete Examples

Deep learning maps inputs over outputs and finds correlations between them. It is known as "a universal function derivative and solver" because it can learn to use an unknown function $f(x) = y$ between any input x and any output y, assuming that they are all related (e.g., correlated). In the learning process, when the neural network is fed with $f(x) = 3x + 12$ or $f(x) = 9x - 0.1$, it finds the correct form of the equation by converting f to work for any x to reach y.

1.2 Neural Network Elements

Deep learning is a term for "stacked neural networks," i.e., networks of several layers (Silahtaroğlu, 2008). Layers are made up of nodes that represent and act like neurons. Node refers to the place where the calculation takes place, as a neuron makes activations in the human brain, a node makes activations when it encounters sufficient stimulus. A node combines input from data with a set of coefficients or weights that increase or decrease the effect of this input, thus assigning importance (value coefficient) to the task-related inputs that the algorithm is trying to learn.

Neural networks learn the answers of questions as follows:

Which input is most useful? How can I classify the data set without errors? How can I calculate the final result? What is the best equation to solve the given problem in order to achieve the task? To do all these, an activation function is used for each node. According to the value of the activation function, it is calculated whether the signal will pass through the network and how much information pass through that layer (Silahtaroğlu, 2009). Figure 1.1 illustrates a node (artificial neuron) and its activation function. As it is seen a neuron first sums all values it received from the previous layers and then activates it.

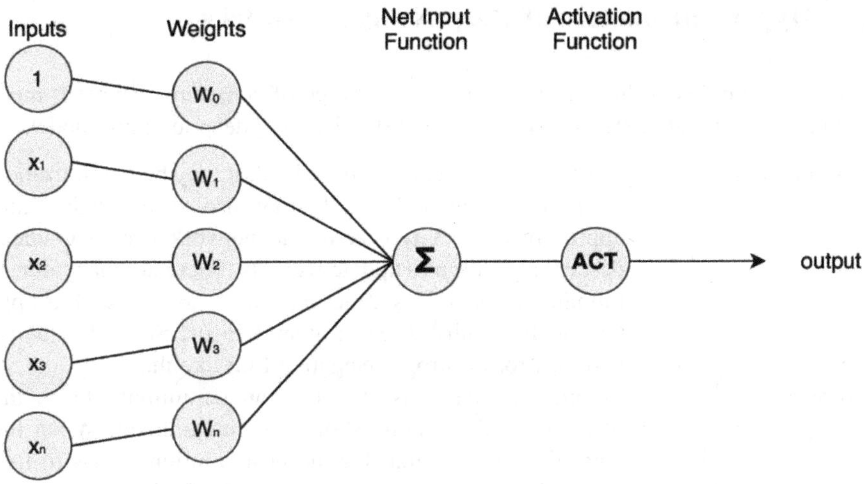

Fig. 1.1 Artificial neural network model

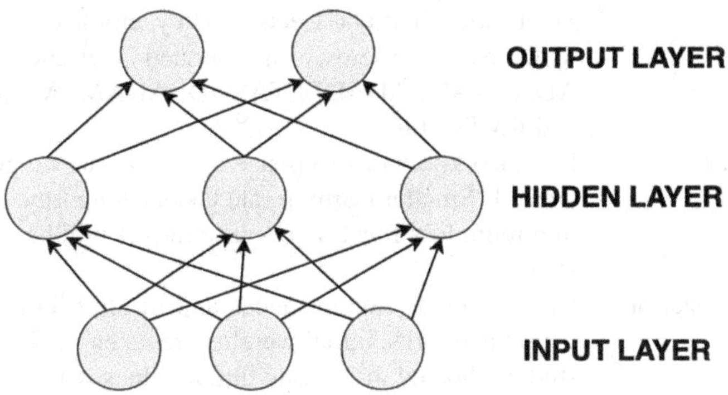

Fig. 1.2 Layers of a typical ANN

Basically, in a simple artificial neural network, x1, x2, x3, . . . xm inputs are given and arbitrarily defined w weights compose an f (x) function. Inputs are simply the dataset. Hidden layers are made up of many hidden layers each has got many nodes or neurons. All hidden layers are interconnected via neurons. Each neuron has its own SUM and ACTIVATION functions (Hambarde et al., 2020). Output layers are the labels. A deep learning model tries to learn by creating a huge equation by the help of the hidden layers in order to establish a rational among labels. The model finds an equation to solve a nonlinear and sometimes chaotic correlation between inputs (data) and outputs (labels) (Fig. 1.2).

1.3 Hyper Parameters of Deep Neural Networks

Besides the number of hidden layers, nodes, and type of activation functions there are some other parameters to consider when establishing a deep learning model.

Loss Function: It is the main function to be solved. It may be maximization or minimization problem. It may also be a certain value approximation. A typical neural network uses a gradient descent algorithm to update weights. There are many others though. Typical loss functions used are Cross Entropy, Cosine Proximity, Mean Squared Error, Sum of Squared Errors, Cross Entropy, Negative Log likelihood.

Optimizer: In order to keep loss function at a minimum level, the weights of all neurons should be streamlined. When the algorithm is searching for the best solution, it has to find the right direction for a fast and efficient downward movement. Most common optimizer algorithms are Line Gradient Decent, Conjugate Gradient Decent, and Stochastic Gradient Decent. They employ the following updaters: Nesterov accelerated gradient (NAG), ADAGRAD, ADADELTASGD, ADAM, MOMENTUM, and RMSPROP.

Learning Rate: It is also known as step-size and its value ranges between 0 and 1. Smaller learning rate takes a long time to reach the minimum loss function because moves will be with smaller steps.

Weight Initialization: Under normal circumstances and in the original model of neural networks, initial weights are taken randomly. Recent studies showed that taking initial values which are closer to the final weights to found through the model dramatically reduces the learning time. XAVIER (Glorot & Bengio, 2010), SIGMOID, RELU, Softsign are some of the algorithms (functions), which are used to choose initial weights.

1.4 Support Vector Machine

A Support Vector Machine (SVM) is a distinctive classifier normally defined by a differential hyperplane. In other words, when labelled training data (for supervised learning) is given, the algorithm extracts the most appropriate hyperplane that categorizes the new samples (Amari & Wu, 1999). In the two-dimensional space, this hyperplane is a line that divides a plane into two parts on each side of each class. Let us assume that two classes are given in the graph, as shown in the Fig. 1.3. The process of finding the most suitable line to separate classes is actually the essence of

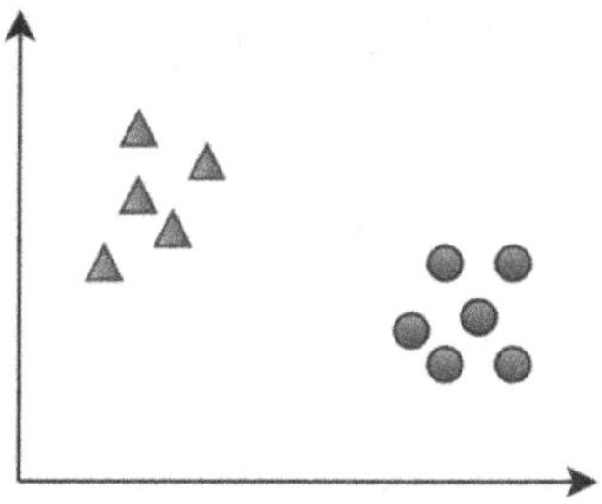

Fig. 1.3 Classes on a 2D hyperplane

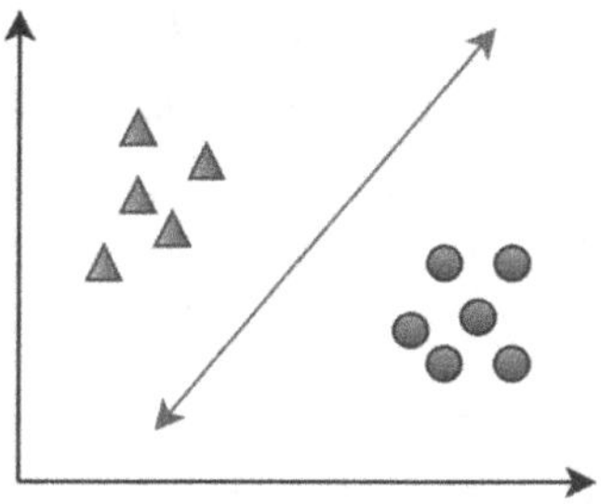

Fig. 1.4 Hyperplane linear division

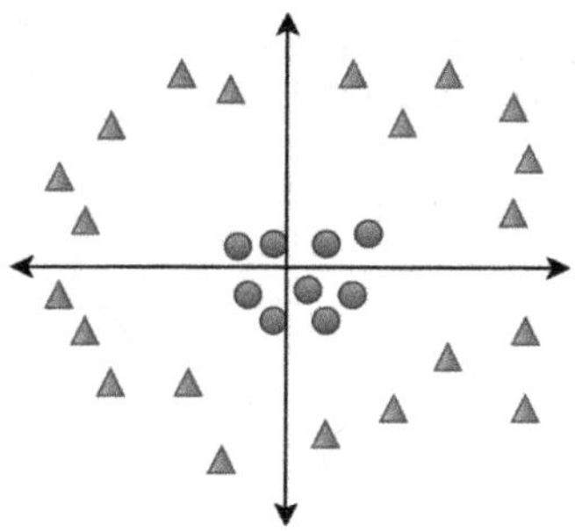

Fig. 1.5 Data set which cannot be divided linearly

SVM. SVM performs this process in the form of linear, hyperbolic, cubic, etc. This is also called KERNEL (Oreški & Oreški, 2014).

The line in the Fig. 1.4 separates the two classes. As it is clearly seen, one class is on one side of the other class members are on the other side of the hyperplane. However, in the real life, data are not separated so evenly as in the figure.

Please see Fig. 1.5 to image how data may be separated from one another in terms of classes given. All representations are done in two-dimensional hyperplane, which is the easiest one and can also be achieved by data visualization. SVM achieves it for multidimensional hyperplanes (Bai et al., 2019).

When achieving the separations SVM exercises some conversions:

For conversion, another dimension is added, as we call the *z*-axis. Let us assume the value of the points in the *z* plane, $w = x^2 + y^2$. In this case, it can be arranged as the distance from point *z* to all other points. Now if we draw on the *z*-axis, a clear separation appears, and a line can be drawn (Fig. 1.6).

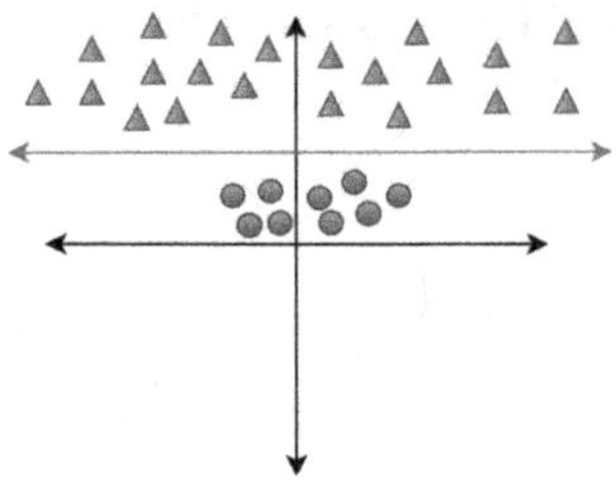

Fig. 1.6 After conversion

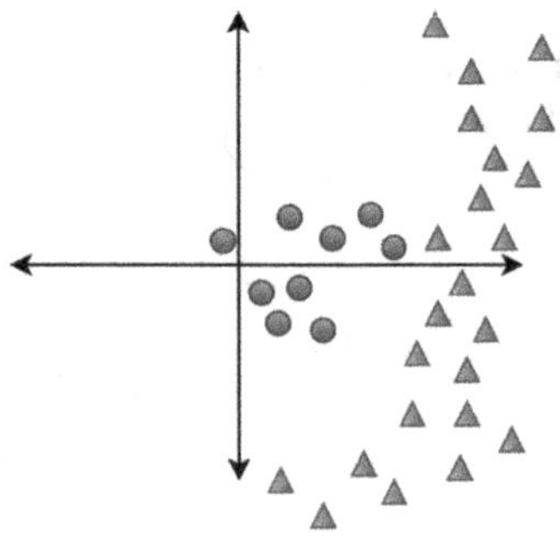

Fig. 1.7 Reorganizing the data on the 2D hyperplane

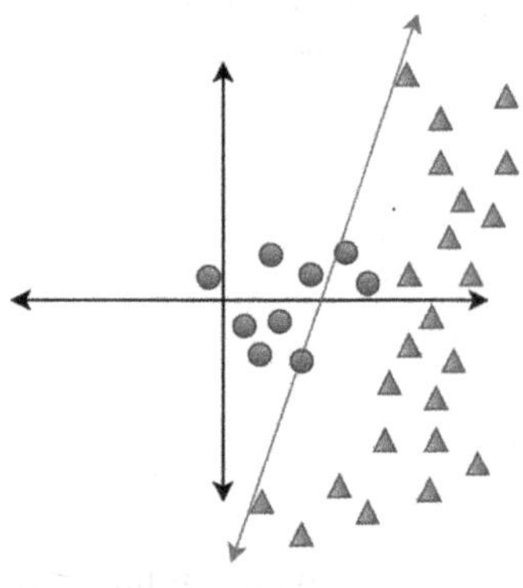

Fig. 1.8 An apparent conflict when dividing

When we convert this line to the original plane, it matches the circular boundary as shown in the Fig. 1.7. These transformations are called kernels.

SVM's attitude will be different if there is a conflict between data or if different classes share the very same coordinates (Fig. 1.8).

Both of the above answers are correct. The first tolerates some outliers. The second one tries to achieve 0 tolerance with perfect partitioning.

However, it takes a lot of time to find the perfect class for millions of training data in the real-world applications. To prevent this, SVM uses the concept of normalization. At this stage, using parameters such as GAMA, MARGIN, it can reach a remarkably nonlinear classification line with greater accuracy in a reasonable time.

1.5 Kernel

Learning the hyperplane in linear SVM is done by transforming the problem using some linear algebra (Bai et al., 2019). This is where the kernel plays its role. For linear kernel, the estimation equation of a new input using the dot product between input (x) and each support vector (xi) is calculated as follows:

$$\mathrm{f}\ (\mathrm{x}) = \mathrm{B0} + \mathrm{sum}\ (\mathrm{ai} * (\mathrm{x}, \mathrm{xi}))$$

This is an equation to calculate the inner products of a new input vector (x) with all the support vectors in the training data. B0 and ai coefficients (for each entry) should be estimated from the training data by the learning algorithm.

The polynomial nucleus can be exponentially defined as K (x, xi) = 1 + sum (x * xi) ^ d and K (x, xi) = exp. (−gamma * sum ((x − xi^2))). Polynomial and exponential kernels calculate the separation line at a higher dimension.

1.6 Regularization

The regulation parameter which is usually represented as C in programing environment tells SVM optimization module that it wants to avoid misclassifying each training sample. For large C values, if the hyperplane does a better job of classifying all training points correctly, optimization will select a smaller part of hyperplane. On the contrary, a very small C value causes the optimizer to search for hyperplanes with a larger margin even if more points are misclassified in this hyperplane. The images below are examples of two different editing parameters. There are some misclassifications on the left due to the low normalization value. A higher value leads to results such as the correct one (Fig. 1.9). Please, compare.

Fig. 1.9 Nonlinear separation

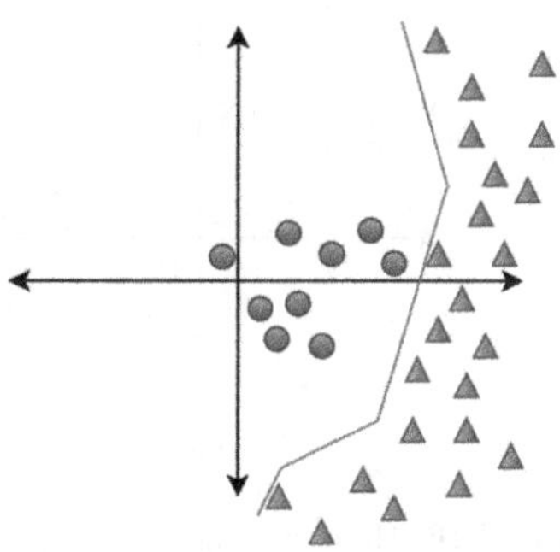

1.7 Gamma

The gamma parameter calculates the effect of a single training sample as low values "far" and high values "close." In other words, points that are far from the reasonable separation line are taken into account when calculating the separation line with low gamma. On the other hand, high gamma scores that are near the reasonable line are taken into account in the calculation (Fig. 1.10).

1.8 Margin

Last but not least, a very important feature of the SVM classifier. SVM tries to provide a good margin to the Kernel. Margin is the division of the line into the closest class points. Good margin is the area where this separation is greater for both classes. Figure 1.11 provides a visual example of good and bad margins. A good margin allows points to be in their class before moving to another class.

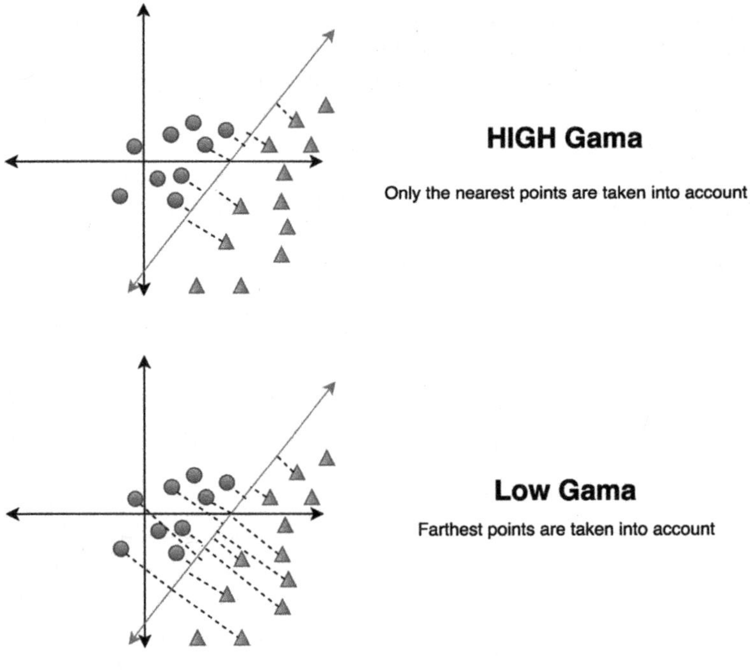

Fig. 1.10 High gamma and low gamma representations

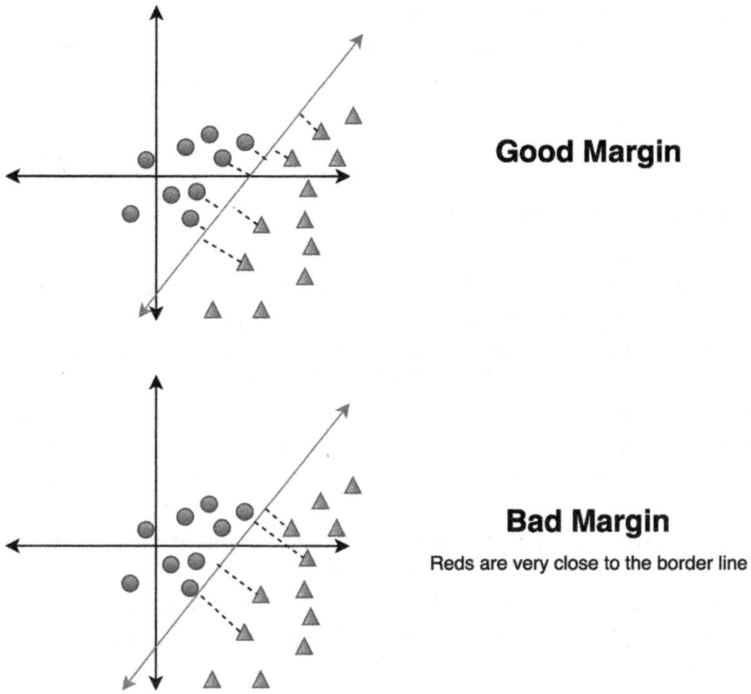

Fig. 1.11 Good and bad margin representations

1.9 Decision Trees

Decision trees are one of the most frequently used algorithms in classification problems. Compared to other methods, it can be said that decision trees are easier to configure, and they are also understood by humans. In this technique, a tree is created for classification; Then, each record in the database is applied to this tree and this record is classified according to the result. Basically, it can be said that it consists of two steps: The first is the building of the tree, and the second is the implementation of the classification by applying the data to the tree one by one.

In order to understand the decision trees more clearly, it can be defined mathematically as follows:

Let D = {t1, t2, t3 ... tn} be a database.

Each ti here consists of ti = <ti ... ti2 > and this database consists of {A1, A2, A3 ... An} fields.

Apart from this, C = {C1, C2, C3, ... Cn} is also given a class. In this case, a decision tree can be defined as follows:

It is a tree structure where

- Each node is labelled with the A_i field
- Each branching node answers a question about this field
- Each leaf is a class.

1.10 Sample Decision Tree

Figure 1.12 shows a sample decision tree. Each node of the tree is split into two branches. During this separation process, a question is asked about the Ai node in the database, and a branch is followed according to the response to make a rule. A typical decision tree creates IF-ELSE-THEN rules for decision making.

Decision trees produce rules but also calculate some parameters to enhance the rules. One of the most important of these is the concept of lift. Lift is the value that indicates how much of the records in any node belong to the target class compared to the whole tree. For example, the 255% lift value indicates that the rule is 2.55 times stronger to predict a class compared to the initial probability to predict the same class under the same conditions (Silahtaroğlu, 2019).

A group of decision tree algorithms takes advantage of the concept of entropy (Silahtaroğlu, 2009). Entropy is the digitization of the information extracted. If all the data used belonged to a single class, we would not be surprised when we encountered the class; in this case, the entropy would be zero (0). Entropy has got a value between 0 and 1. When all possibilities are equal, entropy will reach its maximum value. Entropy can be defined mathematically as follows (Fig. 1.13).

Entropy is calculated as follows:

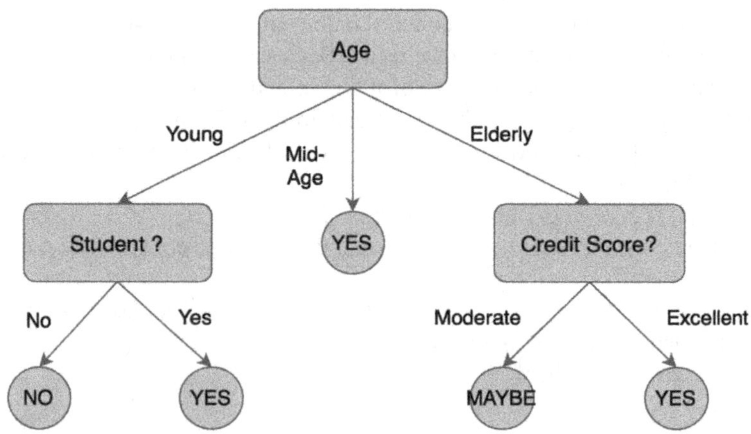

Fig. 1.12 A sample decision tree

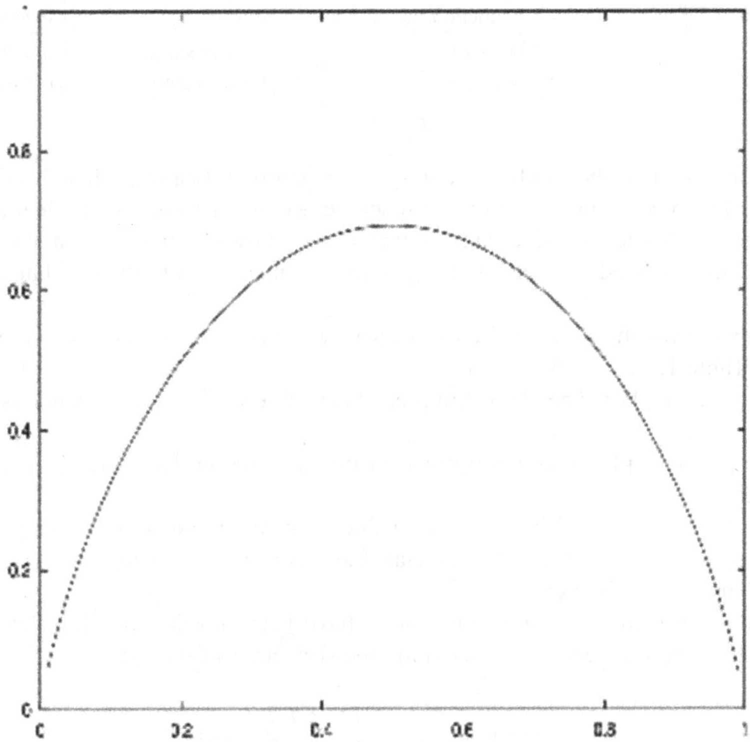

Fig. 1.13 Representation of entropy

$$H(\mathrm{P}_1, \mathrm{P}_2 \ldots \mathrm{P}_\mathrm{n}) = \sum \left(p_i \log \left({}^1\!/_{p_i}\right)\right)$$

The GINI index is another parameter used to create trees. The gini (K) index of any K dataset is calculated as follows:

$$gini\,(K) = 1 - \sum p_j^2$$

where p_j is the frequency of class j within the K set.

1.11 Testing Learning

The data should be divided into two groups as learning and testing of learning. There are a number of preprocesses for testing both supervised and unsupervised learning. In supervised learning, the data set should be divided into two parts: 60% to 80% learning and 20% to 40% supervision data (Oreški & Oreški, 2014).

Table 1.1 Truth table

Prediction/Real class	Positive	Negative
Positive	True positive	False positive
Negative	False negative	True negative

After completing the machine training in the learning data set, it handles the test data set. The predictions made by the machine according to the model learned are compared and the actual values are compared to test how much the machine learned. The machine is kind of graded using some parametric techniques (Hauskrecht, 2019).

For this, estimation and real class values are compared in a confusion or truth matrix (Table 1.1).

True positive (TP): The algorithm predicts positive while the class value is really positive.

False positive (FP): The algorithm's positive prediction when the class value is negative.

False negative (FN): When the class value is negative, the algorithm is positive.

True negative (TN): When the true class value is negative, the algorithm correctly predicts the class as negative.

Various performance evaluation criteria have been developed using these four parameters. These criteria and calculation methods are as follows:

$$Accuracy = \frac{TP \times TN}{TP + TN + FP + FN}$$

$$Error\ Rate = \frac{FP + FN}{TP + TN + FP + FN}$$

$$Specificity = \frac{TN}{TN + FP}$$

$$Recall = \frac{TP}{TP + FN}$$

$$Precision = \frac{TP}{TP + FP}$$

1.12 Text Mining

Text mining is a general term which embodies all models, methods, algorithms, and techniques that are used to retrieve or extract useful information from unstructured texts. Text mining may be defined as structuring free-style text data in various formats and analyze them with machine learning tools or algorithms in order to get valuable information (Hauskrecht, 2019).

Most of the machine learning or data mining tools employ data in a tabular form. However, text data is different from the data in a tabular form; and thus, text data should be converted into tabular form expressed with numbers. This is called "vector presentation" or "vectorising" (Hauskrecht, 2019).

Text mining is supported by Machine Learning algorithms like Artificial Intelligence and decision trees. Text mining is used for the following purposes (Hauskrecht, 2019):

- Information retrieval
- Information extraction
- Concept extraction
- Classification
- Clustering
- Sentiment analysis
- Topic extraction
- Text summarization
- Web mining

Information retrieval (IR) is to get a predefined piece of information in a large data set. What search engine tools are doing is IR.

Information extraction (IE) is a more complicated process than IR. It needs to understand the real meaning of words in context with a detailed discourse analysis. To do that an IE process needs to use clustering, classification, and sentiment analysis as well.

Concept extraction is to mine abstract ideas or general notions that occur in a document.

Classification as in data mining is to find the category of the given text.

Clustering differs from classification by not having predefined classes. So, it is to group given texts according to the information they have.

Sentiment analysis is deriving the mood of a sentence, paragraph, page, chapter, or the whole text. If sentiment analysis is done to tell whether the given piece of text has a positive or negative mood, this is called polarity extraction (Hauskrecht, 2019).

Topic extraction is a general term of the process which results in getting the gist of the given text. This may be done in two ways: Classification and clustering (Hauskrecht, 2019).

Text summarization is rewriting the text in a shorter length. It may be done as extraction based, abstraction based, or aided (Hauskrecht, 2019).

Web mining may sound like performing text mining on web pages. Well, this is partly true; Text mining uses any kind of text (or speech) including web pages. However, web mining itself is different from that. It has some other components, these are:

Web Content Mining.
Web Usage Mining.
Web Structure Mining.

In order to perform a text mining study or analysis, there are certain steps to be followed (Hauskrecht, 2019).

Suggested steps for text analysis:

1. Obtaining data
2. Converting data into a single (readable) format
3. Transforming text data
    (a) Vectorizing
    (b) Tokenization
    (c) Bag of words creation
    (d) Stemming
    (e) Translation
4. Feature selection
    (a) N-Gram elimination
    (b) Stop words elimination
    (c) Part of speech filtering
5. Information retrieval
    (a) Keywords extraction
    (b) Similarity calculation
6. Information extraction
    (a) Sentiment analysis
    (b) Topic extraction
    (c) Classification.
    (d) Clustering
    (e) Pattern recognition
7. Merging texts with structured datasets for other data mining or machine learning purposes

Appendix

Key Terms and Definitions

NAG: Nesterov Accelerated Gradient
SVM: Support Vector Machine

References

Amari, S. I., & Wu, S. (1999). Improving support vector machine classifiers by modifying kernel functions. *Neural Networks, 12*(6), 783–789.

Bai, Y., Sun, Z., Zeng, B., Long, J., Li, L., de Oliveira, J. V., & Li, C. (2019). A comparison of dimension reduction techniques for support vector machine modeling of multi-parameter manufacturing quality prediction. *Journal of Intelligent Manufacturing, 30*(5), 2245–2256.

Glorot, X., & Bengio, Y. (2010). Understanding the difficulty of training deep feedforward neural networks. In *Proceedings of the Thirteenth International Conference on Artificial Intelligence and Statistics (AISTATS)* (Vol. 9, pp. 249–256). Chia Laguna Resort, Sardinia, Italy.

Hambarde, K., et al. (2020). Data analytics implemented over E-commerce data to evaluate performance of supervised learning approaches in relation to customer behavior. In *Soft computing for problem solving* (pp. 285–293). Springer.

Hauskrecht, M. (2019). Decision trees. https://people.cs.pitt.edu/milos/courses/cs2750-Spring03/lectures/class19.pdf

Oreški, G., & Oreški, S. (2014, January). An experimental comparison of classification algorithm performances for highly imbalanced datasets. In *25th Central European Conference on Information and Intelligent Systems*. Varaždin, Croatia.

Silahtaroğlu, G. (2008). *Data mining concepts and algorithms*. Papatya Publishing.

Silahtaroğlu, G. (2009). An attribute-centre based decision tree classification algorithm. *World Academy of Science, Engineering and Technology, 56*, 302–306.

Silahtaroğlu, G. (2019). *Concepts of text mining with python and real life exercises*. Amazon.

Chapter 2
Identifying Indicators of Global Financial Crisis with Fuzzy Logic and Data Science: A Comparative Analysis Between Developing and Developed Economies

Abstract The main purpose of this study is to define the leading indicators of the 2008 global financial crisis for both developing and developed economies. In this context, 16 different variables are defined with the help of literature review. These variables are weighted by considering the fuzzy DEMATEL approach and the most significant 8 variables are identified. In addition to this analysis, decision tree methodology is also taken into consideration to understand main determinants of the financial crisis. The findings show that growth rate and capital adequacy of the banking industry are accepted as the leading indicators of the global crisis for developed economies. On the other hand, it is also concluded that inflation and industry development are accepted as the indicator of the financial crisis in addition to the economic growth and capital adequacy of the banks for developing economies. While considering the results, it is recommended that developed countries should periodically control economic growth rate and capital adequacy ratio of the banks to understand whether they have a financial crisis risk or not. Furthermore, for developing countries, it is also recommended that inflation rate should be periodically controlled, and they should identify necessary actions in order to minimize inflation rate.

Keywords Global financial crisis · Data science · Fuzzy DEMATEL

2.1 Introduction

The crisis is the result of some unforeseen developments occurrence of undesirable events. At the time of the crisis, the financial system in the country has deteriorated and cannot fulfill its basic function of providing financing to the real sector. In other words, banks are becoming more reluctant to lend, and as a result, firms find it difficult to find resources. Companies that cannot find resources reduce their investments. This situation not only puts the country into recession but also causes unemployment. The most important reason for this is the decrease in the profits of

G. Silahtaroğlu et al., *Data Science and Multiple Criteria Decision Making Approaches in Finance*, Multiple Criteria Decision Making,
https://doi.org/10.1007/978-3-030-74176-1_2

the firms, which have lost their investment and therefore want to reduce the costs of the related companies.

In the last two decades, financial crises have increased dramatically. Although many of these crises are in developing countries, there are important crises in developed countries. In addition, some of the financial crises are limited to the country in which they occur, while a significant portion has spread to other countries. Another important point is that some of these crises became a global crises because it affected lots of countries in a negative manner. 1929 Great Depression and 2008 Global Mortgage Crisis can be given as the examples of this devastating global financial crisis.

Considering the aforementioned issues, it is seen that the crisis poses a serious threat to the country in which it occurs. It is highly probable that the country experiencing a crisis will have serious problems both socially and financially. With respect to the social factors, financial crises cause high unemployment in the countries. Thus, people, who do not have a regular income, may commit an illegal act to manage their financial problems. Therefore, the crisis must be managed successfully, in other words, emergency intervention is necessary.

Early warning systems are the systems used to prevent this negativity by identifying the necessary clues before a negative event occurs. The use of early warning systems has many benefits in terms of the countries. With the mentioned systems, it is possible to prevent the occurrence of crises in cases where they can be predicted correctly. In this way, the damage caused by the crises to both the banks and the national economy is prevented.

In this study, it is aimed to examine the main factors of the 2008 global financial crisis. For this purpose, an analysis is made for both developing and developed economies. Additionally, fuzzy DEMATEL and decision tree approaches are considered. In the first aspect, 16 different variables are defined by examining similar studies in the literature. These criteria are weighted by using fuzzy DEMATEL methodology and the most important 8 criteria are selected. In addition, the decision tree method is also taken into consideration to understand the main indicators of the financial crisis.

2.2 General Information About the Financial Crises and 2008 Global Mortgage Crisis

2.2.1 Types of the Financial Crises

Financial crises may be classified into three different types. The first type of the financial crisis is named as the currency crisis. The foreign currency crisis is defined as the excessive depreciation of the domestic currency of a country and consequently the fall of the central banks' reserves. It has mainly occurred in the countries that implement fixed exchange rate systems. In these countries, when the amount of foreign currency goes down, central banks try to sell these currencies to the market in order to save the value of the local currencies. However, this situation causes important decreases in the amount of foreign reserves of the central banks.

As can be seen from the above-mentioned definitions, the currency of the country during the exchange crisis is depreciating significantly. Expectations that the national currency will lose value in this process can be very effective. The speculators, which think that the national currency will depreciate, buy foreign currency from the market. In order to prevent this loss, the central bank sells foreign currency to the market. In this process, the central bank loses a significant portion of its international reserves.

The central bank, which wants to prevent the depreciation of the national currency, needs to intervene in the market by using other means than selling foreign currency. The most important reason for this is that the central bank does not tolerate losing more of its reserves. Therefore, the central bank will begin to raise interest rates. With the rising interest rate, the national currency will gain importance for the investors and thus the depreciation of the national currency will be prevented.

An increase in the value of the foreign currency has also significant negative impacts on the companies that have foreign debts. Some companies can prefer to take foreign debt because of the low-interest payment advantage. However, in case of the depreciation of the national currency, the value of the foreign currency goes up. In other words, the debt amount of these countries increases at the same time. In this situation, if this increase in the debt amount is too much, this issue may cause these companies to go bankrupt.

Banking crisis is the second type of the financial crisis. In this crisis type, banks firstly go bankrupt in the country and it leads to other companies to have significant difficulties. The main reason behind this issue is that companies cannot make investment effectively because they do not take loans from the banks in this crisis period. The decrease in the investment amount also causes the decrease in the profitability of these companies. Because of that condition, these companies, which have lower profitability, decide to fire some employees in order to minimize the costs. It is obvious that this condition has an increasing effect on the unemployment problem.

As it was defined in the previous paragraph, a banking crisis can be defined as the situation in which banks cannot fulfill their responsibilities. There can be many different reasons for this situation. For example, very low capital amount of the banks can cause an important crisis for the banking sector. Therefore, regulating authority should make an effective audit to prevent this situation. Another important reason for the banking crisis can be higher nonperforming loans ratio of the banks. It is obvious that in order not to have significant problems, banks should be very careful to select the customers while giving loans.

In summary, banks play an essential role in the sustainability of the economies. Hence, in a country, banks' bankruptcy or high losses can cause serious losses for the country. With the emergence of the banking crisis, the flow of funds in the country may come to a halt. As a result, firms in the country will not be able to find resources for investment and will have to shrink. Shrinking firms will lay off their employees and thus the crisis in the country will become deeper.

The third type of financial crisis can be defined as the debt crisis. Foreign debt crisis is expressed as a country's inability to pay its debts abroad. Most of the countries can take some debts from abroad owing to many different aspects. For instance, in order to finance the current account deficit, countries get foreign debt. Another important reason for taking financial debt is to provide sustainable economic growth by making new investments.

In such a case, the essential point is that these countries should evaluate these debts effectively so as not to face difficulties in the future. That is to say, if these foreign debts provided by countries cannot be used in beneficial investments, the situation will create problems for the countries. Especially with the effect of globalization, it has become much easier to find external resources. This situation may cause some countries to borrow excessively and unconsciously. Therefore, some countries may have difficulty paying these debts.

2.2.2 2008 Global Financial Crisis

According to many researchers, the basis of the 2008 crisis was taken after the dot. com crisis in 2000. In order to prevent the aforementioned crisis, FED has lowered its interest rates to the lowest level of the last 45 years. It is obvious that this action played a key role to minimize the negative impacts of the dot.com crisis that occurred in 2000. However, because this situation led to an increase in housing loans in an uncontrolled manner, it is also thought that this radical strategy created the ground for a more devastating crisis that will be occurred in the future.

In this process, only persons with high creditworthiness have not been taken the loans. The size of high-risk loans, referred to as "subprime" and used by low-income people, was about $ 1.5 trillion. Subsequently, the banks issued real estate bonds, showing collateral due to loans given to this risky group in order to give more credit. As a result, buying housing for investment purposes, which is called residential speculation, became more important than the purpose of obtaining housing. During this period, FED decided to increase the interest rate and this situation also increased the installment amount of the loans. As a result, unexpected problems arose in loan repayments due to this situation.

After the reasons mentioned above, the return of mortgage loans has been disrupted. As a result, banks have narrowed down their loans. This led to a decline in mortgage loan demand and house prices. Houses, which are the guarantee of real estate bonds, cannot meet the nominal value of the papers. When the banks could not collect the loans they gave, they were in a shortage of resources. This situation caused the financial system to stop.

2.3 Literature Review

There is a broad literature on the subject of the financial crisis. Most of these studies focused on the macroeconomic factors as the indicators of the financial crisis. High unemployment rate is accepted as a significant determinant of the financial crisis. For example, Drydakis (2015) tried to evaluate the Greek debt crisis after the period of 2008. In this study, descriptive statistics between the years 2008 and 2015 are used. As a result, it is stated that high unemployment rate is an important factor for this crisis. Economou et al. (2016), Parmar et al. (2016), Pavli et al. (2019), Theodossiou et al. (2017), and Christodoulou et al. (2017) also examined the Greek financial crisis and reached the same conclusions. Similar to these studies, Hall (2015) also focused on global mortgage crisis that occurred in the United States. It is concluded that lots of people became unemployed after this crisis period. In addition to these studies, Torrubiano-Domínguez et al. (2015), Yüksel and Adalı (2017), Yüksel (2016a), Polyakova and Fligstein (2016), Dijkstra et al. (2015), Foster and Frieden (2017), and Laanani et al. (2015) tried to find the effects of global mortgage crisis to the Europe and determined that unemployment rate is a very important factor.

In addition to the unemployment rate, economic growth is also accepted as a significant indicator for many different researchers. For instance, Bartz and Winkler (2016) aimed to understand the economic performance of the countries before financial crisis period. In this scope, the German economy was evaluated in the study. It is determined that lower economic growth is an important factor in the financial crisis. Also, Kunieda and Shibata (2016), Lee et al. (2015), Lins et al. (2017), Yüksel (2017a), and Perles-Ribes et al. (2017) also concluded that before the financial crisis period, countries had very low economic growth. On the other side, Asteriou and Spanos (2019), Dinçer, Yüksel and Adalı (2018a), Rafindadi and Ozturk (2016), Dinçer, Yüksel and Şenel (2018b), and Floyd et al. (2015) concluded that uncontrolled economic growth caused the countries to have a financial crisis and during this crisis period, countries have economic recession. Additionally, Hall (2015) and Stiglitz (2016) are also other studies that examined global financial crisis and defined that economic recession is occurred before countries have financial crisis.

The current account deficit was also accepted as an indicator of the financial crisis. A country pays foreign exchange to the countries for the goods and services imported from abroad. On the other hand, the country receives foreign exchange income in return for goods and services exported abroad. In addition to this, a foreign exchange may enter or leave the country due to reasons such as interest income / expense other than imports and exports (Yüksel, 2016b). As a result, the difference between the amount of foreign currency entered into a country for export or other reasons and the amount of foreign exchange due to import or other reasons gives us the current account balance. Ahmed et al. (2018), Griffiths (2019), Baimbridge et al. (2017), Borio (2016), Yüksel and Zengin (2016), and Lane (2015) underlined the importance of the current account deficit in the financial crisis. In the related studies, the unresolved current account deficit problem led to the devaluation of the countries and this would cause crises.

In addition to these variables, a sudden change in exchange rates is accepted as an important danger for the companies. Bénétrix et al. (2015), Fatum and Yamamoto (2016), Chuen (2015), Dinçer, Hacıoğlu, and Yüksel (2018), Sui and Sun (2016), Yüksel, Özsarı and Canöz (2016b) and Dua and Tuteja (2016) stated that the companies, which have foreign currency debt, have a significant amount of losses in case of any devaluation. The bankruptcies of these banks lead to financial recession for the countries. Moreover, Alessandri and Mumtaz (2017), Dinçer et al. (2017), Asongu and De Moor (2017), Yüksel and Özsarı (2016a), Friedrich (2016) and Chen et al. (2016) identified that high inflation rates can cause financial crisis, especially in developing countries. These researchers defined that if the inflation is too high in an economy, the confidence of individuals in the national currency will disappear. Increasing foreign currency demand will also lower the value of the national currency. This is likely to lead to negativity in the country's economy (Yüksel & Özsarı, 2016b).

Additionally, the conditions of the banking industry are also accepted as the leading indicators of the financial crisis. For instance, Bekiros et al. (2018), Mukhtarov et al. (2018), Oktar and Yüksel (2015a), Apergis and Cooray (2018), Zia et al. (2018), Yüksel (2017b), and Basheer et al. (2019) showed that low capital amount of the banks is an important determinant of the financial crisis. On the other hand, nonperforming loans ratio is accepted another indicator of the financial crisis. In this framework, Ho et al. (2016), Dinçer, Yüksel, Adalı, and Aydın (2019e), Dinçer and Yüksel (2018), Mohaddes et al. (2017), Yüksel, Mukhtarov, Mahmudlu, et al. (2018a), Morgan and Zhang (2017), Yüksel (2016c) and Ozili (2019) determined that the high level of nonperforming loans has negative effects on the real sector. In this situation, the asset quality of the banks will decrease and as a result, banks will be more reluctant to lend. This situation will make it difficult for the real sector to find resources in the country.

Also, Doumpos et al. (2015), de Haan et al. (2018), Yüksel and Özsarı (2017), and Garriga (2016) indicated that the problems related to the central bank independence cause financial crisis in the country. According to these researchers, central banks should be independent with respect to the economic, political, and financial instrument. The significance of the environmental factors for the financial crisis were also underlined in some studies. For instance, Baumeister and Kilian (2016), Tsai (2015), and Kocaarslan et al. (2018) concluded that oil price volatility can cause a financial crisis, especially for oil importing countries. Similarly, Byun and Chang (2015), Yüksel and Zengin (2016) and Chernov et al. (2018) indicated that the USD interest rate is an important factor that can cause financial crisis for developing economies. Karanikolos et al. (2016), Kim et al. (2015), and Lennartz et al. (2016) accepted global financial crisis as a main reason for the local crisis. Also, Ben Ayed et al. (2018), Kentikelenis (2018), Yüksel, Mukhtarov, Mammadov, and Özsarı (2018b), and Cerna and Czaika (2016) focused on the negative effects of the external migration on the financial crisis.

In some studies, the importance of the internal factors was considered as a reason for the financial crisis. For example, Fraser (2017), Alessandri and Mumtaz (2017), and Marques et al. (2016) reached a conclusion that decrease in industrial production is an indicator of the financial crisis. Parallel to these studies, Hobolt and De Vries (2016), Funke et al. (2016), and Hernández and Kriesi (2016) also concluded that the election period causes too much expenditure, which leads to financial recession. On the other hand, Ehrmann and Fratzscher (2017), Lane and Milesi-Ferretti (2018), and Cooper and Nikolov (2018) demonstrated that in case of high government debt, there is a risk of financial recession for the countries. In addition to these factors, Bhagat (2016), Palomares-Linares and van Ham (2018), Yüksel, Eroğlu and Özsarı (2016a), and An et al. (2017) showed that internal migration is a crucial factor of the financial crisis.

This literature review demonstrates that financial crisis subject was taken into consideration with various purposes. In most of the studies, it was aimed to find the determinants of the financial crisis. Additionally, lots of different financial crises were evaluated, such as the 2008 global mortgage crisis, 1998 Asia crisis, 2001 Turkey crisis, and 1929 great recession. Moreover, probit, logit, regression, multivariate adaptive regression spline, and decision tree approaches were used in the analysis process. Hence, it is concluded that a new evaluation should be made to identify the indicators of the financial crisis with an original methodology. In this framework, data science and fuzzy logic can contribute to the originality of the study.

2.4 An Application on Turkish Banking Industry

2.4.1 Data Set and Variables

This study aims to evaluate the leading indicators of the 2008 global mortgage crisis for both developing and developed economies. First of all, 16 different variables are identified as a result of literature review. The details of these variables are given in Table 2.1.

Out of these 16 variables, the fuzzy DEMATEL approach is performed to select the most important 8 different variables. After that, gain entropy methodology is used to understand the indicators of the financial crisis for both developing and developed economies. The data of the variables is obtained from World Bank.

2.4.2 Fuzzy DEMATEL

DEMATEL approach is a type of multi-criteria decision-making model. The purpose of this method is to make decisions when there is uncertainty. In addition to this issue, the causal relationship between the criteria can be identified by using this

Table 2.1 Indicators of the financial crisis

Group	Indicator	References
Macroeconomic factors	Unemployment rate	Drydakis (2015), Economou et al. (2016), Parmar et al. (2016), Pavli et al. (2019), Theodossiou et al. (2017) and Christodoulou et al. (2017), Hall (2015), Torrubiano-Domínguez et al. (2015), Yüksel and Adalı (2017), Yüksel (2016a, b, c), Polyakova and Fligstein (2016), Dijkstra et al. (2015), Foster and Frieden (2017), Laanani et al. (2015)
	Economic growth	Bartz and Winkler (2016), Kunieda and Shibata (2016), Lee et al. (2015), Lins et al. (2017), Yüksel (2017a, b), Perles-Ribes et al. (2017), Asteriou and Spanos (2019), Dinçer et al. (2018a), Rafindadi and Ozturk (2016), Dinçer et al. (2018b), Floyd et al. (2015), Hall (2015), Stiglitz (2016)
	Current account deficit	Ahmed et al. (2018), Griffiths (2019), Baimbridge et al. (2017), Borio (2016), Yüksel and Zengin (2016), Yüksel (2016c), Lane (2015)
	Inflation	Alessandri and Mumtaz (2017), Dinçer et al. (2017), Asongu and De Moor (2017), Yüksel and Özsarı (2016a), Friedrich (2016), Chen et al. (2016)
Financial factors	Bank capital-to-asset ratio	Bekiros et al. (2018), Mukhtarov et al. (2018), Oktar and Yüksel (2015b), Apergis and Cooray (2018), Zia et al. (2018), Yüksel (2017b), Basheer et al. (2019)
	Currency exchange rate	Bénétrix et al. (2015), Fatum and Yamamoto (2016), Chuen (2015), Dinçer, Hacıoğlu, and Yüksel (2018), Sui and Sun (2016), Yüksel, Özsarı and Canöz (2016b), Dua and Tuteja (2016)
	NPL Ratio	Ho et al. (2016), Dinçer, Yüksel, Korsakienė, Raišienė, and Bilan (2019f), Dinçer and Yüksel (2018), Mohaddes et al. (2017), Yüksel Mukhtarov, Mahmudlu, et al. (2018a), Morgan and Zhang (2017), Yüksel (2016a, b, c), Ozili (2019)
	Central bank independence	Doumpos et al. (2015), de Haan et al. (2018), Yüksel and Özsarı (2017), Garriga (2016)
External factors	Oil price	Baumeister and Kilian (2016), Tsai (2015), Kocaarslan et al. (2018)
	USD interest rate	Byun and Chang (2015), Yüksel and Zengin (2016), Chernov et al. (2018)
	Foreign financial crisis	Karanikolos et al. (2016), Kim et al. (2015), Lennartz et al. (2016)
	External migration	Ben Ayed et al. (2018), Kentikelenis (2018), Yüksel, Mukhtarov, Mammadov, and Özsarı (2018b), Cerna and Czaika (2016)
Internal factors	Industrial production	Fraser (2017), Alessandri and Mumtaz (2017), Marques et al. (2016)
	elections	Hobolt and De Vries (2016), Funke et al. (2016), Hernández and Kriesi (2016)
	Government debt	Ehrmann and Fratzscher (2017), Lane and Milesi-Ferretti (2018), Cooper and Nikolov (2018)
	Internal migration	Bhagat (2016), Palomares-Linares and van Ham (2018), Yüksel, Eroğlu and Özsarı (2016a), An et al. (2017)

methodology. Moreover, it is also possible to understand impact relationship analysis with the help of DEMATEL approach. The first step of this method includes the identification of the main purpose. Also, different criteria are determined in the second step. For this purpose, five different aspects (no, low, medium, high, and very high) are used in the evaluation of the experts. On the other side, the initial direct-relation fuzzy matrix ($\widetilde{Z}$) is created in the third step by using expert evaluations. This process is shown in Eqs. (2.1) and (2.2).

$$\widetilde{Z} = \begin{bmatrix} 0 & \widetilde{z}_{12} & \cdots & \cdots & \widetilde{z}_{1n} \\ \widetilde{z}_{21} & 0 & \cdots & \cdots & \widetilde{z}_{2n} \\ \vdots & \vdots & \ddots & \cdots & \cdots \\ \vdots & \vdots & \vdots & \ddots & \vdots \\ \widetilde{z}_{n1} & \widetilde{z}_{n2} & \cdots & \cdots & 0 \end{bmatrix} \tag{2.1}$$

$$\widetilde{Z} = \frac{\widetilde{Z}^1 + \widetilde{Z}^2 + \widetilde{Z}^3 + \ldots \widetilde{Z}^n}{n} \tag{2.2}$$

Furthermore, the fourth step is related to the normalization of this matrix by using Eqs. (2.3)–(2.5).

$$\widetilde{X} = \begin{bmatrix} \widetilde{x}_{11} & \widetilde{x}_{12} & \cdots & \cdots & \widetilde{x}_{1n} \\ \widetilde{x}_{21} & \widetilde{x}_{22} & \cdots & \cdots & \widetilde{x}_{2n} \\ \vdots & \vdots & \ddots & \cdots & \cdots \\ \vdots & \vdots & \vdots & \ddots & \vdots \\ \widetilde{x}_{n1} & \widetilde{x}_{n2} & \cdots & \cdots & \widetilde{x}_{nn} \end{bmatrix} \tag{2.3}$$

$$\widetilde{x}_{ij} = \frac{\widetilde{z}_{ij}}{r} = \left(\frac{l_{ij}}{r}, \frac{m_{ij}}{r}, \frac{u_{ij}}{r}\right) \tag{2.4}$$

$$r = max_{1 \leq i \leq n}\left(\sum_{j=1}^{n} u_{ij}\right) \tag{2.5}$$

In the fifth step, the total influence fuzzy matrix is defined with the help of Eqs. (2.5)–(2.12).

$$X_l = \begin{bmatrix} 0 & l'_{12} & \cdots & \cdots & l'_{1n} \\ l'_{21} & 0 & \cdots & \cdots & l'_{2n} \\ \vdots & \vdots & \ddots & \cdots & \cdots \\ \vdots & \vdots & \vdots & \ddots & \vdots \\ l'_{n1} & l'_{n2} & \cdots & \cdots & 0 \end{bmatrix} X_m = \begin{bmatrix} 0 & m'_{12} & \cdots & \cdots & m'_{1n} \\ m'_{21} & 0 & \cdots & \cdots & m'_{2n} \\ \vdots & \vdots & \ddots & \cdots & \cdots \\ \vdots & \vdots & \vdots & \ddots & \vdots \\ m'_{n1} & m'_{n2} & \cdots & \cdots & 0 \end{bmatrix} X_u = \begin{bmatrix} 0 & u'_{12} & \cdots & \cdots & u'_{1n} \\ u'_{21} & 0 & \cdots & \cdots & u'_{2n} \\ \vdots & \vdots & \ddots & \cdots & \cdots \\ \vdots & \vdots & \vdots & \ddots & \vdots \\ u'_{n1} & u'_{n2} & \cdots & \cdots & 0 \end{bmatrix} \tag{2.6}$$

$$\widetilde{T} = \lim_{k \to \infty} \widetilde{X} + \widetilde{X}^2 + \ldots + \widetilde{X}^k \tag{2.7}$$

$$\widetilde{T} = \begin{bmatrix} \widetilde{t}_{11} & \widetilde{t}_{12} & \cdots & \cdots & \widetilde{t}_{1n} \\ \widetilde{t}_{21} & \widetilde{t}_{22} & \cdots & \cdots & \widetilde{t}_{2n} \\ \vdots & \vdots & \ddots & \cdots & \cdots \\ \vdots & \vdots & \vdots & \ddots & \vdots \\ \widetilde{t}_{n1} & \widetilde{t}_{n2} & \cdots & \cdots & \widetilde{t}_{nn} \end{bmatrix} \tag{2.8}$$

$$\widetilde{t}_{ij} = \left(l''_{ij}, m''_{ij}, u''_{ij}\right) \tag{2.9}$$

$$\left[l''_{ij}\right] = X_l \times (I - X_l)^{-1} \tag{2.10}$$

$$\left[m''_{ij}\right] = X_m \times (I - X_m)^{-1} \tag{2.11}$$

$$\left[u''_{ij}\right] = X_u \times (I - X_u)^{-1} \tag{2.12}$$

In the last step, the defuzzified total influence matrix is determined. For this purpose, $\widetilde{R}_i^{def}$ and $\widetilde{D}_i^{def}$ demonstrate the sum of all vector columns and the rows. In this framework, $\left(\widetilde{D}_i + \widetilde{R}_i\right)^{def}$ gives information about the total degree of the influence between the different criteria. Also, the value of $\left(\widetilde{D}_i - \widetilde{R}_i\right)^{def}$ shows the degree of causality. The Eqs. (2.13)–(2.21) summarize this process.

$$u_i^{max} = max\, u_i, l_i^{min} = \underset{j}{min}\, l_i \tag{2.13}$$

$$\Delta_{min}^{max} = u_i^{max} - l_i^{min} \tag{2.14}$$

$$x_{lj} = \left(l_{ij} - l_i^{min}\right)/\Delta_{min}^{max} \tag{2.15}$$

$$x_{mj} = \left(m_{ij} - l_i^{min}\right)/\Delta_{min}^{max} \tag{2.16}$$

$$x_{uj} = \left(u_{ij} - l_i^{min}\right)/\Delta_{min}^{max} \tag{2.17}$$

$$x_j^{ls} = x_{mj}/\left(1 + x_{mj} - x_{lj}\right) \tag{2.18}$$

$$x_j^{rs} = x_{uj}/\left(1 + x_{uj} - x_{mj}\right) \tag{2.19}$$

$$x_j^{crisp} = \left[x_j^{ls}\left(1 - x_j^{ls}\right) + x_j^{rs}x_j^{rs}\right]/\left[1 - x_j^{ls} + x_j^{rs}\right] \tag{2.20}$$

$$f_{ij} = l_i^{min} + x_j^{crisp}\Delta_{min}^{max} \tag{2.21}$$

Researchers used fuzzy DEMATEL approach for different industries, such as logistics (Tian et al., 2019; Yang et al., 2019), energy (Addae et al., 2019; Dinçer, Yüksel, & Pınarbaşı, 2019d; Abdullah et al., 2019; Cui et al., 2019; Dinçer & Yüksel, 2019a, 2019b; Yüksel et al., 2019), construction (Hatefi & Tamošaitienė, 2019), and banking (Dinçer, Yüksel, Pınarbaşı, and Çetiner 2019g; Dinçer, Yüksel, Yazici, and Pınarbaşı 2019h; Dinçer, Yüksel, & Çetiner, 2019b; Sepehri-Rad et al., 2019; Dinçer, Yüksel, & Martínez, 2019c; Dinçer, Uzunkaya, & Yüksel, 2019a; Dinçer & Yüksel, 2019c).

2.4.3 Analysis Results

In the first stage of the analysis process, the fuzzy DEMATEL approach is performed to select the most important indicators of the financial crisis. For this purpose, linguistic evaluations provided from a group of decision makers are used for analyzing the criteria and dimensions. Linguistic evaluations are constructed by using the influence level in Table 2.2.

Additionally, Tables 2.8–2.11 represent the weighting process of the macroeconomic factors. Accordingly, same procedure is also applied for the dimensions and their criteria. The overall weighting and ranking results are defined in Table 2.3.

According to the results of the fuzzy DEMATEL, the weights of the dimensions and criteria are defined. The findings show that macroeconomic factors (Dimension 1) have the highest importance. On the other side, external factors (Dimension 3) have a lower effect on the financial performance of the countries in comparison with

Table 2.2 Linguistic variables of the impact-relationship degrees

Influence level	Triangular fuzzy numbers		
No (N)	0	0	0.25
Low (L)	0	0.25	0.5
Medium (M)	0.25	0.5	0.75
High (H)	0.5	0.75	1
Very high (VH)	0.75	1	1

Source: Uygun et al. (2015); Uygun and Dede (2016); Khorasaninejad et al. (2016)

Table 2.3 Overall weighting and ranking results for the criteria

Dimensions	Weights	Criteria	Weights	Overall results	Ranking
Macroeconomic factors (Dimension 1)	0.282	Unemployment Rate (Criterion 1)	0.243	0.069	4
		Economic Growth (Criterion 2)	0.246	0.069	3
		Current Account Deficit (Criterion 3)	0.258	0.073	1
		Inflation Rate (Criterion 4)	0.253	0.071	2
Financial factors (Dimension 2)	0.239	Bank Capital to Asset Ratio (Criterion 5)	0.266	0.064	6
		Currency Exchange Rate (Criterion 6)	0.245	0.059	13
		NPL Ratio (Criterion 7)	0.260	0.062	8
		Central Bank Independence (Criterion 8)	0.228	0.055	16
External factors (Dimension 3)	0.231	Oil Price (Criterion 9)	0.243	0.056	15
		USD Interest Rate (Criterion 10)	0.247	0.057	14
		Foreign Financial Crisis (Criterion 11)	0.256	0.059	10
		External Migration (Criterion 12)	0.255	0.059	12
Internal factors (Dimension 4)	0.248	Industrial Production (Criterion 13)	0.262	0.065	5
		Elections (Criterion 14)	0.248	0.062	9
		Government Debt (Criterion 15)	0.253	0.063	7
		Internal Migration (Criterion 16)	0.238	0.059	11

other dimensions. In addition to the dimensions, 16 different criteria are weighted regarding their significance. As a result, the most important 8 criteria are selected which are Unemployment Rate (Criterion 1), Economic Growth (Criterion 2), Current Account Deficit (Criterion 3), Inflation Rate (Criterion 4), Bank Capital to Asset Ratio (Criterion 5), NPL Ratio (Criterion 7), Industrial Production (Criterion 13) and Government Debt (Criterion 15). Moreover, decision tree methodology is taken into consideration for these selected 8 criteria in order to understand the leading indicators of the global financial crisis for both developing and developed economies.

In this study growth, CAD, inflation, industry values of developed and undeveloped countries have been used to train machines about unemployment rate prediction. Values span years between 1991 and 2007. The machine has trained to predict the 2008 unemployment rate of each country whether it is less than the group average or not. Developed and developing countries grouped separately and algorithms have been run separately. During training machine discarded missing values which are more than 25%. Trainings of the machine have been conducted through two different algorithms: Decision Trees and Artificial Neural Networks.

Decision tree algorithms are supervised machine learning models, which generate a tree data structure that can be implemented to classify new cases or make predictions. Each predicted case is described by a set of features. These features or attributes may both be numeric or string values. The most widely used techniques to train a machine throughout the decision tree learning process are entropy gain or gini index calculations. In this study, we used the entropy gain technique which is known as C4.5 algorithm developed by Quinlan. Decision trees have been used to train machines for a great deal of real-world domains such as prediction of wine quality before fermentation is finished, heart disease diagnosis, credit—loan approval and so on.

At Artificial Neural Network training session, we used RPROP learning algorithm, which is developed for multilayer feedforward networks. RPROP avoids the common disadvantages of pure gradient-descent algorithms by performing a local adaptation of the weight-updates. In addition, RPROP also overcomes the problem of "blurred adaptivity," by changing the size of the weight-update directly. In this study, we used an Artificial Neural Networks with three hidden layers each contains ten neurons. The maximum number of iteration has been set as 1000. The detailed tables are given in the appendix part.

As it is seen in Tables 2.12–2.15, after the training session machine has selected the following attributes to predict if 2008 unemployment rate is above or below the average unemployment rate of developed countries. 1993 Growth, 1999 Inflation, 2000 Growth, 2006 CAD. They may be considered as the hidden factors or motive behind the 2008 unemployment rate. For developing countries, the machine has extracted a different motive. 2006 Inflation, 2007 Inflation, $2005 CAD, 2002 Industry, 2006 Industry, 2001 Inflation, 1999 Growth, 1999 Growth, 1994 Growth, 2003 Growth, 2000 Growth, 2007 Growth are the attributes selected by the machine and used for learning. The detailed results are also indicated in the appendix part.

2.5 Conclusion

In this study, it is aimed to identify the main determinants of the global financial crisis that occurred in 2008. Within this context, an evaluation is performed with the help of fuzzy DEMATEL and decision tree methods for both developing and developed economies. In the first part of the analysis, 16 different indicators are defined by making literature review. After that, these criteria are weighted with the help of fuzzy DEMATEL and the most significant 8 criteria are identified. In the final stage of the analysis, decision tree methodology is considered in order to understand the main factors of the financial crisis for both developing and developed economies.

As a result of the fuzzy DEMATEL, it is stated that macroeconomic factors (Dimension 1) have the highest importance whereas external factors (Dimension 3) have a lower effect on the financial performance of the countries. Additionally, the most important 8 criteria are selected which are Unemployment Rate (Criterion 1), Economic Growth (Criterion 2), Current Account Deficit (Criterion 3), Inflation Rate (Criterion 4), Bank Capital to Asset Ratio (Criterion 5), NPL Ratio (Criterion 7), Industrial Production (Criterion 13), and Government Debt (Criterion 15).

Moreover, decision tree methodology is taken into consideration for these selected 8 criteria in order to understand the leading indicators of the global financial crisis for both developing and developed economies. It is concluded that the growth rate and capital adequacy of the banking industry are accepted as the leading indicators of the global crisis for developed economies. Moreover, inflation and industry development are accepted as the indicator of the financial crisis in addition to the economic growth and capital adequacy of the banks regarding the developing economies.

The findings show that the growth rate and capital adequacy of the banking industry are accepted as the leading indicators of the global crisis for developed economies. While looking at these results, it is recommended that developed countries should periodically control economic growth rates to understand whether they have a financial crisis risk or not. In addition to this situation, it is also defined that capital adequacy ratio of the banks should also be taken into consideration. On the other side, with respect to the developing economies, inflation, and industry development are accepted as the indicator of the financial crisis in addition to the economic growth and capital adequacy of the banks. For these countries, it is recommended that inflation rate should be periodically controlled, and they should identify necessary actions in order to minimize inflation rate.

In this study, the main determinants of the financial crisis are identified. In this circumstance, fuzzy DEMATEL and decision tree methods are taken into consideration so that an original methodology is used. On the other hand, in future studies, different methods can be considered, such as interval type-2 fuzzy VIKOR. Owing to this issue, it can be possible to compare the results between different studies.

Appendix 1

Key Term and Definition

GDP: It is gross domestic product that can be calculated as the sum of consumption, private investment, government expenditure, and net export amount.

Appendix 2

Table 2.4 Rule set for developed countries which is generated by machine after training

Rule	Unemployment rate	Record count	Number of correct
($1993 Growth$ < = −0.5652863423208672)	Above average	10	9
($1999 Inflation$ < = 1.6309618820726448 AND $1993 Growth $ > −0.5652863423208672)	Below average	11	11
($2006 CAD$ < = −2.816890927219842 AND $2000 Growth$ < = 4.892841187163789 AND $1999 Inflation $ > 1.6309618820726448 AND $1993 Growth $ > −0.5652863423208672)	Above average	4	3
($2006 CAD$ > −2.816890927219842 AND $2000 Growth$ < = 4.892841187163789 AND $1999 Inflation $ > 1.6309618820726448 AND $1993 Growth $ > −0.5652863423208672)	Below average	6	6
($2000 Growth$ > 4.892841187163789 AND $1999 Inflation $ > 1.6309618820726448 AND $1993 Growth $ > −0.5652863423208672)	Above average	5	5

Table 2.5 Rule set for developing countries which is generated by machine after training

Rule	Unemployment rate	Record count	Number of correct
($2003 Growth$ < = −0.42996380535500833 AND $1999 Growth$ < = 2.9965766514127097 AND $2000 Growth$ < = 4.5894680655235955 AND $1994 Growth$ < = 3.865152800274579)	Below average	4	3
($2003 Growth$ > −0.42996380535500833 AND $1999 Growth$ < = 2.9965766514127097 AND $2000 Growth$ < = 4.5894680655235955 AND $1994 Growth$ < = 3.865152800274579)	Above average	25	24
($2005 CAD$ < = −7.2875681093217075 AND $1999 Growth $ > 2.9965766514127097 AND $2000 Growth$ < = 4.5894680655235955 AND $1994 Growth$ < = 3.865152800274579)	Below average	5	5
($2007 Inflation$ < = 1.1898880683354265 AND $2007 Growth$ < = 9.136795046349853 AND $2005 CAD $ > −7.2875681093217075 AND $1999 Growth $ > 2.9965766514127097 AND $2000 Growth$ < = 4.5894680655235955 AND $1994 Growth$ < = 3.865152800274579)	Below average	2	2
($2005 Industry$ < = 21.263062220357305 AND $2002 Industry$ < = 22.278529392209613 AND $2007 Inflation $ > 1.1898880683354265 AND $2007 Growth$ < = 9.136795046349853 AND $2005 CAD $ > −7.2875681093217075 AND $1999 Growth $ > 2.9965766514127097 AND $2000 Growth$ < = 4.5894680655235955 AND $1994 Growth$ < = 3.865152800274579)	Above average	3	3

(continued)

Table 2.5 (continued)

Rule	Unemployment rate	Record count	Number of correct
($2005 Industry$ > 21.263062220357305 AND $2002 Industry$ < = 22.278529392209613 AND $2007 Inflation $ > 1.1898880683354265 AND $2007 Growth$ < = 9.136795046349853 AND $2005 CAD $ > −7.2875681093217075 AND $1999 Growth $ > 2.9965766514127097 AND $2000 Growth$ < = 4.5894680655235955 AND $1994 Growth$ < = 3.865152800274579)	Below average	3	3
($2002 Industry$ > 22.278529392209613 AND $2007 Inflation $ > 1.1898880683354265 AND $2007 Growth$ < = 9.136795046349853 AND $2005 CAD $ > −7.2875681093217075 AND $1999 Growth $ > 2.9965766514127097 AND $2000 Growth$ < = 4.5894680655235955 AND $1994 Growth$ < = 3.865152800274579)	Above average	11	11
($2007 Growth$ > 9.136795046349853 AND $2005 CAD $ > −7.2875681093217075 AND $1999 Growth $ > 2.9965766514127097 AND $2000 Growth$ < = 4.5894680655235955 AND $1994 Growth$ < = 3.865152800274579)	Below average	4	4
($2002 Growth$ < = 1.8237542395982942 AND $2005 Growth$ < = 3.894378315914274 AND $2002 Inflation$ < = 8.192065762707895 AND $2000 Growth $ > 4.5894680655235955 AND $1994 Growth$ < = 3.865152800274579)	Above average	3	3
($2002 Growth$ > 1.8237542395982942 AND $2005 Growth$ < =	Below average	3	3

(continued)

Table 2.5 (continued)

Rule	Unemployment rate	Record count	Number of correct
3.894378315914274 AND \$2002 Inflation\$ < = 8.192065762707895 AND \$2000 Growth \$ > 4.5894680655235955 AND \$1994 Growth\$ < = 3.865152800274579)			
(\$2005 Growth\$ > 3.894378315914274 AND \$2002 Inflation\$ < = 8.192065762707895 AND \$2000 Growth \$ > 4.5894680655235955 AND \$1994 Growth\$ < = 3.865152800274579)	Below average	21	20
(\$2005 Inflation\$ < = 9.15186771421736 AND \$2002 Inflation \$ > 8.192065762707895 AND \$2000 Growth \$ > 4.5894680655235955 AND \$1994 Growth\$ < = 3.865152800274579)	Above average	8	8
(\$2005 Inflation\$ > 9.15186771421736 AND \$2002 Inflation \$ > 8.192065762707895 AND \$2000 Growth \$ > 4.5894680655235955 AND \$1994 Growth\$ < = 3.865152800274579)	Below average	6	5
(\$1996 Growth\$ < = 1.8938011133155328 AND \$1999 Growth\$ < = −1.8641107990029369 AND \$1999 Growth\$ < = 11.083889257093936 AND \$1994 Growth \$ > 3.865152800274579)	Below average	4	3
(\$1996 Growth\$ > 1.8938011133155328 AND \$1999 Growth\$ < = −1.8641107990029369 AND \$1999 Growth\$ < = 11.083889257093936 AND \$1994 Growth \$ > 3.865152800274579)	Above average	5	5
(\$2001 Inflation\$ < = −4.815302094061063 AND \$1999 Growth \$ > −1.8641107990029369 AND \$1999 Growth\$ < = 11.083889257093936	Above average	2	2

(continued)

Table 2.5 (continued)

Rule	Unemployment rate	Record count	Number of correct
AND $1994 Growth $ > 3.865152800274579)			
($2006 Industry$ < = 19.39700183758328 AND $2001 Inflation $ > −4.815302094061063 AND $1999 Growth $ > −1.8641107990029369 AND $1999 Growth$ < = 11.083889257093936 AND $1994 Growth $ > 3.865152800274579)	Below average	18	18
($2006 Inflation$ < = 7.5823218312795255 AND $2005 CAD$ < = −10.187316098345043 AND $2006 Industry $ > 19.39700183758328 AND $2001 Inflation $ > −4.815302094061063 AND $1999 Growth $ > −1.8641107990029369 AND $1999 Growth$ < = 11.083889257093936 AND $1994 Growth $ > 3.865152800274579)	Above average	5	5
($2006 Inflation$ > 7.5823218312795255 AND $2005 CAD$ < = −10.187316098345043 AND $2006 Industry $ > 19.39700183758328 AND $2001 Inflation $ > −4.815302094061063 AND $1999 Growth $ > −1.8641107990029369 AND $1999 Growth$ < = 11.083889257093936 AND $1994 Growth $ > 3.865152800274579)	Below average	2	2
($2004 Growth$ < = 4.485156340099337 AND $2007 Growth$ < = 5.163473687871964 AND $2005 CAD $ > −10.187316098345043 AND $2006 Industry $ > 19.39700183758328 AND $2001 Inflation $ > −4.815302094061063 AND $1999 Growth $ > −1.8641107990029369	Below average	6	5

(continued)

Table 2.5 (continued)

Rule	Unemployment rate	Record count	Number of correct
AND $1999 Growth$ < = 11.083889257093936 AND $1994 Growth $ > 3.865152800274579)			
($2004 Growth$ > 4.485156340099337 AND $2007 Growth$ < = 5.163473687871964 AND $2005 CAD $ > −10.187316098345043 AND $2006 Industry $ > 19.39700183758328 AND $2001 Inflation $ > −4.815302094061063 AND $1999 Growth $ > −1.8641107990029369 AND $1999 Growth$ < = 11.083889257093936 AND $1994 Growth $ > 3.865152800274579)	Above average	4	4
($2007 Growth$ > 5.163473687871964 AND $2005 CAD $ > −10.187316098345043 AND $2006 Industry $ > 19.39700183758328 AND $2001 Inflation $ > −4.815302094061063 AND $1999 Growth $ > −1.8641107990029369 AND $1999 Growth$ < = 11.083889257093936 AND $1994 Growth $ > 3.865152800274579)	Below average	32	30
($1999 Growth$ > 11.083889257093936 AND $1994 Growth $ > 3.865152800274579)	Above average	3	3

Table 2.6 The developed countries analyzed in the study

Country name
United Arab Emirates
Australia
Austria
Belgium
Canada
Switzerland
Cyprus
Czech Republic
Germany
Denmark
Spain
Estonia
Finland
France
United Kingdom
Greece
Hong Kong SAR, China
Ireland
Iceland
Israel
Italy
Japan
Korea, Rep.
Liechtenstein
Luxembourg
Monaco
Malta
Netherlands
Norway
New Zealand
Korea, Dem. People's Rep.
Portugal
Slovak Republic
Slovenia
Sweden
United States

Table 2.7 The developing countries analyzed in the study

Country name
Aruba
Afghanistan
Angola
Albania
Andorra
Argentina
Armenia
American Samoa
Antigua and Barbuda
Azerbaijan
Burundi
Benin
Burkina Faso
Bangladesh
Bulgaria
Bahrain
Bahamas, The
Bosnia and Herzegovina
Belarus
Belize
Bermuda
Bolivia
Brazil
Barbados
Brunei Darussalam
Bhutan
Botswana
Central African Republic
Channel Islands
Chile
China
Cote d'Ivoire
Cameroon
Congo, Dem. Rep.
Congo, Rep.
Colombia
Comoros
Cabo Verde
Costa Rica
Caribbean small states
Cuba
Curacao

(continued)

Table 2.7 (continued)

Country name
Cayman Islands
Djibouti
Dominica
Dominican Republic
Algeria
Ecuador
Egypt, Arab Rep.
Eritrea
Ethiopia
Fiji
Faroe Islands
Micronesia, Fed. Sts.
Gabon
Georgia
Ghana
Gibraltar
Guinea
Gambia, The
Guinea-Bissau
Equatorial Guinea
Grenada
Greenland
Guatemala
Guam
Guyana
Honduras
Croatia
Haiti
Hungary
Indonesia
India
Iran, Islamic Rep.
Iraq
Jamaica
Jordan
Kazakhstan
Kenya
Kyrgyz Republic
Cambodia
Kiribati
St. Kitts and Nevis
Kuwait

(continued)

Table 2.7 (continued)

Country name
Lao PDR
Lebanon
Liberia
Libya
St. Lucia
Sri Lanka
Lesotho
Lithuania
Latvia
Macao SAR, China
St. Martin (French part)
Morocco
Moldova
Madagascar
Maldives
Mexico
Marshall Islands
North Macedonia
Mali
Myanmar
Montenegro
Mongolia
Northern Mariana Islands
Mozambique
Mauritania
Mauritius
Malawi
Malaysia
Namibia
New Caledonia
Niger
Nigeria
Nicaragua
Nepal
Nauru
Oman
Pakistan
Panama
Peru
Philippines
Palau
Papua New Guinea

(continued)

Table 2.7 (continued)

Country name
Poland
Puerto Rico
Paraguay
Qatar
Romania
Russian Federation
Rwanda
South Asia
Saudi Arabia
Sudan
Senegal
Singapore
Solomon Islands
Sierra Leone
El Salvador
San Marino
Somalia
Serbia
South Sudan
Sao Tome and Principe
Suriname
Eswatini
Sint Maarten (Dutch part)
Seychelles
Syrian Arab Republic
Turks and Caicos Islands
Chad
Togo
Thailand
Tajikistan
Turkmenistan
Timor-Leste
Tonga
Trinidad and Tobago
Tunisia
Turkey
Tuvalu
Tanzania
Uganda
Ukraine
Uruguay
Uzbekistan

(continued)

Table 2.7 (continued)

Country name
St. Vincent and the Grenadines
Venezuela, RB
Virgin Islands (USA)
Vietnam
Vanuatu
Samoa
Kosovo
Yemen, Rep.
South Africa
Zambia
Zimbabwe

Table 2.8 Initial direct-relation fuzzy matrix

	C1			C2			C3			C4		
Unemployment rate (C1)	0.000	0.000	0.000	0.200	0.450	0.700	0.350	0.600	0.850	0.300	0.550	0.800
Economic growth (C2)	0.300	0.550	0.800	0.000	0.000	0.000	0.450	0.700	0.950	0.350	0.600	0.850
Current account deficit (C3)	0.250	0.500	0.750	0.250	0.500	0.750	0.000	0.000	0.000	0.300	0.550	0.800
Inflation (C4)	0.300	0.550	0.800	0.250	0.500	0.650	0.450	0.700	0.950	0.000	0.000	0.000

Table 2.9 Normalized direct-relation fuzzy matrix

	C1			C2			C3			C4		
C1	0.000	0.000	0.000	0.077	0.173	0.269	0.135	0.231	0.327	0.115	0.212	0.308
C2	0.115	0.212	0.308	0.000	0.000	0.000	0.173	0.269	0.365	0.135	0.231	0.327
C3	0.096	0.192	0.288	0.096	0.192	0.288	0.000	0.000	0.000	0.115	0.212	0.308
C4	0.115	0.212	0.308	0.096	0.192	0.250	0.173	0.269	0.365	0.000	0.000	0.000

Table 2.10 Total-relation fuzzy matrix

	C1			C2			C3			C4		
C1	0.050	0.297	2.805	0.114	0.423	2.790	0.188	0.544	3.408	0.158	0.487	3.132
C2	0.166	0.510	3.270	0.054	0.311	2.789	0.237	0.616	3.689	0.188	0.541	3.380
C3	0.135	0.452	2.989	0.128	0.430	2.764	0.067	0.349	3.116	0.156	0.480	3.090
C4	0.161	0.494	3.080	0.137	0.457	2.816	0.229	0.597	3.475	0.063	0.336	2.938

Table 2.11 Defuzzified total relation matrix and weights

	C1	C2	C3	C4	$\left(\widetilde{D}_i + \widetilde{R}_i\right)^{def}$	$\left(\widetilde{D}_i - \widetilde{R}_i\right)^{def}$	Weights
C1	0.732	0.831	1.021	0.936	7.048	−0.008	0.243
C2	0.982	0.743	1.128	1.023	7.143	0.609	0.246
C3	0.879	0.828	0.814	0.916	7.473	−0.601	0.258
C4	0.936	0.864	1.075	0.785	7.320	0.000	0.253

Table 2.12 Developed countries Decision Tree Accuracy Statistics of prediction

	True pos	False pos	True neg	False neg
Less than average	19.00	0.00	17.00	0.00
Equal or higher than average	17.00	0.00	19.00	0.00
Overall	18.00	0.00	18.00	0.00
	Recall	Precision	Sensitivity	Specifity
Less than average	1.00	1.00	1.00	1.00
Equal or higher than average	1.00	1.00	1.00	1.00
Overall	1.00	1.00	1.00	1.00
	F-Measure	Over all accuracy	Overall Cohen's Kappa	
Less than average	1.00	–	–	
Equal or higher than average	1.00	–	–	
Overall	1.00	1.00	1.00	

Table 2.13 Developing countries Decision Tree Accuracy Statistics of prediction

	True pos	False pos	True neg	False neg
Less than average	103.00	7.00	68.00	1.00
Equal or higher than average	68.00	1.00	103.00	7.00
Overall	85.50	4.00	85.50	4.00
	Recall	Precision	Sensitivity	Specificity
Less than average	0.99	0.94	0.99	0.91
Equal or higher than average	0.91	0.99	0.91	0.99
Overall	0.95	0.96	0.95	0.95
	F-Measure	Over all accuracy	Overall Cohen's Kappa	
Less than average	0.96	–	–	
Equal or higher than average	0.94	–	–	
Overall	0.95	0.96	0.91	

Table 2.14 Developed countries Artificial Neural Networks Accuracy Statistics

	True pos	False pos	True neg	False neg
Less than average	19.00	0.00	17.00	0.00
Equal or higher than average	17.00	0.00	19.00	0.00
Overall	18.00	0.00	18.00	0.00
	Recall	Precision	Sensitivity	Specificity
Less than average	1.00	1.00	1.00	1.00
Equal or higher than average	1.00	1.00	1.00	1.00
Overall	1.00	1.00	1.00	1.00
	F-Measure	Overall accuracy	Overall Cohen's Kappa	
Less than average	1.00	–	–	
Equal or higher than average	1.00	–	–	
Overall	1.00	1.00	1.00	

Table 2.15 Developing countries Artificial Neural Networks Accuracy Statistics

	True pos	False pos	True neg	False neg
Less than average	103.00	5.00	70.00	1.00
Equal or higher than average	70.00	1.00	103.00	5.00
Overall	86.50	3.00	86.50	3.00
	Recall	Precision	Sensitivity	Specificity
Less than average	0.99	0.95	0.99	0.93
Equal or higher than average	0.93	0.99	0.93	0.99
Overall	0.96	0.97	0.96	0.96
	F-Measure	Over all accuracy	Overall Cohen's Kappa	
Less than average	0.97	–	–	
Equal or higher than average	0.96	–	–	
Overall	0.97	0.97	0.93	

References

Abdullah, L., Zulkifli, N., Liao, H., Herrera-Viedma, E., & Al-Barakati, A. (2019). An interval-valued intuitionistic fuzzy DEMATEL method combined with Choquet integral for sustainable solid waste management. *Engineering Applications of Artificial Intelligence, 82*, 207–215.

Addae, B. A., Zhang, L., Zhou, P., & Wang, F. (2019). Analyzing barriers of Smart Energy City in Accra with two-step fuzzy DEMATEL. *Cities, 89*, 218–227.

Ahmed, S., Bertaut, C., Liu, J., & Vigfusson, R. (2018). Should we be concerned again about US current account sustainability?. *IFDP Notes*. Board of Governors of the Federal Reserve System.

Alessandri, P., & Mumtaz, H. (2017). Financial conditions and density forecasts for US output and inflation. *Review of Economic Dynamics, 24*, 66–78.

An, G., Becker, C. M., & Cheng, E. (2017). Economic crisis, income gaps, uncertainty, and inter-regional migration responses: Kazakhstan 2000–2014. *The Journal of Development Studies, 53* (9), 1452–1470.

Apergis, N., & Cooray, A. (2018). The behaviour of interest rate spreads prior to and after the financial crisis: Evidence across OECD countries. *The Manchester School, 86*(5), 559–585.

Asongu, S. A., & De Moor, L. (2017). Financial globalisation dynamic thresholds for financial development: evidence from Africa. *The European Journal of Development Research, 29*(1), 192–212.

Asteriou, D., & Spanos, K. (2019). The relationship between financial development and economic growth during the recent crisis: Evidence from the EU. *Finance Research Letters, 28*, 238–245.

Baimbridge, M., Litsios, I., Jackson, K., & Lee, U. R. (2017). The Eurozone Crisis: Current account imbalances, budget deficits and national debt. In *The segmentation of Europe* (pp. 119–140). Palgrave Macmillan.

Bartz, W., & Winkler, A. (2016). Flexible or fragile? The growth performance of small and young businesses during the global financial crisis—Evidence from Germany. *Journal of Business Venturing, 31*(2), 196–215.

Basheer, M., Ahmad, A., & Hassan, S. (2019). Impact of economic and financial factors on tax revenue: Evidence from the Middle East countries. *Accounting, 5*(2), 53–60.

Baumeister, C., & Kilian, L. (2016). Forty years of oil price fluctuations: Why the price of oil may still surprise us. *Journal of Economic Perspectives, 30*(1), 139–160.

Bekiros, S., Nilavongse, R., & Uddin, G. S. (2018). Bank capital shocks and countercyclical requirements: Implications for banking stability and welfare. *Journal of Economic Dynamics and Control, 93*, 315–331.

Ben Ayed, M., Karaa, A., & Prigent, J. L. (2018). Duration models for credit rating migration: Evidence from the financial crisis. *Economic Inquiry, 56*(3), 1870–1886.

Bénétrix, A. S., Lane, P. R., & Shambaugh, J. C. (2015). International currency exposures, valuation effects and the global financial crisis. *Journal of International Economics, 96*, S98–S109.

Bhagat, R. B. (2016). Changing pattern of internal migration in India. In *Contemporary demographic transformations in China, India and Indonesia* (pp. 239–254). Springer.

Borio, C. (2016). On the centrality of the current account in international economics. *Journal of International Money and Finance, 68*, 266–274.

Byun, S. J., & Chang, K. C. (2015). Volatility risk premium in the interest rate market: Evidence from delta-hedged gains on USD interest rate swaps. *International Review of Financial Analysis, 40*, 88–102.

Cerna, L., & Czaika, M. (2016). European policies to attract talent: The crisis and highly skilled migration policy changes. In *High-skill migration and recession* (pp. 22–43). Palgrave Macmillan.

Chen, Q., Filardo, A., He, D., & Zhu, F. (2016). Financial crisis, US unconventional monetary policy and international spillovers. *Journal of International Money and Finance, 67*, 62–81.

Chernov, M., Graveline, J., & Zviadadze, I. (2018). Crash risk in currency returns. *Journal of Financial and Quantitative Analysis, 53*(1), 137–170.

Christodoulou, C., Efstathiou, V., Michopoulos, I., Ferentinos, P., Korkoliakou, P., Gkerekou, M., … Douzenis, A. (2017). A case-control study of hopelessness and suicidal behavior in the city of Athens, Greece. The role of the financial crisis. *Psychology, Health & Medicine, 22*(7), 772–777.

Chuen, D. L. K. (Ed.). (2015). *Handbook of digital currency: Bitcoin, innovation, financial instruments, and big data*. Academic Press.

Cooper, R., & Nikolov, K. (2018). Government debt and banking fragility: The spreading of strategic uncertainty. *International Economic Review, 59*(4), 1905–1925.

Cui, L., Chan, H. K., Zhou, Y., Dai, J., & Lim, J. J. (2019). Exploring critical factors of green business failure based on Grey-Decision Making Trial and Evaluation Laboratory (DEMATEL). *Journal of Business Research, 98*, 450–461.

Dijkstra, L., Garcilazo, E., & McCann, P. (2015). The effects of the global financial crisis on European regions and cities. *Journal of Economic Geography, 15*(5), 935–949.

Dinçer, H., & Yüksel, S. (2018). Financial sector-based analysis of the G20 economies using the integrated decision-making approach with DEMATEL and TOPSIS. In *Emerging trends in banking and finance* (pp. 210–223). Springer.

Dinçer, H., & Yüksel, S. (2019a). Multidimensional evaluation of global investments on the renewable energy with the integrated fuzzy decision-making model under the hesitancy. *International Journal of Energy Research*. https://doi.org/10.1002/er.4400.

Dinçer, H., & Yüksel, S. (2019b). Balanced scorecard-based analysis of investment decisions for the renewable energy alternatives: A comparative analysis based on the hybrid fuzzy decision-making approach. *Energy, 175*, 1259–1270.

Dinçer, H., & Yüksel, S. (2019c). IT2-based fuzzy hybrid decision making approach to soft computing. *IEEE Access, 7*, 15932–15944.

Dinçer, H., Hacıoğlu, Ü., & Yüksel, S. (2017). A strategic approach to global financial crisis in banking sector: A critical appraisal of banking strategies using fuzzy ANP and fuzzy TOPSIS methods. *International Journal of Sustainable Economies Management (IJSEM), 6*(1), 1–21.

Dinçer, H., Hacıoğlu, Ü., & Yüksel, S. (2018). Determining influencing factors of currency exchange rate for decision making in global economy using MARS method. In *Geopolitics and strategic management in the global economy* (pp. 261–273). IGI Global.

Dinçer, H., Yüksel, S., & Adalı, Z. (2018a). Relationship between non-performing loans, industry, and economic growth of the African economies and policy recommendations for global growth. In *Globalization and trade integration in developing countries* (pp. 203–228). IGI Global.

Dinçer, H., Yüksel, S., & Şenel, S. (2018b). Analyzing the global risks for the financial crisis after the great depression using comparative hybrid hesitant fuzzy decision-making models: Policy recommendations for sustainable economic growth. *Sustainability, 10*(9), 3126.

Dinçer, H., Uzunkaya, S. S., & Yüksel, S. (2019a). An IT2-based hybrid decision-making model using hesitant fuzzy linguistic term sets for selecting the development plan of financial economics. *International Journal of Computational Intelligence Systems, 12*(2), 460–473.

Dinçer, H., Yüksel, S., & Çetiner, İ. T. (2019b). Strategy selection for organizational performance of Turkish banking sector with the integrated multi-dimensional decision-making approach. In *Handbook of research on contemporary approaches in management and organizational strategy* (pp. 273–291). IGI Global.

Dinçer, H., Yüksel, S., & Martínez, L. (2019c). Interval type 2-based hybrid fuzzy evaluation of financial services in E7 economies with DEMATEL-ANP and MOORA methods. *Applied Soft Computing, 79*, 186–202.

Dinçer, H., Yüksel, S., & Pınarbaşı, F. (2019d). SERVQUAL-based evaluation of service quality of energy companies in Turkey: Strategic policies for sustainable economic development. In *The circular economy and its implications on sustainability and the green supply chain* (pp. 142–167). IGI Global.

Dinçer, H., Yüksel, S., Adalı, Z., & Aydın, R. (2019e). Evaluating the role of research and development and technology investments on economic development of E7 countries. In *Organizational transformation and managing innovation in the fourth industrial revolution* (pp. 245–263). IGI Global.

Dinçer, H., Yüksel, S., Korsakienė, R., Raišienė, A. G., & Bilan, Y. (2019f). IT2 hybrid decision-making approach to performance measurement of internationalized firms in the baltic states. *Sustainability, 11*(1), 296.

Dinçer, H., Yüksel, S., Pınarbaşı, F., & Çetiner, İ. T. (2019g). Measurement of economic and banking stability in emerging markets by considering income inequality and nonperforming loans. In *Maintaining financial stability in times of risk and uncertainty* (pp. 49–68). IGI Global.

Dinçer, H., Yüksel, S., Yazici, M., & Pınarbaşı, F. (2019h). Assessing corporate social responsibilities in the banking sector: As a tool of strategic communication during the global financial crisis. In *Handbook of research on global issues in financial communication and investment decision making* (pp. 1–27). IGI Global.

Doumpos, M., Gaganis, C., & Pasiouras, F. (2015). Central bank independence, financial supervision structure and bank soundness: An empirical analysis around the crisis. *Journal of Banking & Finance, 61*, S69–S83.

Drydakis, N. (2015). The effect of unemployment on self-reported health and mental health in Greece from 2008 to 2013: A longitudinal study before and during the financial crisis. *Social Science & Medicine, 128*, 43–51.

Dua, P., & Tuteja, D. (2016). Financial crises and dynamic linkages across international stock and currency markets. *Economic Modelling, 59*, 249–261.

Economou, M., Angelopoulos, E., Peppou, L. E., Souliotis, K., & Stefanis, C. (2016). Major depression amid financial crisis in Greece: Will unemployment narrow existing gender differences in the prevalence of the disorder in Greece? *Psychiatry Research, 242*, 260–261.

Ehrmann, M., & Fratzscher, M. (2017). Euro area government bonds—Fragmentation and contagion during the sovereign debt crisis. *Journal of International Money and Finance, 70*, 26–44.

Fatum, R., & Yamamoto, Y. (2016). Intra-safe haven currency behavior during the global financial crisis. *Journal of International Money and Finance, 66*, 49–64.

Floyd, E., Li, N., & Skinner, D. J. (2015). Payout policy through the financial crisis: The growth of repurchases and the resilience of dividends. *Journal of Financial Economics, 118*(2), 299–316.

Foster, C., & Frieden, J. (2017). Crisis of trust: Socio-economic determinants of Europeans' confidence in government. *European Union Politics, 18*(4), 511–535.

Fraser, N. (2017). A triple movement? Parsing the politics of crisis after Polanyi. In *Beyond neoliberalism* (pp. 29–42). Palgrave Macmillan.

Friedrich, C. (2016). Global inflation dynamics in the post-crisis period: What explains the puzzles? *Economics Letters, 142*, 31–34.

Funke, M., Schularick, M., & Trebesch, C. (2016). Going to extremes: Politics after financial crises, 1870–2014. *European Economic Review, 88*, 227–260.

Garriga, A. C. (2016). Central bank independence in the world: A new data set. *International Interactions, 42*(5), 849–868.

Griffiths, J. F. (2019). *Latin American political economy: Financial crisis and political change*. Routledge.

de Haan, J., Bodea, C., Hicks, R., & Eijffinger, S. C. (2018). Central bank independence before and after the crisis. *Comparative Economic Studies, 60*(2), 183–202.

Hall, R. E. (2015). Quantifying the lasting harm to the US economy from the financial crisis. *NBER Macroeconomics Annual, 29*(1), 71–128.

Hatefi, S. M., & Tamošaitienė, J. (2019). An integrated fuzzy DEMATEL-fuzzy ANP model for evaluating construction projects by considering interrelationships among risk factors. *Journal of Civil Engineering and Management, 25*(2), 114–131.

Hernández, E., & Kriesi, H. (2016). The electoral consequences of the financial and economic crisis in Europe. *European Journal of Political Research, 55*(2), 203–224.

Ho, P. H., Huang, C. W., Lin, C. Y., & Yen, J. F. (2016). CEO overconfidence and financial crisis: Evidence from bank lending and leverage. *Journal of Financial Economics, 120*(1), 194–209.

Hobolt, S. B., & De Vries, C. (2016). Turning against the Union? The impact of the crisis on the Eurosceptic vote in the 2014 European Parliament elections. *Electoral Studies, 44*, 504–514.

Karanikolos, M., Heino, P., McKee, M., Stuckler, D., & Legido-Quigley, H. (2016). Effects of the global financial crisis on health in high-income OECD countries: A narrative review. *International Journal of Health Services, 46*(2), 208–240.

Kentikelenis, A. (2018). Intersecting crises: Migration, the economy and the right to health in Europe. *European Journal of Public Health, 28*(Suppl_5), 61–62.

Khorasaninejad, E., Fetanat, A., & Hajabdollahi, H. (2016). Prime mover selection in thermal power plant integrated with organic Rankine cycle for waste heat recovery using a novel multi criteria decision making approach. *Applied Thermal Engineering, 102*, 1262–1279.

Kim, B. H., Kim, H., & Lee, B. S. (2015). Spillover effects of the US financial crisis on financial markets in emerging Asian countries. *International Review of Economics & Finance, 39*, 192–210.

Kocaarslan, B., Soytas, U., Sari, R., & Ugurlu, E. (2018). The changing role of financial stress, oil price, and gold price in financial contagion among US and BRIC markets. *International Review of Finance, 19*(3), 541–574.

Kunieda, T., & Shibata, A. (2016). Asset bubbles, economic growth, and a self-fulfilling financial crisis. *Journal of Monetary Economics, 82*, 70–84.

Laanani, M., Ghosn, W., Jougla, E., & Rey, G. (2015). Impact of unemployment variations on suicide mortality in Western European countries (2000–2010). *Journal of Epidemiology and Community Health, 69*(2), 103–109.

Lane, P. R. (2015). A financial perspective on the UK current account deficit. *National Institute Economic Review, 234*(1), F67–F72.

Lane, P. R., & Milesi-Ferretti, G. M. (2018). The external wealth of nations revisited: International financial integration in the aftermath of the global financial crisis. *IMF Economic Review, 66*(1), 189–222.

Lee, N., Sameen, H., & Cowling, M. (2015). Access to finance for innovative SMEs since the financial crisis. *Research Policy, 44*(2), 370–380.

Lennartz, C., Arundel, R., & Ronald, R. (2016). Younger adults and homeownership in Europe through the global financial crisis. *Population, Space and Place, 22*(8), 823–835.

Lins, K. V., Servaes, H., & Tamayo, A. (2017). Social capital, trust, and firm performance: The value of corporate social responsibility during the financial crisis. *The Journal of Finance, 72* (4), 1785–1824.

Marques, A. C., Fuinhas, J. A., & Menegaki, A. N. (2016). Renewable vs non-renewable electricity and the industrial production nexus: Evidence from an ARDL bounds test approach for Greece. *Renewable Energy, 96*, 645–655.

Mohaddes, K., Raissi, M., & Weber, A. (2017). Can Italy grow out of its NPL overhang? A panel threshold analysis. *Economics Letters, 159*, 185–189.

Morgan, P. J., & Zhang, Y. (2017). Mortgage lending, banking crises, and financial stability in Asia and Europe. *Asia Europe Journal, 15*(4), 463–482.

Mukhtarov, S., Yüksel, S., & Mammadov, E. (2018). Factors that increase credit risk of Azerbaijani banks. *Journal of International Studies, 11*(2), 63–75.

Oktar, S., & Yüksel, S. (2015a). 1998 Yılında Rusya'da Yaşanan Bankacılık Krizi Ve Öncü Göstergeleri. *Marmara University Journal of Economic & Administrative Sciences, 37*(2), 327–340.

Oktar, S., & Yüksel, S. (2015b). *Bankacılık krizlerinin erken uyarı sinyalleri: Türkiye üzerine bir uygulama*. Academic Press.

Ozili, P. K. (2019). Non-performing loans and financial development: New evidence. *The Journal of Risk Finance, 20*(1), 59–81.

Palomares-Linares, I., & van Ham, M. (2018). Understanding the effects of homeownership and regional unemployment levels on internal migration during the economic crisis in Spain. *Regional Studies*, 1, 515–12, 526.

Parmar, D., Stavropoulou, C., & Ioannidis, J. P. (2016). Health outcomes during the 2008 financial crisis in Europe: systematic literature review. *BMJ, 354*, i4588.

Pavli, A., Lymperi, I., Minitsios, T., Katerelos, P., Souli, M., Ouzounidou, Z., & Maltezou, H. C. (2019). Changing trends and pretravel preparation of business travelers from Greece during the financial crisis. *Public Health, 168*, 168–171.

Perles-Ribes, J. F., Ramón-Rodríguez, A. B., Rubia, A., & Moreno-Izquierdo, L. (2017). Is the tourism-led growth hypothesis valid after the global economic and financial crisis? The case of Spain 1957–2014. *Tourism Management, 61*, 96–109.

Polyakova, A., & Fligstein, N. (2016). Is European integration causing Europe to become more nationalist? Evidence from the 2007–9 financial crisis. *Journal of European Public Policy, 23* (1), 60–83.

Rafindadi, A. A., & Ozturk, I. (2016). Effects of financial development, economic growth and trade on electricity consumption: Evidence from post-Fukushima Japan. *Renewable and Sustainable Energy Reviews, 54*, 1073–1084.

Sepehri-Rad, A., Sadjadi, S., & Sadi-Nezhad, S. (2019). An application of DEMATEL for transaction authentication in online banking. *International Journal of Data and Network Science, 3*(2), 71–76.

Stiglitz, J. E. (2016). How to restore equitable and sustainable economic growth in the United States. *American Economic Review, 106*(5), 43–47.

Sui, L., & Sun, L. (2016). Spillover effects between exchange rates and stock prices: Evidence from BRICS around the recent global financial crisis. *Research in International Business and Finance, 36*, 459–471.

Theodossiou, G., Rigas, I., Thanou, E., & Goulas, A. (2017, April). Financial crisis and brain drain: An investigation of the emigration intentions of Greek scientists. In *9th International Conference: 'The Economies of Balkan and Eastern Europe Countries in the Changed World'* EBEEC (pp. 28–30). Athens, Greece.

Tian, G., Liu, X., Zhang, M., Yang, Y., Zhang, H., Lin, Y., . . . Li, Z. (2019). Selection of take-back pattern of vehicle reverse logistics in China via Grey-DEMATEL and Fuzzy-VIKOR combined method. *Journal of Cleaner Production, 220*, 1088–1100.

Torrubiano-Domínguez, J., Vives-Cases, C., San-Sebastián, M., Sanz-Barbero, B., Goicolea, I., & Álvarez-Dardet, C. (2015). No effect of unemployment on intimate partner-related femicide during the financial crisis: A longitudinal ecological study in Spain. *BMC Public Health, 15*(1), 990.

Tsai, C. L. (2015). How do US stock returns respond differently to oil price shocks pre-crisis, within the financial crisis, and post-crisis? *Energy Economics, 50*, 47–62.

Uygun, Ö., & Dede, A. (2016). Performance evaluation of green supply chain management using integrated fuzzy multi-criteria decision making techniques. *Computers & Industrial Engineering, 102*, 502–511.

Uygun, Ö., Kahveci, T. C., Taşkın, H., & Piriştine, B. (2015). Readiness assessment model for institutionalization of SMEs using fuzzy hybrid MCDM techniques. *Computers & Industrial Engineering, 88*, 217–228.

Yang, C., Lan, S., & Tseng, M. L. (2019). Coordinated development path of metropolitan logistics and economy in Belt and Road using DEMATEL–Bayesian analysis. *International Journal of Logistics Research and Applications, 22*(1), 1–24.

Yüksel, S. (2016a). Bankaların Takipteki Krediler Oranını Belirleyen Faktörler: Türkiye İçin Bir Model Önerisi. *Bankacılar Dergisi, 98*, 41–56.

Yüksel, S. (2016b). Rusya Ekonomisinde Büyüme, Issizlik ve Enflasyon Arasindaki Nedensellik Iliskileri/The Causality Relationship Between Growth, Unemployment and Inflation in Russian Economy. *Finans Politik & Ekonomik Yorumlar, 53*(614), 43.

Yüksel, S. (2016c). Türkiye'de Cari İşlemler Açığının Belirleyicileri: Mars Yöntemi ile Bir İnceleme. *Bankacılar Dergisi, 96*(27), 102–121.

Yüksel, S. (2017a). Determinants of the credit risk in developing countries after economic crisis: A case of Turkish banking sector. In *Global financial crisis and its ramifications on capital markets* (pp. 401–415). Springer.

Yüksel, S. (2017b). Strategies out of global recession in emerging markets: An application for 2008 global crisis. In *Global business strategies in crisis* (pp. 57–75). Springer.

Yüksel, S., & Adalı, Z. (2017). Determining influencing factors of unemployment in Turkey with MARS method. *International Journal of Commerce and Finance, 3*(2), 25–36.

Yüksel, S., & Özsarı, M. (2016a). Impact of consumer loans on inflation and current account deficit: A Toda Yamamoto Causality Test for Turkey. *World Journal of Applied Economics, 2*(2), 3–14.
Yüksel, S., & Özsarı, M. (2016b). *Türkiye'deki Bireysel Krediler ile Enflasyon ve Cari İşlemler Açığı Arasındaki Nedensellik İlişkisinin İncelenmesi.* Econworld Konferansı.
Yüksel, S., & Özsarı, M. (2017). Türkiye Cumhuriyet Merkez Bankası'nın Döviz Rezervlerine Etki Eden Makroekonomik Faktörlerin Belirlenmesi. *Finans Politik & Ekonomik Yorumlar, 54*(631), 41–53.
Yüksel, S., & Zengin, S. (2016). Identifying the determinants of interest rate risk of the banks: A case of Turkish banking sector. *International Journal of Research in Business and Social Science, 5*(6), 12–28.
Yüksel, S., Eroğlu, S., & Ozsarı, M. (2016a). An analysis of the reasons of internal migration in Turkey with logit method. *Business and Management Horizons, 4*(2), 34–45.
Yüksel, S., Özsarı, M., & Canöz, İ. (2016b). Influencing factors of currency risk of deposit banks in Turkey by using probit method. *International Journal of Commerce and Finance, 2*, 85–95.
Yüksel, S., Mukhtarov, S., Mahmudlu, C., Mikayilov, J., & Iskandarov, A. (2018a). Measuring international migration in Azerbaijan. *Sustainability, 10*(1), 132.
Yüksel, S., Mukhtarov, S., Mammadov, E., & Özsarı, M. (2018b). Determinants of profitability in the banking sector: An analysis of post-Soviet countries. *Economies, 6*(3), 41.
Yüksel, S., Dinçer, H., & Meral, Y. (2019). Financial analysis of international energy trade: A strategic outlook for EU-15. *Energies, 12*(3), 431.
Zia, M., Karafiath, I., & Tripathy, N. (2018). Bank capital, the announcement of the federal reserve's term auction facility, and bank borrowing during the financial crisis of 2007–2008. *Journal of Financial Research, 41*(4), 485–506.

Chapter 3
Determining the Ways to Increase Economic Growth of Developing and Developed Economies: An Application with Data Mining and Fuzzy TOPSIS

Abstract This study aims to identify the influencing factors of economic growth for both developing and developed economies. Firstly, literature is reviewed, and 7 different variables are selected as leading indicators of the economic growth. In this framework, 155 developing and 31 developed economies are evaluated. After that, decision tree approach is taken into consideration and the most significant 4 variables are determined for each country group. In the final process, fuzzy TOPSIS approach is used to weigh E7 and G7 economies with respect to the economic development. The findings indicate that for developing economies, the most important determinants are foreign direct investment, interest rate, domestic credit, and research and development. On the other side, inflation, domestic credit, foreign direct investment, and unemployment play a more significant role in the economic growth of developed economies. Hence, it is recommended that developing economies should mainly focus on the strategies to attract the attention of the foreign investors and to increase research and development.

Keywords Economic growth · Decision tree · Fuzzy TOPSIS

3.1 Introduction

Every state wants its citizens to live in good conditions. In this context, they develop strategies to ensure that the best technological conditions exist in their countries. On the other hand, conditions such as education and health are demanded to be very good. In addition to the aforementioned issues, each state desires that the economic populations in the country be good. In this context, the main expectations are that there are no unemployed people in the country, everyone is above a certain income level and the citizens of the country can easily access the products and services they demand. However, it is quite difficult for all of these demands to be fulfilled at the same time. In order to meet these conditions, the country's economy needs to grow continuously (Morakinyo & Sibanda, 2016).

G. Silahtaroğlu et al., *Data Science and Multiple Criteria Decision Making Approaches in Finance*, Multiple Criteria Decision Making,
https://doi.org/10.1007/978-3-030-74176-1_3

It is possible to talk about many factors that affect the economic growth of a country. First of all, the development of a country's financial system is a prerequisite for economic growth. An efficient financial system will ensure that the flow of funds in the country operates in a healthy way. In this way, investments in the country will increase and new business opportunities will emerge. In this case, it can contribute to the growth of the national economy (Wang & Zeng, 2016). Parallel to the financial system, foreign direct investments in the country serve this purpose positively. Therefore, a significant number of governments are implementing a number of practices to encourage foreign investors to come to the country (Duarte et al., 2017; Zhu et al., 2016).

On the other hand, there are some issues that negatively affect a country's economic growth. For example, in an environment of high inflation, investors will not want to invest. The main reason for this is the increase in the costs of investments as a result of the increase in intermediate goods prices (Aloui et al., 2018; Bittencourt et al., 2015). Similarly, high unemployment affects economic growth negatively. In a country where many people do not have income, trade volume will decrease. This situation will cause the economic shrinkage of the country (Chand et al., 2017; Sadiku et al., 2015; Tegep et al., 2019).

In this study, what affects the economic growth of developing and developed countries is investigated. In this framework, 155 developing and 31 developed countries were included in the study. On the other hand, as a result of the literature review, 7 different variables that are thought to affect economic growth were determined. These variables were analyzed by decision tree method and four of them were determined. Subsequently, taking into account the four variables mentioned, E7 and G7 countries are ranked according to their economic growth performance. In this process, fuzzy TOPSIS method was used.

The study consists of four different parts. In the first part, general information about the concept of economic growth is given. The second part consists of literature review. In this context, similar studies in the literature have been examined. In the third part of the study, the details of two different analyzes are shared. In the last section, the recommendations developed for the results are mentioned.

3.2 Literature Review

There is a wide literature on economic growth. A significant part of the studies focused on the factors affecting economic growth. Bank loans are the most prominent issues affecting economic growth (Ahmad et al., 2016; Dinçer, Yüksel, & Adalı 2018a). In order for an economy to grow effectively, financial markets must operate effectively. The banking system plays a very important role in this process (Morakinyo & Sibanda, 2016; Wang & Zeng, 2016). Banks bring together those who have surplus funds and those who need funds. Therefore, in an environment where banks effectively operate the credit mechanism, investments in the country will increase and this will contribute to the growth of the economy (Černohorská &

Kula, 2017; Makinde, 2016). Additionally, Ionescu and Negurita (2017), Pourmonazah (2015), and Hanişoğlu and Azer (2017) also determined that the economy of the country can be improved mainly with the help of the bank loans.

The impact of inflation on economic growth has also been discussed by many researchers. Inflation means an increase in the general level of prices (Higgins et al., 2016; Pradhan et al., 2015). In a country where inflation has increased, it is understood that the prices of products have continuously increased. This is not a highly preferred issue by investors (Baharumshah et al., 2016; Chu et al., 2017). The main reason for this is that inflation increases the uncertainty in the economy. In an environment where prices are constantly increasing, investors' raw material costs are also increasing. As a result, the costs of investments will increase (Behera & Mishra, 2017; Dinç et al., 2019; Pradhan et al., 2017). As a result, investors will be reluctant to make new investments. This situation will cause the economic shrinkage of the country (Aloui et al., 2018; Bittencourt et al., 2015). Moreover, Mohseni and Jouzaryan (2016), Loganathan et al. (2017), Khan and Hanif (2018), and Lu et al. (2017) focused on the leading indicators of economic growth in different regions and concluded that inflation plays a key role in this issue.

On the other hand, some studies focused on the relationship between foreign direct investment and economic growth. Foreign direct investment is the investment of a company or individual in one country for commercial purposes in another country (Budiharto et al., 2017; Duarte et al., 2017; Zhu et al., 2016). As can be seen from this definition, foreign direct investment is a long-term investment (Pegkas, 2015; Siddique et al., 2017). In this respect, it differs from financial investments. As it is a long-term continuous investment, it is accepted that foreign direct investments have a continuous impact on the economic growth of the country (Gökmenoğlu & Taspinar, 2016; Gunby et al., 2017). In this framework, Nwaogu and Ryan (2015), Shahzad et al. (2016), Hakimi and Hamdi (2016), and Abdouli and Hammami (2017) reached a conclusion that foreign direct investment has a contributing effect on the economic development of a country so that governments should take necessary actions to attract the attention of the foreign investors.

In addition, the interest rate is considered to have a significant impact on economic growth. In a country with high interest rates, the costs of investments will increase (Ayopo et al., 2016; Tan & Tang, 2016). This situation will negatively affect the economic growth of the country (Jelilov et al., 2016; Ogawa et al., 2016). Additionally, Ajayi et al. (2017) and Low and Chan (2017) also defined that in order to have sustainable economic growth, interest rates should be low. Similarly, a significant majority of the authors in the literature emphasized the negative impact of unemployment on economic growth (Sadiku et al., 2015; Sinha & Tseladikae, 2018). In a situation where the number of unemployed in the country increases, trade volume will decrease (Chand et al., 2017; Mucuk et al., 2017; Tegep et al., 2019). This decreasing trade will adversely affect the profitability of companies.

In addition to these variables, it has been emphasized in many studies that research and development performance has an impact on economic growth. In a country where emphasis is placed on research and development activities, it is possible to develop qualified products and services (Bozkurt, 2015; Choi & Yi,

2018; Inekwe, 2015). On the other hand, research and development activities also enable the development of the technological infrastructure of the country (Kahouli, 2018; Hong, 2017; Gumus & Celikay, 2015. As a result of this, both domestic trade will develop and export figures of the country will increase (Edquist & Henrekson, 2017; Prettner & Trimborn, 2017; Sokolov-Mladenović et al., 2016; Song et al., 2019). As a result of the literature review, it has been determined that there are many studies on the factors affecting economic growth. Therefore, using a different method in a new study will provide innovation to the study. In addition to this, the separation of the country groups and the analysis will contribute to the literature.

3.3 An Application on Developing and Developed Economies

3.3.1 Data Set and Variables

In this study, the factors that affect the economic growth of developing and developed countries are tried to be determined. In this framework, 155 developing and 31 developed countries whose data can be accessed are included in the scope of the review. In this context, as a result of literature review, 7 different variables were determined. In the aforementioned study, the data for 2018 were used and the relevant data were obtained from the World Bank. Details of these variables are given in Table 3.1.

Table 3.1 The main indicators of economic growth

Indicator	References
Inflation	Bittencourt et al. (2015), Aloui et al. (2018), Baharumshah et al. (2016), Chu et al. (2017)
Domestic credit to private sector	Dinçer, Yüksel, and Şenel (2018b), Ahmad et al. (2016), Morakinyo and Sibanda (2016), Wang and Zeng (2016)
Foreign direct investment	Gökmenoğlu and Taspinar (2016), Gunby et al. (2017), Budiharto et al. (2017), Duarte et al. (2017), Zhu et al. (2016)
Interest rate	Ayopo et al. (2016), Tan and Tang (2016), Ogawa et al. (2016), Jelilov et al. (2016)
Unemployment rate	Mucuk et al. (2017), Chand et al. (2017), Tegep et al. (2019), Sadiku et al. (2015), Sinha and Tseladikae (2018)
Government expenditure on education	Morakinyo and Sibanda (2016), Wang and Zeng (2016), Aloui et al. (2018), Baharumshah et al. (2016)
Research and development expenditure	Choi and Yi (2018), Bozkurt (2015), Inekwe (2015), Kahouli (2018), Hong (2017), Gumus and Celikay (2015)

3.3.2 *Fuzzy TOPSIS*

TOPSIS can be derived from the expression of "The Technique for Order of Preference by Similarity to Ideal Solution." This approach is one of the most popular multicriteria decision-making methods. It is mainly used to rank different alternatives according to the criteria. Therefore, the criteria should be defined first. After that, TOPSIS method is performed to understand the better criteria. TOPSIS approach can also be considered with fuzzy logic. It has four different steps in the analysis process. The first step is related to the creation of the fuzzy decision matrix by calculating the fuzzy weights. In this process, Eq. (3.1) is taken into consideration.

$$\widetilde{X}_{ij} = \frac{1}{k}\left(\widetilde{X}_{ij}^{1} + \widetilde{X}_{ij}^{2} + \widetilde{X}_{ij}^{3} + \ldots\ldots + \widetilde{X}_{ij}^{k}\right) \tag{3.1}$$

Moreover, the second step is related to the normalization of this matrix with the help of the Eqs. (3.2) and (3.3). Owing to this situation, the database can be reorganized in order to eliminate redundancy.

$$\widetilde{r}_{ij} = \left(\frac{a_{ij}}{c_{ij}^{*}}, \frac{b_{ij}}{c_{ij}^{*}}, \frac{c_{ij}}{c_{ij}^{*}}\right) \tag{3.2}$$

$$c_{ij}^{*} = \sqrt{\sum_{i=1}^{m} c_{ij}^{2}} \tag{3.3}$$

Furthermore, the fuzzy positive-ideal solution A^{+} and the fuzzy negative-ideal solution A^{-} are identified in the third step. Eq. (3.4) is considered for this purpose.

$$A^{+} = \left(\widetilde{v}_{1}^{*}, \widetilde{v}_{2}^{*}, \widetilde{v}_{3}^{*}, \ldots \widetilde{v}_{n}^{*}\right) \text{ and } A^{-} = \left(\widetilde{v}_{1}^{-}, \widetilde{v}_{2}^{-}, \widetilde{v}_{3}^{-}, \ldots \widetilde{v}_{n}^{-}\right) \tag{3.4}$$

After that, Eqs. (3.5) and (3.6) are used to calculate the distance of each alternative from the ideal solutions.

$$D_{i}^{*} = \sum\nolimits_{j=1}^{n} d\left(\widetilde{v}_{ij}, \widetilde{v}_{j}^{*}\right) \tag{3.5}$$

$$D_{i}^{-} = \sum\nolimits_{j=1}^{n} d\left(\widetilde{v}_{ij}, \widetilde{v}_{j}^{-}\right) \tag{3.6}$$

In this framework, $\widetilde{v}_{j}^{*}$ gives information about $(1, 1, 1)$ and $\widetilde{v}_{1}^{-}$ shows $(0, 0, 0)$. Furthermore, the final step explains the defining of the closeness coefficient with the aim of ranking the alternatives. Eq. (3.7) is used for this issue.

$$CC_i = \frac{D_i^-}{D_i^+ + D_i^-}. \tag{3.7}$$

There are lots of studies in the literature in which fuzzy TOPSIS model is considered. For example, Dinçer and Yüksel (2018), Bulgurcu (2012), Dinçer et al. (2016), Wang (2014), Dinçer and Hacıoğlu (2014), Kazan and Ozdemir (2014), Dinçer and Hacıoğlu (2015), Islamoglu et al. (2015), Dinçer and Yüksel (2019c), Bai et al. (2014), and Dinçer et al. (2019a, 2019b) made an analysis about the effectiveness of the financial system. On the other side, Seçme et al. (2009), Dinçer (2019), Hosseini and Keshavarz (2017), Dinçer et al. (2017), Pal and Choudhury (2009), Dinçer et al. (2019c, 2019d), Akkoç and Vatansever (2013), Dinçer and Yüksel (2019a), Çelen (2014), Hemmati et al. (2013), and Dinçer et al. (2018a, b) made various analysis related to banking industry. Additionally, Kaya and Kahraman (2011), Dinçer, Yüksel, Kartal, and Alpman (2019e), Şengül et al. (2015), Yüksel et al. (2019), Chamodrakas and Martakos (2012), Dinçer and Yüksel (2019a, 2019b), Cavallaro (2010), Boran et al. (2012), and Tang and Dinçer (2019) focused on the energy industry.

3.3.3 *Analysis Results*

As a result of literature review, 2018 data of 7 different variables were tested with decision tree approach. The main purpose of this analysis is to determine the four most important variables. The results of the analysis are shown in Table 3.2.

Table 3.2 indicates that for developing economies, the most important determinants are foreign direct investment, interest rate, domestic credit, and research and development. On the other side, inflation, domestic credit, foreign direct investment, and unemployment play more significant role in the economic growth of developed economies. In the next process, E7 and G7 economies are ranked according to the economic growth performance based on these 4 different determinants. For this purpose, linguistic scales are taken into consideration which is given in Table 3.3.

The details of fuzzy TOPSIS analysis are given in the Appendix part. On the other side, the ranking results of G7 economies are demonstrated in Table 3.4.

Table 3.4 indicates that the United States is the best country with respect to economic growth. In addition, Germany has the second-best place in this framework.

Table 3.2 Most significant indicators of economic growth

Important variables for developing economies	Important variables for developed economies
Foreign direct investment	Inflation
Interest rates	Domestic credit to private sector
Domestic credit to private sector	Foreign direct investment
Research and development expenditure	Unemployment rate

Table 3.3 Linguistic scales for rating of alternatives

Definition	Triangular fuzzy numbers		
Worst (W)	0	0	2.5
Poor (P)	0	2.5	5
Fair (F)	2.5	5	7.5
Good (G)	5	7.5	10
Best (B)	7.5	10	10

Source: Dinçer et al. (2016)

Table 3.4 The values of closeness coefficient and ranking results of G7 economies

	D_i^*	D_i^-	CC_i	Ranking
A1 (Canada)	3.775	0.244	0.0608	7
A2 (France)	3.712	0.303	0.0755	3
A3 (Germany)	3.702	0.312	0.0777	2
A4 (Italy)	3.775	0.245	0.0609	6
A5 (Japan)	3.752	0.266	0.0661	4
A6 (United Kingdom)	3.764	0.255	0.0634	5
A7 (United States)	3.648	0.361	0.0901	1

Table 3.5 The values of closeness coefficient and ranking results of E7 economies

	D_i^*	D_i^-	CC_i	Ranking
A1 (Brazil)	3.785	0.238	0.0591	6
A2 (Russia)	3.713	0.304	0.0757	2
A3 (India)	3.755	0.265	0.0659	4
A4 (China)	3.667	0.348	0.0867	1
A5 (Mexico)	3.785	0.237	0.0590	7
A6 (Indonesia)	3.755	0.265	0.0659	3
A7 (Turkey)	3.755	0.265	0.0659	5

On the other side, Italy and Canada have the lowest rank. Moreover, the ranking results of E7 economies are illustrated in Table 3.5.

It can be understood from Table 3.5 that, China is the best country regarding economic growth. Similarly, Russia has the second-best performance for this issue. Nevertheless, Brazil and Mexico are in the last ranks with respect to the economic growth.

3.4 Conclusion

The aim of this study is to determine the factors that affect the economic growth of countries. In this framework, 155 developing and 31 developed economies were examined. The analysis process consisted of 3 different stages. First, similar studies in the literature have been examined in detail and 7 different variables have been identified that may affect economic growth. In order to determine which of these 7 variables are more important, the decision trees were analyzed. As a result of the analysis conducted for both developing and developed countries, four variables that had more impact on economic growth were identified. In the last stage of the analysis process of the study, taking into account these variables, E7 and G7 countries are listed within the scope of economic growth.

According to the results of the analysis made with the decision trees approach, the most important determinants are foreign direct investment, interest rate, domestic credit, and research and development for developing economies. In addition to this situation, inflation, domestic credit, foreign direct investment, and unemployment play more significant role for the economic growth of developed economies. These results demonstrate that the important variables are quite different for these country groups. On the other side, the results of fuzzy TOPSIS method indicate that China and Russia are the most successful developing countries regarding economic development. Moreover, with respect to the developed countries, Germany and the United States take place on the first ranks for this issue.

The results of the study show that the factors affecting economic growth are different for developing and developed countries. Therefore, developing countries need to produce strategies that will attract the interest of foreign investors. In this context, issues such as tax relief and ground support may make it easier for these countries to achieve this objective. On the other hand, it would be appropriate for these countries to give importance to research and development activities. In this way, it will be possible to produce qualified products in the country. Exporting these products to foreign countries will affect the foreign trade balance positively and contribute to the growth of the economy. It is believed that these strategy proposals will contribute to the economic development of developing countries.

In this study, it is examined how economic growth of countries can be increased. In this context, different analyzes have been conducted for both developed and developing countries in order to reach more specific results. In a new study, it is thought that the study of smaller country groups such as MINT and BRICS will contribute to the literature. In addition, in the analysis process of the study, it was aimed to make an original evaluation by using decision trees and fuzzy TOPSIS approaches. However, using a different method in a new study will allow comparison of the results.

Appendix 1

Key Terms and Definitions

BRICS: Brazil, Russia, India, China, South Africa
E7: Brazil, China, India, Indonesia, Mexico, Turkey, Russia
G7: Germany, Italy, France, Japan, United Kingdom, United States, Canada
MINT: Mexico, Indonesia, Nigeria, Turkey
TOPSIS: The Technique for Order of Preference by Similarity to Ideal Solution

Appendix 2

Table 3.6 Linguistic evaluations of decision makers for fuzzy decision matrix

	C1 (Foreign direct investment)					C2 (Interest rates)					C3 (Domestic credit to private sector)					C4 (Research and development expenditure)				
	DM1	DM2	DM3	DM4	DM5	DM1	DM2	DM3	DM4	DM5	DM1	DM2	DM3	DM4	DM5	DM1	DM2	DM3	DM4	DM5
A1 (Brazil)	F	F	P	F	P	G	F	F	G	F	F	F	F	G	F	G	G	B	G	G
A2 (Russia)	F	F	F	F	F	F	F	G	F	F	F	F	F	F	F	G	G	G	F	G
A3 (India)	P	F	F	F	F	F	F	G	G	F	F	F	P	F	F	F	G	G	G	F
A4 (China)	P	F	F	F	F	F	F	G	G	G	F	F	F	G	F	G	F	G	F	G
A5 (Mexico)	F	F	P	F	P	G	F	F	G	F	F	F	F	G	F	G	G	B	G	G
A6 (Indonesia)	F	F	F	F	F	F	F	G	F	F	F	F	F	F	F	G	G	G	F	G
A7 (Turkey)	P	F	F	F	F	F	F	G	G	F	F	F	P	F	F	F	G	G	G	F

Table 3.7 Fuzzy decision matrix of decision makers for Alternative 1

Criteria	DM1			DM2			DM3			DM4			DM5		
C1	2.5	5	7.5	2.5	5	7.5	0	2.5	5	2.5	5	7.5	0	2.5	5
C2	2.5	5	7.5	2.5	5	7.5	2.5	5	7.5	2.5	5	7.5	2.5	5	7.5
C3	0	2.5	5	2.5	5	7.5	2.5	5	7.5	2.5	5	7.5	2.5	5	7.5
C4	0	2.5	5	2.5	5	7.5	2.5	5	7.5	2.5	5	7.5	2.5	5	7.5

Table 3.8 Fuzzy decision matrix of decision makers for Alternative 2

Criteria	DM1			DM2			DM3			DM4			DM5		
C1	5	7.5	10	2.5	5	7.5	2.5	5	7.5	5	7.5	10	2.5	5	7.5
C2	2.5	5	7.5	2.5	5	7.5	5	7.5	10	2.5	5	7.5	2.5	5	7.5
C3	2.5	5	7.5	2.5	5	7.5	5	7.5	10	5	7.5	10	2.5	5	7.5
C4	2.5	5	7.5	2.5	5	7.5	5	7.5	10	5	7.5	10	5	7.5	10

Table 3.9 Fuzzy decision matrix of decision makers for Alternative 3

Criteria	DM1			DM2			DM3			DM4			DM5		
C1	2.5	5	7.5	2.5	5	7.5	2.5	5	7.5	5	7.5	10	2.5	5	7.5
C2	2.5	5	7.5	2.5	5	7.5	2.5	5	7.5	2.5	5	7.5	2.5	5	7.5
C3	2.5	5	7.5	2.5	5	7.5	0	2.5	5	2.5	5	7.5	2.5	5	7.5
C4	2.5	5	7.5	2.5	5	7.5	2.5	5	7.5	5	7.5	10	2.5	5	7.5

Table 3.10 Fuzzy decision matrix of decision makers for Alternative 4

Criteria	DM1			DM2			DM3			DM4			DM5		
C1	5	7.5	10	5	7.5	10	7.5	10	10	5	7.5	10	5	7.5	10
C2	5	7.5	10	5	7.5	10	5	7.5	10	2.5	5	7.5	5	7.5	10
C3	2.5	5	7.5	5	7.5	10	5	7.5	10	5	7.5	10	2.5	5	7.5
C4	5	7.5	10	2.5	5	7.5	5	7.5	10	2.5	5	7.5	5	7.5	10

Table 3.11 Fuzzy decision matrix of decision makers for Alternative 5

Criteria	DM1			DM2			DM3			DM4			DM5		
C1	0	2.5	5	0	2.5	5	2.5	5	7.5	2.5	5	7.5	2.5	5	7.5
C2	0	2.5	5	2.5	5	7.5	2.5	5	7.5	2.5	5	7.5	2.5	5	7.5
C3	2.5	5	7.5	2.5	5	7.5	5	7.5	10	2.5	5	7.5	0	2.5	5
C4	0	2.5	5	2.5	5	7.5	2.5	5	7.5	2.5	5	7.5	2.5	5	7.5

Table 3.12 Fuzzy decision matrix of decision makers for Alternative 6

Criteria	DM1			DM2			DM3			DM4			DM5		
C1	2.5	5	7.5	2.5	5	7.5	2.5	5	7.5	2.5	5	7.5	0	2.5	5
C2	2.5	5	7.5	2.5	5	7.5	2.5	5	7.5	2.5	5	7.5	2.5	5	7.5
C3	2.5	5	7.5	2.5	5	7.5	5	7.5	10	2.5	5	7.5	2.5	5	7.5
C4	5	7.5	10	2.5	5	7.5	2.5	5	7.5	2.5	5	7.5	2.5	5	7.5

Table 3.13 Fuzzy decision matrix of decision makers for Alternative 7

Criteria	DM1			DM2			DM3			DM4			DM5		
C1	2.5	5	7.5	2.5	5	7.5	5	7.5	10	2.5	5	7.5	2.5	5	7.5
C2	2.5	5	7.5	0	2.5	5	2.5	5	7.5	2.5	5	7.5	2.5	5	7.5
C3	2.5	5	7.5	2.5	5	7.5	2.5	5	7.5	2.5	5	7.5	2.5	5	7.5
C4	5	7.5	10	2.5	5	7.5	2.5	5	7.5	2.5	5	7.5	2.5	5	7.5

Table 3.14 Averaged fuzzy decision matrix

	C1			C2			C3			C4		
A1	1.50	4.00	6.50	2.50	5.00	7.50	2.00	4.50	7.00	2.00	4.50	7.00
A2	3.50	6.00	8.50	3.00	5.50	8.00	3.50	6.00	8.50	4.00	6.50	9.00
A3	3.00	5.50	8.00	2.50	5.00	7.50	2.00	4.50	7.00	3.00	5.50	8.00
A4	5.50	8.00	10.00	4.50	7.00	9.50	4.00	6.50	9.00	4.00	6.50	9.00
A5	1.50	4.00	6.50	2.00	4.50	7.00	2.50	5.00	7.50	2.00	4.50	7.00
A6	2.00	4.50	7.00	2.50	5.00	7.50	3.00	5.50	8.00	3.00	5.50	8.00
A7	3.00	5.50	8.00	2.00	4.50	7.00	2.50	5.00	7.50	3.00	5.50	8.00

Table 3.15 The values of c_{ij}^*

Alternatives	Values			
A1	42.25	56.25	49.00	49.00
A2	72.25	64.00	72.25	81.00
A3	64.00	56.25	49.00	64.00
A4	100.00	90.25	81.00	81.00
A5	42.25	49.00	56.25	49.00
A6	49.00	56.25	64.00	64.00
A7	64.00	49.00	56.25	64.00
Total	20.83	20.52	20.68	21.26

Table 3.16 Normalized fuzzy decision matrix

	C1			C2			C3			C4		
A1	0.07	0.19	0.31	0.12	0.24	0.37	0.10	0.22	0.34	0.09	0.21	0.33
A2	0.17	0.29	0.41	0.15	0.27	0.39	0.17	0.29	0.41	0.19	0.31	0.42
A3	0.14	0.26	0.38	0.12	0.24	0.37	0.10	0.22	0.34	0.14	0.26	0.38
A4	0.26	0.38	0.48	0.22	0.34	0.46	0.19	0.31	0.44	0.19	0.31	0.42
A5	0.07	0.19	0.31	0.10	0.22	0.34	0.12	0.24	0.36	0.09	0.21	0.33
A6	0.10	0.22	0.34	0.12	0.24	0.37	0.15	0.27	0.39	0.14	0.26	0.38
A7	0.14	0.26	0.38	0.10	0.22	0.34	0.12	0.24	0.36	0.14	0.26	0.38

Table 3.17 Weighted normalized fuzzy decision matrix

	C1			C2			C3			C4		
A1	0.02	0.05	0.08	0.03	0.06	0.09	0.02	0.05	0.08	0.02	0.05	0.08
A2	0.04	0.07	0.10	0.04	0.07	0.10	0.04	0.07	0.10	0.05	0.08	0.11
A3	0.04	0.07	0.10	0.03	0.06	0.09	0.02	0.05	0.08	0.04	0.06	0.09
A4	0.07	0.10	0.12	0.05	0.09	0.12	0.05	0.08	0.11	0.05	0.08	0.11
A5	0.02	0.05	0.08	0.02	0.05	0.09	0.03	0.06	0.09	0.02	0.05	0.08
A6	0.02	0.05	0.08	0.03	0.06	0.09	0.04	0.07	0.10	0.04	0.06	0.09
A7	0.04	0.07	0.10	0.02	0.05	0.09	0.03	0.06	0.09	0.04	0.06	0.09

Table 3.18 Linguistic evaluations of decision makers for fuzzy decision matrix

	C1 (Inflation)					C2 (Domestic credit to private sector)					C3 (Foreign direct investment)					C4 (Unemployment rate)				
	DM1	DM2	DM3	DM4	DM5	DM1	DM2	DM3	DM4	DM5	DM1	DM2	DM3	DM4	DM5	DM1	DM2	DM3	DM4	DM5
A1 (Canada)	G	F	P	F	P	G	F	F	G	F	F	F	F	G	F	F	F	P	P	F
A2 (France)	G	F	F	F	F	G	F	G	F	G	G	G	B	G	F	F	F	F	F	F
A3 (Germany)	P	G	F	G	F	G	F	G	G	F	B	B	G	G	F	F	F	F	F	F
A4 (Italy)	P	F	F	F	F	F	F	G	G	G	F	F	G	G	F	F	F	G	F	G
A5 (Japan)	G	F	P	F	P	G	F	F	G	F	F	F	F	G	F	F	F	P	P	F
A6 (United Kingdom)	G	F	F	F	F	G	F	G	F	G	G	G	B	G	F	F	F	F	F	F
A7 (United States)	P	G	F	G	F	G	F	G	G	F	B	B	G	G	F	F	F	F	F	F

Table 3.19 Fuzzy decision matrix of decision makers for Alternative 1

Criteria	DM1			DM2			DM3			DM4			DM5		
C1	5	7.5	10	2.5	5	7.5	0	2.5	5	2.5	5	7.5	0	2.5	5
C2	5	7.5	10	2.5	5	7.5	2.5	5	7.5	2.5	5	7.5	2.5	5	7.5
C3	0	2.5	5	5	7.5	10	2.5	5	7.5	5	7.5	10	2.5	5	7.5
C4	0	2.5	5	2.5	5	7.5	2.5	5	7.5	2.5	5	7.5	2.5	5	7.5

Table 3.20 Fuzzy decision matrix of decision makers for Alternative 2

Criteria	DM1			DM2			DM3			DM4			DM5		
C1	5	7.5	10	2.5	5	7.5	2.5	5	7.5	5	7.5	10	2.5	5	7.5
C2	5	7.5	10	2.5	5	7.5	5	7.5	10	2.5	5	7.5	5	7.5	10
C3	5	7.5	10	2.5	5	7.5	5	7.5	10	5	7.5	10	2.5	5	7.5
C4	2.5	5	7.5	2.5	5	7.5	5	7.5	10	5	7.5	10	5	7.5	10

Table 3.21 Fuzzy decision matrix of decision makers for Alternative 3

Criteria	DM1			DM2			DM3			DM4			DM5		
C1	2.5	5	7.5	2.5	5	7.5	2.5	5	7.5	5	7.5	10	2.5	5	7.5
C2	5	7.5	10	5	7.5	10	7.5	10	10	5	7.5	10	2.5	5	7.5
C3	7.5	10	10	7.5	10	10	5	7.5	10	5	7.5	10	2.5	5	7.5
C4	2.5	5	7.5	2.5	5	7.5	5	7.5	10	5	7.5	10	2.5	5	7.5

Table 3.22 Fuzzy decision matrix of decision makers for Alternative 4

Criteria	DM1			DM2			DM3			DM4			DM5		
C1	2.5	5	7.5	2.5	5	7.5	0	2.5	5	0	2.5	5	2.5	5	7.5
C2	2.5	5	7.5	2.5	5	7.5	2.5	5	7.5	2.5	5	7.5	2.5	5	7.5
C3	2.5	5	7.5	2.5	5	7.5	2.5	5	7.5	2.5	5	7.5	2.5	5	7.5
C4	2.5	5	7.5	2.5	5	7.5	5	7.5	10	2.5	5	7.5	5	7.5	10

Table 3.23 Fuzzy decision matrix of decision makers for Alternative 5

Criteria	DM1			DM2			DM3			DM4			DM5		
C1	2.5	5	7.5	2.5	5	7.5	2.5	5	7.5	2.5	5	7.5	2.5	5	7.5
C2	5	7.5	10	5	7.5	10	2.5	5	7.5	2.5	5	7.5	2.5	5	7.5
C3	2.5	5	7.5	2.5	5	7.5	5	7.5	10	2.5	5	7.5	2.5	5	7.5
C4	5	7.5	10	2.5	5	7.5	2.5	5	7.5	2.5	5	7.5	2.5	5	7.5

Table 3.24 Fuzzy decision matrix of decision makers for Alternative 6

Criteria	DM1			DM2			DM3			DM4			DM5		
C1	2.5	5	7.5	2.5	5	7.5	2.5	5	7.5	2.5	5	7.5	0	2.5	5
C2	2.5	5	7.5	5	7.5	10	2.5	5	7.5	2.5	5	7.5	2.5	5	7.5
C3	2.5	5	7.5	2.5	5	7.5	5	7.5	10	2.5	5	7.5	2.5	5	7.5
C4	5	7.5	10	2.5	5	7.5	2.5	5	7.5	2.5	5	7.5	2.5	5	7.5

Table 3.25 Fuzzy decision matrix of decision makers for Alternative 7

Criteria	DM1			DM2			DM3			DM4			DM5		
C1	5	7.5	10	5	7.5	10	5	7.5	10	5	7.5	10	7.5	10	10
C2	5	7.5	10	7.5	10	10	7.5	10	10	7.5	10	10	7.5	10	10
C3	2.5	5	7.5	7.5	10	10	7.5	10	10	7.5	10	10	5	7.5	10
C4	5	7.5	10	2.5	5	7.5	5	7.5	10	5	7.5	10	2.5	5	7.5

Table 3.26 Averaged fuzzy decision matrix

	C1			C2			C3			C4		
A1	2.00	4.50	7.00	3.00	5.50	8.00	3.00	5.50	8.00	2.00	4.50	7.00
A2	3.50	6.00	8.50	4.00	6.50	9.00	4.00	6.50	9.00	4.00	6.50	9.00
A3	3.00	5.50	8.00	5.00	7.50	9.50	5.50	8.00	9.50	3.50	6.00	8.50
A4	1.50	4.00	6.50	2.50	5.00	7.50	2.50	5.00	7.50	3.50	6.00	8.50
A5	2.50	5.00	7.50	3.50	6.00	8.50	3.00	5.50	8.00	3.00	5.50	8.00
A6	2.00	4.50	7.00	3.00	5.50	8.00	3.00	5.50	8.00	3.00	5.50	8.00
A7	5.50	8.00	10.00	7.00	9.50	10.00	6.00	8.50	9.50	4.00	6.50	9.00

Table 3.27 The values of c_{ij}^*

Alternatives	Values			
A1	49.00	64.00	64.00	49.00
A2	72.25	81.00	81.00	81.00
A3	64.00	90.25	90.25	72.25
A4	42.25	56.25	56.25	72.25
A5	56.25	72.25	64.00	64.00
A6	49.00	64.00	64.00	64.00
A7	100.00	100.00	90.25	81.00
Total	20.80	22.97	22.58	21.99

Table 3.28 Normalized fuzzy decision matrix

	C1			C2			C3			C4		
A1	0.10	0.22	0.34	0.13	0.24	0.35	0.13	0.24	0.35	0.09	0.20	0.32
A2	0.17	0.29	0.41	0.17	0.28	0.39	0.18	0.29	0.40	0.18	0.30	0.41
A3	0.14	0.26	0.38	0.22	0.33	0.41	0.24	0.35	0.42	0.16	0.27	0.39
A4	0.07	0.19	0.31	0.11	0.22	0.33	0.11	0.22	0.33	0.16	0.27	0.39
A5	0.12	0.24	0.36	0.15	0.26	0.37	0.13	0.24	0.35	0.14	0.25	0.36
A6	0.10	0.22	0.34	0.13	0.24	0.35	0.13	0.24	0.35	0.14	0.25	0.36
A7	0.26	0.38	0.48	0.30	0.41	0.44	0.27	0.38	0.42	0.18	0.30	0.41

Table 3.29 Weighted normalized fuzzy decision matrix

	C1			C2			C3			C4		
A1	0.02	0.05	0.08	0.03	0.06	0.09	0.03	0.06	0.09	0.02	0.05	0.08
A2	0.04	0.07	0.10	0.04	0.07	0.10	0.04	0.07	0.10	0.05	0.07	0.10
A3	0.04	0.07	0.10	0.05	0.08	0.10	0.06	0.09	0.11	0.04	0.07	0.10
A4	0.02	0.05	0.08	0.03	0.05	0.08	0.03	0.06	0.08	0.04	0.07	0.10
A5	0.03	0.06	0.09	0.04	0.07	0.09	0.03	0.06	0.09	0.03	0.06	0.09
A6	0.02	0.05	0.08	0.03	0.06	0.09	0.03	0.06	0.09	0.03	0.06	0.09
A7	0.07	0.10	0.12	0.08	0.10	0.11	0.07	0.09	0.11	0.05	0.07	0.10

References

Abdouli, M., & Hammami, S. (2017). Economic growth, FDI inflows and their impact on the environment: An empirical study for the MENA countries. *Quality & Quantity, 51*(1), 121–146.

Ahmad, M. I., Guohui, W., Hasan, M., Ali, R., & Rafiq, M. Y. (2016). Non-performing loans and economic growth. *Scholars Journal of Economics, Business and Management, 3*(10), 584–586.

Ajayi, S. A., Oladipo, O. A., Ajayi, L. B., & Nwanji, T. I. (2017). Interest rate and economic growth: The case of Nigeria. *International Review of Business Research Papers, 13*(1), 141–150.

Akkoç, S., & Vatansever, K. (2013). Fuzzy performance evaluation with AHP and Topsis methods: Evidence from Turkish banking sector after the global financial crisis. *Eurasian Journal of Business and Economics, 6*(11), 53–74.

Aloui, C., Hkiri, B., Hammoudeh, S., & Shahbaz, M. (2018). A multiple and partial wavelet analysis of the oil price, inflation, exchange rate, and economic growth nexus in Saudi Arabia. *Emerging Markets Finance and Trade, 54*(4), 935–956.

Ayopo, B. A., Isola, L. A., & Olukayode, S. R. (2016). Stock market response to economic growth and interest rate volatility: Evidence from Nigeria. *International Journal of Economics and Financial Issues, 6*(1), 354–360.

Baharumshah, A. Z., Slesman, L., & Wohar, M. E. (2016). Inflation, inflation uncertainty, and economic growth in emerging and developing countries: Panel data evidence. *Economic Systems, 40*(4), 638–657.

Bai, C., Dhavale, D., & Sarkis, J. (2014). Integrating fuzzy C-means and TOPSIS for performance evaluation: An application and comparative analysis. *Expert Systems with Applications, 41*(9), 4186–4196.

Behera, J., & Mishra, A. K. (2017). The recent inflation crisis and long-run economic growth in India: An empirical survey of threshold level of inflation. *South Asian Journal of Macroeconomics and Public Finance, 6*(1), 105–132.

Bittencourt, M., Van Eyden, R., & Seleteng, M. (2015). Inflation and economic growth: Evidence from the Southern African Development Community. *South African Journal of Economics, 83*(3), 411–424.

Boran, F. E., Boran, K., & Menlik, T. (2012). The evaluation of renewable energy technologies for electricity generation in Turkey using intuitionistic fuzzy TOPSIS. *Energy Sources, Part B: Economics, Planning, and Policy, 7*(1), 81–90.

Bozkurt, C. (2015). R&D expenditures and economic growth relationship in Turkey. *International Journal of Economics and Financial Issues, 5*(1), 188–198.

Budiharto, A., Suyanto, M., & Aluisius, H. P. (2017, October). The relationship between economic growth, FDI, trade, labor, and capital formation in Indonesia. In *Mulawarman International Conference on Economics and Business (MICEB 2017)*. Atlantis Press.

Bulgurcu, B. K. (2012). Application of TOPSIS technique for financial performance evaluation of technology firms in Istanbul stock exchange market. *Procedia-Social and Behavioral Sciences, 62*, 1033–1040.

Cavallaro, F. (2010). Fuzzy TOPSIS approach for assessing thermal-energy storage in concentrated solar power (CSP) systems. *Applied Energy, 87*(2), 496–503.

Çelen, A. (2014). Comparative analysis of normalization procedures in TOPSIS method: With an application to Turkish deposit banking market. *Informatica, 25*(2), 185–208.

Černohorská, L., & Kula, V. (2017). *The effect of M3 monetary aggregates and bank loans on the economic growth of countries in the Eurozone, the USA and Japan*. Scientific papers of the University of Pardubice. Series D, Faculty of Economics and Administration. 40/2017.

Chamodrakas, I., & Martakos, D. (2012). A utility-based fuzzy TOPSIS method for energy efficient network selection in heterogeneous wireless networks. *Applied Soft Computing, 12*(7), 1929–1938.

Chand, K., Tiwari, R., & Phuyal, M. (2017). Economic growth and unemployment rate: An empirical study of Indian economy. *PRAGATI: Journal of Indian Economy, 4*(2), 130–137.

Choi, C., & Yi, M. H. (2018). The internet, R&D expenditure and economic growth. *Applied Economics Letters, 25*(4), 264–267.

Chu, A. C., Cozzi, G., Furukawa, Y., & Liao, C. H. (2017). Inflation and economic growth in a Schumpeterian model with endogenous entry of heterogeneous firms. *European Economic Review, 98*, 392–409.

Dinç, D. T., Gökmen, A., & Üstündağ, K. (2019). Economic growth-inflation nexus and its impact on the development of the automotive industry: The case of Turkey. *International Journal of Economics and Business Research, 18*(1), 94–111.

Dinçer, H. (2019). *HHI-based evaluation of the European banking sector using an integrated fuzzy approach*. Kybernetes.

Dinçer, H., & Hacıoğlu, Ü. (2014). A comparative hybrid method in technical analysis for stock selection process in banking sector by fuzzy AHP-TOPSIS and VIKOR method. In *Global strategies in banking and finance* (pp. 187–204). IGI Global.

Dinçer, H., & Hacıoğlu, U. (2015). A comparative performance evaluation on bipolar risks in emerging capital markets using fuzzy AHP-TOPSIS and VIKOR approaches. *Engineering Economics, 26*(2), 118–129.

Dinçer, H., & Yüksel, S. (2018). Financial sector-based analysis of the G20 economies using the integrated decision-making approach with DEMATEL and TOPSIS. In *Emerging trends in banking and finance* (pp. 210–223). Springer.

Dinçer, H., & Yüksel, S. (2019a). Balanced scorecard-based analysis of investment decisions for the renewable energy alternatives: A comparative analysis based on the hybrid fuzzy decision-making approach. *Energy, 175*, 1259–1270.

Dinçer, H., & Yüksel, S. (2019b). An integrated stochastic fuzzy MCDM approach to the balanced scorecard-based service evaluation. *Mathematics and Computers in Simulation, 166*, 93–112. https://doi.org/10.1016/j.matcom.2019.04.008.

Dinçer, H., & Yüksel, S. (2019c). IT2-based fuzzy hybrid decision making approach to soft computing. *IEEE Access, 7*, 15932–15944.

Dinçer, H., Hacıoğlu, U., Tatoglu, E., & Delen, D. (2016). A fuzzy-hybrid analytic model to assess investors' perceptions for industry selection. *Decision Support Systems, 86*, 24–34.

Dinçer, H., Hacıoğlu, Ü., & Yüksel, S. (2017). A strategic approach to global financial crisis in banking sector: A critical appraisal of banking strategies using fuzzy ANP and fuzzy Topsis methods. *International Journal of Sustainable Economies Management (IJSEM), 6*(1), 1–21.

Dinçer, H., Yüksel, S., & Adalı, Z. (2018a). Relationship between non-performing loans, industry, and economic growth of the African economies and policy recommendations for global growth. In *Globalization and trade integration in developing countries* (pp. 203–228). IGI Global.

Dinçer, H., Yüksel, S., & Şenel, S. (2018b). Analyzing the global risks for the financial crisis after the great depression using comparative hybrid hesitant fuzzy decision-making models: Policy recommendations for sustainable economic growth. Sustainability, 10(9), 3126.

Dinçer, H., Yüksel, S., & Martinez, L. (2019a). Balanced scorecard-based analysis about European energy investment policies: A hybrid hesitant fuzzy decision-making approach with quality function deployment. *Expert Systems with Applications, 115*, 152–171.

Dinçer, H., Yüksel, S., & Martínez, L. (2019b). Interval type 2-based hybrid fuzzy evaluation of financial services in E7 economies with DEMATEL-ANP and MOORA methods. *Applied Soft Computing, 79*, 186–202.

Dinçer, H., Yüksel, S., & Çetiner, İ. T. (2019c). Strategy selection for organizational performance of Turkish banking sector with the integrated multi-dimensional decision-making approach. In *Handbook of research on contemporary approaches in management and organizational strategy* (pp. 273–291). IGI Global.

Dinçer, H., Yüksel, S., Korsakienė, R., Raišienė, A. G., & Bilan, Y. (2019d). IT2 hybrid decision-making approach to performance measurement of internationalized firms in the Baltic states. *Sustainability, 11*(1), 296.

Dinçer, H., Yüksel, S., Kartal, M. T., & Alpman, G. (2019e). Corporate governance-based evaluation of alternative distribution channels in the Turkish banking sector using quality function deployment with an integrated fuzzy MCDM method. In *Intergenerational governance and leadership in the corporate world: Emerging research and opportunities* (pp. 39–77). IGI Global.

Duarte, L. D. R. V., Kedong, Y., & Xuemei, L. (2017). The relationship between FDI, economic growth and financial development in Cabo Verde. *International Journal of Economics and Finance, 9*(5), 132–142.

Edquist, H., & Henrekson, M. (2017). Swedish lessons: How important are ICT and R&D to economic growth? *Structural Change and Economic Dynamics, 42*, 1–12.

Gökmenoğlu, K., & Taspinar, N. (2016). The relationship between CO2 emissions, energy consumption, economic growth and FDI: The case of Turkey. *The Journal of International Trade & Economic Development, 25*(5), 706–723.

Gumus, E., & Celikay, F. (2015). R&D expenditure and economic growth: New empirical evidence. *Margin: The Journal of Applied Economic Research, 9*(3), 205–217.

Gunby, P., Jin, Y., & Reed, W. R. (2017). Did FDI really cause Chinese economic growth? A meta-analysis. *World Development, 90*, 242–255.

Hakimi, A., & Hamdi, H. (2016). Trade liberalization, FDI inflows, environmental quality and economic growth: A comparative analysis between Tunisia and Morocco. *Renewable and Sustainable Energy Reviews, 58*, 1445–1456.

Hanişoğlu, G. S., & Azer, Ö. A. (2017). The impact of housing loans on economic growth in Turkey: Times series analysis for 2010–2015 period. *EMAJ: Emerging Markets Journal, 7*(1), 25–30.

Hemmati, M., Dalghandi, S., & Nazari, H. (2013). Measuring relative performance of banking industry using a DEA and TOPSIS. *Management Science Letters, 3*(2), 499–504.

Higgins, P., Zha, T., & Zhong, W. (2016). Forecasting China's economic growth and inflation. *China Economic Review, 41*, 46–61.

Hong, J. P. (2017). Causal relationship between ICT R&D investment and economic growth in Korea. *Technological Forecasting and Social Change, 116*, 70–75.

Hosseini, M. H., & Keshavarz, E. (2017). Using fuzzy AHP and fuzzy TOPSIS for strategic analysis measurement of service quality in banking industry. *International Journal of Applied Management Science, 9*(1), 55–80.

Inekwe, J. N. (2015). The contribution of R&D expenditure to economic growth in developing economies. *Social Indicators Research, 124*(3), 727–745.

Ionescu, E., & Negurita, O. (2017). The evolution of refinancing loans sector within the economic growth. In *International conference on economic sciences and business administration* (Vol. 4, no. 1, pp. 212–219). Spiru Haret University.

Islamoglu, M., Apan, M., & Oztel, A. (2015). An evaluation of the financial performance of REITs in Borsa Istanbul: A case study using the entropy-based TOPSIS method. *International Journal of Financial Research, 6*(2), 124–138.

Jelilov, G., Waziri, F., & Isik, A. (2016). Interest rate behaviour and its relationship with economic growth in Nigeria: An error correction model approach. *The Empirical Economics Letters, 15*(3), 245–255.

Kahouli, B. (2018). The causality link between energy electricity consumption, CO2 emissions, R&D stocks and economic growth in Mediterranean countries (MCs). *Energy, 145*, 388–399.

Kaya, T., & Kahraman, C. (2011). Multicriteria decision making in energy planning using a modified fuzzy TOPSIS methodology. *Expert Systems with Applications, 38*(6), 6577–6585.

Kazan, H., & Ozdemir, O. (2014). Financial performance assessment of large scale conglomerates via TOPSIS and CRITIC methods. *International Journal of Management and Sustainability, 3* (4), 203.

Khan, M., & Hanif, W. (2018). Institutional quality and the relationship between inflation and economic growth. *Empirical Economics, 2*(10), 1–23.

Loganathan, N., Ismail, S., Streimikiene, D., Hassan, A. A. G., Zavadskas, E. K., & Mardani, A. (2017). Tax reform, inflation, financial development and economic growth in Malaysia. *Romanian Journal of Economic Forecasting, 20*(4), 152–165.

Low, Y. W., & Chan, T. H. (2017). Foreign exchange rate, interest rate, inflation rate and economic growth in Malaysia. *Global Business and Management Research, 9*(4s), 110–127.

Lu, X., Guo, K., Dong, Z., & Wang, X. (2017). Financial development and relationship evolvement among money supply, economic growth and inflation: A comparative study from the US and China. *Applied Economics, 49*(10), 1032–1045.

Makinde, H. O. (2016). Implications of commercial bank loans on economic growth in Nigeria (1986–2014). *Journal of Emerging Trends in Economics and Management Sciences, 7*(3), 124–136.

Mohseni, M., & Jouzaryan, F. (2016). Examining the effects of inflation and unemployment on economic growth in Iran (1996–2012). *Procedia Economics and Finance, 36*, 381–389.

Morakinyo, A., & Sibanda, M. (2016). Non-performing loans and economic growth in Nigeria: A dynamic analysis. *SPOUDAI-Journal of Economics and Business, 66*(4), 61–81.

Mucuk, M., Edirneligil, A., & Gerçeker, M. (2017). The relationship between unemployment rate and economic growth: The case of Turkey. *Siyaset, Ekonomi ve Yönetim Araştırmaları Dergisi, 5*(1), 1–8.

Nwaogu, U. G., & Ryan, M. J. (2015). FDI, foreign aid, remittance and economic growth in developing countries. *Review of Development Economics, 19*(1), 100–115.

Ogawa, K., Sterken, E., & Tokutsu, I. (2016). *Public debt, economic growth and the real interest rate: A panel VAR approach to EU and OECD countries*. Economic Growth and the Real Interest Rate: A Panel VAR Approach to EU and OECD Countries (January 29, 2016).

Pal, M. N., & Choudhury, K. (2009). Exploring the dimensionality of service quality: An application of topsis in the Indian banking industry. *Asia-Pacific Journal of Operational Research, 26* (01), 115–133.

Pegkas, P. (2015). The impact of FDI on economic growth in Eurozone countries. *The Journal of Economic Asymmetries, 12*(2), 124–132.

Pourmonazah, A. (2015). An investigation into the influence of Bank loans granted to agriculture sector on Iranian economic growth. *Mediterranean Journal of Social Sciences*, *6*(6 S2), 722.

Pradhan, R. P., Arvin, M. B., & Bahmani, S. (2015). Causal nexus between economic growth, inflation, and stock market development: The case of OECD countries. *Global Finance Journal, 27*, 98–111.

Pradhan, R. P., Nishigaki, Y., & Hall, J. H. (2017). The multivariate dynamic causal relations between financial depth, inflation, and economic growth. *Philippine Review of Economics, 54* (1), 63–93.

Prettner, K., & Trimborn, T. (2017). Demographic change and R&D-based economic growth. *Economica, 84*(336), 667–681.

Sadiku, M., Ibraimi, A., & Sadiku, L. (2015). Econometric estimation of the relationship between unemployment rate and economic growth of FYR of Macedonia. *Procedia Economics and Finance, 19*, 69–81.

Seçme, N. Y., Bayrakdaroğlu, A., & Kahraman, C. (2009). Fuzzy performance evaluation in Turkish banking sector using analytic hierarchy process and TOPSIS. *Expert Systems with Applications, 36*(9), 11699–11709.

Şengül, Ü., Eren, M., Shiraz, S. E., Gezder, V., & Şengül, A. B. (2015). Fuzzy TOPSIS method for ranking renewable energy supply systems in Turkey. *Renewable Energy, 75*, 617–625.

Shahzad, S. J. H., Zakaria, M., Rehman, M. U., Ahmed, T., & Fida, B. A. (2016). Relationship between FDI, terrorism and economic growth in Pakistan: Pre and post 9/11 analysis. *Social Indicators Research, 127*(1), 179–194.

Siddique, H. M. A., Ansar, R., Naeem, M. M., & Yaqoob, S. (2017). Impact of FDI on economic growth: Evidence from Pakistan. *Bulletin of Business and Economics, 6*(3), 111–116.

Sinha, N., & Tseladikae, K. (2018). Economic growth and unemployment rate for the economy of Botswana: An empirical study. *FOCUS: Journal of International Business, 5*(2), 1–25.

Sokolov-Mladenović, S., Cvetanović, S., & Mladenović, I. (2016). R&D expenditure and economic growth: EU28 evidence for the period 2002–2012. *Economic Research-Ekonomska istraživanja, 29*(1), 1005–1020.

Song, X., Zhou, Y., & Jia, W. (2019). How do economic openness and R&D investment affect green economic growth?—Evidence from China. *Resources, Conservation and Recycling, 146*, 405–415.

Tan, B. W., & Tang, C. F. (2016). Examining the causal linkages among domestic investment, FDI, trade, interest rate and economic growth in ASEAN-5 countries. *International Journal of Economics and Financial Issues, 6*(1), 214–220.

Tang, Z., & Dinçer, H. (2019). Selecting the house-of-quality-based energy investment policies for the sustainable emerging economies. *Sustainability, 11*(13), 3514.

Tegep, J., Suratman, E., & Indra, S. (2019). The failure of foreign direct investment to explain unemployment rate and the mediating role of economic growth and minimum wage. *International Journal of Economics and Financial Issues, 9*(2), 154.

Wang, Y. J. (2014). The evaluation of financial performance for Taiwan container shipping companies by fuzzy TOPSIS. *Applied Soft Computing, 22*, 28–35.

Wang, S., & Zeng, N. (2016). Micro and small enterprises, bank loans and economic growth: A coalition strategy. *Journal of Applied Finance & Banking, 6*(2), 93–101.

Yüksel, S., Dinçer, H., & Meral, Y. (2019). Financial analysis of international energy trade: A strategic outlook for EU-15. *Energies, 12*(3), 431.

Zhu, H., Duan, L., Guo, Y., & Yu, K. (2016). The effects of FDI, economic growth and energy consumption on carbon emissions in ASEAN-5: Evidence from panel quantile regression. *Economic Modelling, 58*, 237–248.

Chapter 4
Profitability Prediction of Turkish Banking Industry: A Comparative Analysis with Data Science and Fuzzy ANP

Abstract In this study, it is aimed to estimate the factors affecting the profitability of the Turkish banking sector. For this purpose, 34 different variables were firstly determined by literature review. Then, with the help of decision trees method, the most important 8 variables were selected. These variables were also evaluated with fuzzy ANP approach. As a result, it is understood that the foreign exchange position is the most important variable for the profitability of the Turkish banking sector. Based on this result, it is recommended that Turkish banks take some actions to minimize the currency exchange rate risk. In this context, it is considered that financial derivative products will help the management of this mentioned risk.

Keywords Banking · Decision tree · Fuzzy ANP

4.1 Introduction

All countries aim to develop their economic conditions. The main purpose of this is to increase the quality of life of the citizens living in the country. Individuals with higher quality of life will be much happier. The most important way to achieve this goal is the development of the economy. In a country with high economic activity, trade volume will increase. Further trade will increase the profitability of companies in the country. Companies with increased profitability will also make new investments. New investments will require new employees. In other words, new investments by companies will reduce the unemployment rate in the country (Ergeç & Ersin, 2018).

In order for this process to be successful, the flow of funds should be provided effectively. Companies need funds to make new investments. Otherwise, these companies will have difficulty in increasing their investments. This will prevent the achievement of the above-mentioned objectives. Therefore, financial institutions that can provide the flow of fun in the country play a vital role. Banks also bring together those who are in need of funds and those with surplus funds. In the absence

G. Silahtaroğlu et al., *Data Science and Multiple Criteria Decision Making Approaches in Finance*, Multiple Criteria Decision Making,
https://doi.org/10.1007/978-3-030-74176-1_4

of banks, it is quite difficult for the two groups to come together. As can be seen here, the high performance of banks for an effective financial system is important.

Therefore, banks are very important institutions for the economic development of the country. Those who have more money will invest their savings in banks and can get the opportunity to gain interest. In this case, banks have also obtained funds in this process. In addition to the mentioned process, banks also provide this fund to companies in need. In this way, banks will gain interest and companies will be able to reach the funds they need. As can be seen, the high performance of banks is essential for the effectiveness of the financial system (Tunay & Yüksel, 2017).

In this context, determining the factors affecting the profitability of banks is very important. It is possible to talk about many factors affecting the profitability of banks. In this process, one of the most important factors is the repayment performance of loans granted by the bank. In addition to the mentioned variable, customer satisfaction also increases the profitability of banks (Zengin & Yüksel, 2016a, 2016b). Furthermore, it is accepted that there is a correct relationship between the profitability of banks and technological investments. In addition to bank-specific factors, macroeconomic performance of the country is also influential on banks' profitability. For example, banks can make more profit if the country's economic growth is high. On the other hand, the high unemployment rate of the country will reduce the profitability of banks (Ersin & Ergeç, 2018). Moreover, as the high inflation rate will increase the uncertainty in the country, it will adversely affect the performance of banks (Dinçer et al. 2019aa, 2019b).

Turkey, in 1994 and 2000, has undergone two major financial crises. As a result of these crises, many companies went bankrupt. However, many people have lost their jobs. Consequently, bankrupt companies and unemployed people could not pay their debts to banks (Oktar & Yüksel, 2015). This situation caused the financial crisis to spread to the banking sector. In this context, a large number of banks could not continue their activities. Especially after the 2000 crisis, Turkey has held several reforms for the banking sector. Since then, many actions have been taken in order for the banking sector to continue its activities much healthier (Yüksel, 2017a, 2017b).

The aim of this study is to determine the factors affecting the profitability of the Turkish banking sector. In this context, literature review was done first. As a result, 34 different variables were identified which could affect profitability. Then, these variables were analyzed by decision tree method. As a result of this study, 8 different variables were determined which are more important than others. These selected variables were tested with fuzzy ANP and their significance was determined. The most important novelty of this study is the hybrid usage of fuzzy logic and data science methods for the banking sector. The main reason of selecting fuzzy ANP is that it considers inner dependency between the criteria. Hence, it is believed that the relationship can be evaluated more effectively.

4.2 Literature Review

In the literature, factors affecting the profitability of banks are frequently discussed. In a significant part of these studies, it is suggested that there is a relationship between the capital and profitability of banks. For example, Rahman et al. (2015) focused on banking sector in Bangladesh. In this study, it is stated that banks with high capital ratios may be more profitable. Similarly, Tan (2016) reached the same results for the Chinese banking sector, Menicucci and Paolucci (2016) for the European banking sector, and Ozili (2017) for the African banking sector.

Additionally, Tran et al. (2016), Bikker and Vervliet (2018), and Zheng et al. (2017) also found that the capital amount of banks is very effective on their profitability. In some of these studies, the capital adequacy ratio was considered (De Jonghe & Öztekin, 2015; Gambacorta & Shin, 2018). On the other hand, in some other studies, different ratios such as "equity/total assets" and "equity/total deposits" were also taken into consideration (Bitar et al., 2016; Djalilov & Piesse, 2016; Lee et al., 2015).

In addition, some researchers emphasized that the increase in exchange rate has an effect on the profitability of banks. Osundina et al. (2016) analyzed Nigeria's banking sector. In this study where many different variables were used, the volatility in exchange rate was found to be the most important variable in determining the profitability of banks. Horton et al. (2016), Liu et al. (2015), Jobst and Lin (2016), Bech and Malkhozov (2016), and Akinkunmi (2017) also expressed similar situation in their studies. On the other hand, Trad et al. (2017), Owusu-Antwi et al. (2017), Topak and Talu (2017) and Arteta et al. (2018) stated that banks should not have open foreign exchange position. This is also the case for Khan et al. (2018), Scheiber et al. (2016), Laryea et al. (2016), and Hasanov et al. (2018).

Moreover, Thornton and Vasilakis (2019), Aliyu and Yusof (2016), Islam et al. (2017), and Agbeja et al. (2016) stated that banking sectors of developing countries are more sensitive to exchange rate risk. In addition to the mentioned studies, Rani and Zergaw (2017), Riyadi (2017), Ali and Shahid (2017), Winarso and Salim (2017), Madaschi and Pablos Nuevo (2017), and Jaradat and ALkhazaleh (2018) also concluded that the exchange rate risk negatively affected the entire financial sector.

In some studies, it is stated that there is a relationship between the banks' credit and deposit figures and their profitability. Borio et al. (2017), Chronopoulos et al. (2015), Said (2018), Samad (2015), and Regehr and Sengupta (2016) analyzed the banking sectors of different countries. According to the results, it was concluded that the loan amount of banks is the most important indicator of profitability. In contrast, Bikker and Vervliet (2018), Apergis and Lau (2017), Menicucci and Paolucci (2016), Agoraki and Tsamis (2017), Ramlan and Adnan (2016), Zarrouk et al. (2016), and Duraj and Moci (2015) emphasized that banks should be careful when lending.

On the other side, Ozgur and Gorus (2016), Kassem and Sakr (2018), Regehr and Sengupta (2016), Nys et al. (2015), and Jobst and Lin (2016) also identified that bank deposit amount is a significant indicator of the bank profitability. In addition to the mentioned variables, some researchers also indicated that nonperforming loans are an important indicator of profitability (Al-Khazali & Mirzaei, 2017; Beaton & Myrvoda, 2016; Dimitrios et al., 2016; Ekanayake & Azeez, 2015; Ghosh, 2015; Khan & Ahmad, 2017; Khan et al., 2018; Kumar & Kishore, 2019; Vithessonthi, 2016).

In addition, banks' liquidity level has been suggested to be effective on profitability by many researchers. In a significant part of the studies, the relationship is positive. For example, Tran et al. (2016), Alshatti (2015), and Borio et al. (2017) mentioned this issue and stated that banks with high liquidity are more profitable. Petria et al. (2015) examined 27 European countries and reached the same result. Al Nimer et al. (2015) and Saif-Alyousfi et al. (2017) are other studies that find a positive relationship between liquidity and profitability. In contrast, Moussa (2015), Jiang et al. (2019), and Chronopoulos et al. (2015) concluded that the excess liquidity would decrease the profitability of banks.

In addition, a significant portion of the studies emphasized that interest income and noninterest incomes are important determinants of profitability. In this context, Claessens et al. (2018) tried to determine the factors affecting the profitability of banks in a study that examined a large number of countries. Consequently, they suggested that interest income was an important indicator in this respect. Similarly, Owusu-Antwi et al. (2017), Kassem and Sakr (2018), and Garcia and Guerreiro (2016) examined the banking sector in Ghana, Egypt, and Portugal and emphasized the same results.

Altavilla et al. (2018) and Brighi and Venturelli (2016) stated that high interest income positively affects the profitability of banks. On the other hand, Ahamed (2017) discussed the banking sector in India and stated that noninterest incomes are important in increasing the profitability of banks. Similar to the study, Bikker and Vervliet (2018), Saunders et al. (2016), Jobst and Lin (2016), Chronopoulos et al. (2015), and Akinkunmi (2017) stated that in order to increase the profitability of banks, they should give importance to noninterest income. The review of the literature indicates that there is a need for a new study, which focuses on this subject by an original methodology.

4.3 An Application on Turkish Banking Industry

4.3.1 Data Set and Variables

In this study, 46 different banks of Turkey are taken into consideration. Additionally, annual data for the years between 2007 and 2017 are considered. Furthermore, 34 different indicators are defined based on literature review. The details of these studies are given in Table 4.1.

Table 4.1 Determinants of bank profitability

Indicator	References
Capital adequacy ratio	Tran et al. (2016); Ozili (2017); Bikker and Vervliet (2018)
Shareholders' equity/Total assets	Zheng et al. (2017); Gambacorta and Shin (2018); De Jonghe and Öztekin (2015)
(Equity-fixed assets)/Total assets	Rahman et al. (2015); Tan (2016); Bitar et al. (2016); Osundina et al. (2016)
Shareholders' equity/(All resources)	Djalilov and Piesse (2016); Menicucci and Paolucci (2016); Lee et al. (2015); Liu et al. (2015)
Net balance sheet position/Shareholders' equity	Jobst and Lin (2016); Bech and Malkhozov (2016); Akinkunmi (2017); Horton et al. (2016)
(Net balance sheet position + net off-balance sheet position)/Shareholders' equity	Oktar and Yüksel (2016); Trad et al. (2017); Owusu-Antwi et al. (2017); Topak and Talu (2017)
FX assets/FX liabilities	Winarso and Salim (2017); Madaschi and Pablos Nuevo (2017); Jaradat and ALkhazaleh (2018); Dinçer, Hacıoğlu, and Yüksel (2018aa)
DC assets/Total assets	Arteta et al. (2018); Khan et al. (2018); Scheiber et al. (2016)
DC liabilities/Total liabilities	Yüksel, Mukhtarov, and Mammadov (2016aa); Aliyu and Yusof (2016); Islam et al. (2017); Agbeja et al. (2016)
DC loans and receivables/Total loans and receivables	Borio et al. (2017); Chronopoulos et al. (2015)
FX liabilities/Total liabilities	Yüksel, Özsarı, and Canöz (2016bb); Rani and Zergaw (2017); Riyadi (2017); Dinçer, Hacıoğlu, and Yüksel (2018aa); Ali and Shahid (2017)
FX assets/Total assets	Laryea et al. (2016); Dinçer, Yüksel, and Martínez (2019f); Hasanov et al. (2018); Thornton and Vasilakis (2019); Ersin (2018)
DC deposit/Total deposits	Ozgur and Gorus (2016); Kassem and Sakr (2018)
Total deposits/Total assets	Regehr and Sengupta (2016); Nys et al. (2015); Jobst and Lin (2016); Yüksel et al. (2017aa, 2017b)
Taken loans/Total assets	Dinçer et al. (2019ce, 2019f, 2019g); Said (2018); Samad (2015); Regehr and Sengupta (2016)
Financial assets (net)/Total assets	Bikker and Vervliet (2018); Apergis and Lau (2017); Dinçer and Yüksel (2018a, 2018b)
Consumer loans/Total loans and receivables	Yüksel and Kavak (2019); Menicucci and Paolucci (2016); Dinçer and Yüksel (2019); Yüksel and Özsarı (2016); Yüksel, Zengin, and Kartal (2016cc)
Total loans and receivables/Total assets	Tunay et al. (2019); Agoraki and Tsamis (2017); Kalkavan and Ersin (2019); Ramlan and Adnan (2016); Dinçer, Hacıoğlu, and Yüksel (2016c)
Total loans and receivables/Total deposits	Dinçer, Yüksel, and Şenel (2018cc); Ersin and Yıldırım (2015); Zarrouk et al. (2016); Duraj and Moci (2015)

(continued)

Table 4.1 (continued)

Indicator	References
Nonperforming loans (gross)/Total loans and receivables	Yüksel et al. (2016aa); Ghosh (2015); Vithessonthi (2016); Beaton and Myrvoda (2016)
Non-performing loans (net)/Total loans and receivables	Ekanayake and Azeez (2015); Khan and Ahmad (2017); Dimitrios et al. (2016); Dinçer, Yuksel, and Adalı (2018bb)
Specific provisions/Non-performing loans (gross)	Kumar and Kishore (2019); Al-Khazali and Mirzaei (2017); Khan et al. (2018)
Fixed assets/Total assets	Yüksel, Özsarı, and Canöz (2016b); Tran et al. (2016); Alshatti (2015)
Liquid assets/Total assets	Yüksel and Zengin (2016a, 2016b); Borio et al. (2017); Petria et al. (2015)
Liquid assets/Short-term liabilities	Al Nimer et al. (2015); Saif-Alyousfi et al. (2017)
TP liquid assets/Total assets	Moussa (2015); Jiang et al. (2019)
Liquid assets/(Deposit + Non deposit items)	Alshatti (2015); Chronopoulos et al. (2015)
FX liquid assets/FX liabilities	Saif-Alyousfi et al. (2017); Tran et al. (2016)
Non-interest income/Total assets	Yuksel and Zengin (2017); Claessens et al. (2018); Saunders et al. (2016)
Non-interest income/Other operating expenses	Owusu-Antwi et al. (2017); Jobst and Lin (2016)
Interest income/Total assets	Yüksel and Özsari (2017); Kassem and Sakr (2018); Ahamed (2017)
Total income/Total expenses	Eti (2019); Garcia and Guerreiro (2016); Bikker and Vervliet (2018)
Interest expenses/Total expenses	Altavilla et al. (2018); Brighi and Venturelli (2016)
Noninterest expenses/Total expenses	Chronopoulos et al. (2015); Akinkunmi (2017)

4.3.2 Fuzzy ANP

ANP methodology is one of the multi-criteria decision-making models. It is mainly used to evaluate the significance of the variables by making comparison. In the literature, this approach is considered with fuzzy logic. In this circumstance, expert opinions are taken into consideration by using pairwise comparison matrix stated in Eq. (4.1).

Table 4.2 The fuzzy scale of the pair-wise comparison

Definition	Triangular fuzzy numbers		
Equally important (EI)	0.5	1	1.5
Weakly more important (WI)	1	1.5	2
Strongly more important (SI)	1.5	2	2.5
Very strongly more important (VI)	2	2.5	3
Absolutely more important (AI)	2.5	3	3.5

Source: Chang (1996), Bozbura et al. (2007), Dinçer, Hacioglu, and Yuksel (2016a, 2016b), 2016c)

$$\widetilde{A} = \begin{bmatrix} 1 & \widetilde{a}_{12} & \widetilde{a}_{13} & & \cdots & \widetilde{a}_{1n} \\ \widetilde{a}_{21} & 1 & \widetilde{a}_{23} & & \cdots & \widetilde{a}_{2n} \\ \widetilde{a}_{31} & \widetilde{a}_{32} & 1 & & \cdots & \widetilde{a}_{3n} \\ \vdots & \vdots & \vdots & \ddots & & \vdots \\ \widetilde{a}_{n1} & \widetilde{a}_{n2} & \widetilde{a}_{n3} & & \cdots & 1 \end{bmatrix} = \begin{bmatrix} 1 & \widetilde{a}_{12} & \widetilde{a}_{13} & & \cdots & \widetilde{a}_{1n} \\ 1/\widetilde{a}_{12} & 1 & \widetilde{a}_{23} & & \cdots & \widetilde{a}_{2n} \\ 1/\widetilde{a}_{13} & 1/\widetilde{a}_{23} & 1 & & \cdots & \widetilde{a}_{3n} \\ \vdots & \vdots & \vdots & \ddots & & \vdots \\ 1/\widetilde{a}_{1n} & 1/\widetilde{a}_{2n} & 1/\widetilde{a}_{3n} & & \cdots & 1 \end{bmatrix} \tag{4.1}$$

In the analysis process, triangular fuzzy numbers are used which are stated in Table 4.2.

In the first step, fuzzy synthetic extent value is defined as the Eq. (4.2).

$$S_i = \sum_{j=1}^{m} M_{gi}^{j} \otimes \left[\sum_{j=1}^{n} \sum_{j=1}^{m} \mathrm{M}_{gi}^{j} \right]^{-1} \tag{4.2}$$

In order to get this equation, Eqs. (4.3)–(4.5) are considered.

$$\sum\nolimits_{j=1}^{m} M_{gi}^{j} = \left(\sum\nolimits_{j=1}^{m} l_j, \sum\nolimits_{j=1}^{m} m_j, \sum\nolimits_{j=1}^{m} u_j \right) \tag{4.3}$$

$$\sum\nolimits_{i=1}^{n} \sum\nolimits_{j=1}^{m} M_{gi}^{j} = \left(\sum\nolimits_{j=1}^{m} l_i, \sum\nolimits_{j=1}^{m} m_i, \sum\nolimits_{j=1}^{m} u_i \right) \tag{4.4}$$

$$\left[\sum\nolimits_{i=1}^{n} \sum\nolimits_{j=1}^{m} M_{gi}^{j} \right]^{-1} = \left(\frac{1}{\sum_{i=1}^{n} u_i}, \frac{1}{\sum_{i=1}^{n} m_i}, \frac{1}{\sum_{i=1}^{n} l_i} \right) \tag{4.5}$$

The second step is related to the definition of the degree of the possibility. In this context, Eqs. (4.6)–(4.8) are used.

$$\left[\sum_{i=1}^{n}\sum_{j=1}^{m}M_{gi}^{j}\right]^{-1}=\left(\frac{1}{\sum_{i=1}^{n}u_i},\frac{1}{\sum_{i=1}^{n}m_i},\frac{1}{\sum_{i=1}^{n}l_i}\right) \tag{4.6}$$

$$V(M_2 \geq M_1)=sup\left[min\left(\mu_{M_1}(x),\mu_{M_2}(y)\right)\right] \tag{4.7}$$

$$=\begin{cases} 1, & if \quad m_2 \geq m_1, \\ 0, & if \quad l_1 \geq u_2, \\ \dfrac{l_1-u_2}{(m_2-u_2)-(m_1-l_1)} & otherwise \end{cases} \tag{4.8}$$

The degree possibility for a convex fuzzy number is determined in the third step by using the Eqs. (4.9)–(4.10).

$$\begin{aligned} V(M \geq M_1, M_2, \ldots M_k) &= V[(M \geq M_1)and(M \geq M_2)and\ldots and(M \geq M_k)] \\ &= min\, V(M \geq M_i) \end{aligned} \tag{4.9}$$

$$d'(A_i)=min\, V(S_i \geq S_k) \tag{4.10}$$

$$W'=\left(d'(A_1),d'(A_2),\ \ldots,d'(A_n)\right)^T \tag{4.11}$$

In the final step, normalization process has occurred with the help of the Eq. (4.12).

$$W'=\left(d(A_1),d(A_2),\ \ldots,d(A_n)\right)^T \tag{4.12}$$

Fuzzy ANP approach was considered for many different purposes, such as supplier selection (Aliakbari Nouri et al., 2015; Uygun et al., 2015; Vinodh et al., 2016; Xu et al., 2017), resource management (Ayağ & Yücekaya, 2019; Ignatius et al., 2016), and performance management (Alilou et al., 2019; Dinçer et al., 2017; Dinçer, Yüksel, & Martínez, 2019g; Samanlioglu & Ayağ, 2016).

4.3.3 Analysis Results

In the analysis process, there are two different stages. Firstly, a decision tree model is applied to select more significant variables that have an influence on the profitability of the banking sector. After that, these variables are weighted with the help of fuzzy ANP approach. In this part of the study, a decision tree model has been designed to extract patterns or features that are to be used for predicting Average Return Equity of banks. Gini algorithm has been used in the decision tree model. The study has three parallel parts. In each part, one of the Average Return Equity values in years 2015, 2016, and 2017 has been attained as the class variable. Class variables are binned into percentiles and labelled as Bin1 (Quarter one), Bin2 (Quarter two), Bin3

Table 4.3 Learning accuracy statistics for 2017

	True pos	False pos	True neg	False neg
Bin 1	15.00	1.00	43.00	0.00
Bin 2	14.00	0.00	44.00	1.00
Bin 3	14.00	0.00	45.00	0.00
Bin 4	15.00	0.00	44.00	0.00
	Recall	Precision	Sensitivity	Specificity
Bin 1	1.00	0.94	1.00	0.98
Bin 2	0.93	1.00	0.93	1.00
Bin 3	1.00	1.00	1.00	1.00
Bin 4	1.00	1.00	1.00	1.00
	F-Measure	Overall accuracy	Overall Cohen's kappa	
Bin 1	0.97	–	–	
Bin 2	0.97	–	–	
Bin 3	1.00	–	–	
Bin 4	1.00	–	–	
Overall	0.97	0.98	0.73	

(Quarter three), and Bin4 (Quarter one four). For 2017, the decision tree found the following six variables as the most important ones to predict Average Return Equity. Learning accuracy statistics are given in Table 4.3.

Variables selected by decision tree algorithm are:

1. Interest Income/Total Revenues of two years ago.
2. Last year's Average return on equity.
3. Interest Income/Total Revenues of three years ago.
4. Last year's Non-Interest Income (Net)/Other Operating Expenses.
5. Consumer Loans/Total Loans and Receivables of two years ago.
6. Interest Income/Total Assets of two Years ago.

For 2016, following variables are selected by the decision tree as to predict Average Return Equity. Learning accuracy statistics are given in Table 4.4.

Variables selected by decision tree algorithm are:

1. Average Equity Profitability of two years ago
2. FX Liquid Assets/FX Liabilities of two years ago
3. Average Equity Profitability of eight years ago
4. Last year's FX Assets/Total Assets
5. Last year's Average return on equity one year ago

For 2015, eight variables are selected by the decision tree to predict Average Return Equity. Learning accuracy statistics are given in Table 4.5.

Variables selected by decision tree algorithm are:

1. Last year's Other Operating Expenses/Total Operating Income
2. Last year's Average return on equity
3. Last year's Interest Expenses/Total Expenses

4. Last year's TL Liquid Assets/Total Assets
5. FX Liabilities/Total Liabilities of two years ago
6. Last year's Liquid Assets/Short-Term Liabilities
7. (Net Balance Sheet Position + Net Off-Balance Sheet Position)/Shareholders' Equity of four years ago
8. Interest Income/Total Assets of seven years ago

Table 4.4 Learning accuracy statistics for 2016

	True pos	False pos	True neg	False neg
Bin 1	11.00	0.00	44.00	4.00
Bin 2	14.00	0.00	44.00	1.00
Bin 3	15.00	12.00	32.00	0.00
Bin 4	7.00	0.00	45.00	7.00
	Recall	Precision	Sensitivity	Specificity
Bin 1	0.73	1.00	0.73	1.00
Bin 2	0.93	1.00	0.93	1.00
Bin 3	1.00	0.56	1.00	0.73
Bin 4	0.50	1.00	0.50	1.00
	F-Measure	Overall accuracy	Overall Cohen's kappa	
Bin 1	0.85	–	–	
Bin 2	0.97	–	–	
Bin 3	0.71	–	–	
Bin 4	0.67	–	–	
Overall	0.91	0.80	0.73	

Table 4.5 Learning accuracy statistics for 2015

	True pos	False pos	True neg	False neg
Bin 1	15.00	0.00	44.00	0.00
Bin 2	15.00	0.00	44.00	0.00
Bin 3	14.00	0.00	45.00	0.00
Bin 4	15.00	0.00	44.00	0.00
Overall	15.00	0.00	44.00	0.00
	Recall	Precision	Sensitivity	Specificity
Bin 1	1.00	1.00	1.00	1.00
Bin 2	1.00	1.00	1.00	1.00
Bin 3	1.00	1.00	1.00	1.00
Bin 4	1.00	1.00	1.00	1.00
Overall	1.00	1.00	1.00	1.00
	F-Measure	Overall accuracy	Overall Cohen's kappa	
Bin 1	1.00	–	–	
Bin 2	1.00	–	–	
Bin 3	1.00	–	–	
Bin 4	1.00	–	–	
Overall	1.00	1.00	1.00	

Table 4.6 More significant indicators of bank profitability

Indicators
Interest income/Total revenues
Non-interest income (Net)/Other operating expenses
Consumer loans/Total loans
Interest income/Total assets
FX liquid assets/FX liabilities
FX assets/Total assets
Interest expenses/Total expenses
DC liquid assets/Total assets

As it is seen from Table 4.5, the learning rate of the algorithm 100%. The details of this calculation process are given in the Appendix part. While making these analyses, it is identified that 8 different indicators are more significant in comparison with others in order to predict the profitability of the Turkish banking industry. These variables were also underlined in many different studies in the literature. The details of these indicators are given in Table 4.6.

In the second stage of the analysis process, fuzzy ANP methodology is applied to understand which indicators are more significant by comparing with the others. 8 Criteria are weighted with the fuzzy ANP. For this purpose, Chang's extent method is used for evaluating the pair-wise comparison matrices. An expert team is appointed to obtain the linguistic choices for the criteria in the matrices. Linguistic choices are collected with the consensus and then, the linguistic scales are converted into the triangular fuzzy numbers. Fuzzy pair-wise comparison matrices for overall evaluation and inner dependence matrices of the factors with respect to each criterion are computed. The pair-wise comparison and inner dependence matrices are provided in Tables 4.8–4.16, respectively (Table 4.7).

Table 16 gives information currency exchange rate position is the most important indicator of the profitability of the Turkish banking sector. In addition to this issue, consumer loans are also important for this circumstance.

4.4 Conclusion

In this study, it is aimed to determine the factors affecting the profitability of the Turkish banking sector. All Turkish banks, regardless of ownership, were included in the scope of the review. In the first phase of the study, a large literature review was conducted. As a result, 34 different variables were identified, which could affect the profitability of banks. After that, 8 variables were determined by using decision trees method. In the last stage of the analysis, these variables were weighted with the help of fuzzy ANP model.

According to the results, it was understood that the exchange rate risk was the most influential factor in the profitability of Turkish banks. This situation shows that if the foreign exchange debts of Turkish banks are less than foreign exchange assets,

Table 4.7 Weighting results of the criteria

Criteria	Interdependent weights of the criteria								Local weights	Global weights
C1	1.000	0.145	0.163	0.157	0.155	0.148	0.151	0.137	0.114	0.124
C2	0.140	1.000	0.141	0.151	0.156	0.158	0.138	0.145	0.117	0.124
C3	0.157	0.153	1.000	0.160	0.165	0.167	0.152	0.152	0.151	0.143
C4	0.144	0.148	0.123	1.000	0.134	0.131	0.127	0.141	0.127	0.122
C5	0.179	0.159	0.173	0.176	1.000	0.183	0.158	0.159	0.157	0.151
C6	0.185	0.171	0.187	0.184	0.174	1.000	0.160	0.161	0.160	0.154
C7	0.102	0.118	0.099	0.093	0.119	0.119	1.000	0.104	0.085	0.092
C8	0.093	0.106	0.113	0.078	0.098	0.094	0.114	1.000	0.089	0.090

a significant decrease in the profitability of these banks occurs. Therefore, it is important that these banks manage their exchange rate risks with the help of financial derivative products. In addition to the aforementioned variable, the rapid increase in retail loans also affects the profitability of banks negatively.

According to the results, the foreign exchange position is the most important variable affecting the profitability of banks. Given these results, Turkish banks should primarily manage the exchange rate risk effectively. In this context, it would be appropriate for banks to not borrow too much foreign currency. On the other hand, current exchange rate risks should be minimized by financial derivative products. In order for all these issues to occur, it would be appropriate for Turkish banks to obtain competent persons for treasury departments.

In this study, considering the decision trees and fuzzy ANP approaches, it has been tried to determine what affects the profitability of Turkish banks. With the use of these two different methods mentioned above, it is aimed to increase the authenticity of the study. However, the use of different methods such as fuzzy DEMATEL and VIKOR in a future study will contribute to the literature. In addition, a large number of developing countries may be included in a new study. In this way, it will be possible to make a comparative analysis between these results and the results of this study.

Appendix 1

Key Terms and Definitions

ANP: Analytical Network Process
DC: Domestic Currency
FX: Foreign Currency

Appendix 2

Analysis Details of Decision Tree Approach

Analysis for 2017

$2015 Interest Income/Total Revenues$ <= 19.345237038957485 AND $2016 Average Return on Equity$ <= 14.367034148529822 => "Bin 4"
$2014 Interest Income/Total Assets$ <= 2.388168549834992 AND $2016 Consumer Loans/ Total Loans and Receivables *$ <= 16.4 AND $2016 Non-Interest Income (Net)/Other Operating Expenses$ <= 161.352849651359 AND $2015 Interest Income/Total Revenues$ > 19.345237038957485 AND $2016 Average Return on Equity$ <= 14.367034148529822 => "Bin 3"
$2014 Interest Income/Total Revenues$ <= 65.60039310568996 AND $2016 Average Return on Equity$ <= 8.441450080924444 AND $2014 Interest Income/Total Assets$ > 2.388168549834992 AND $2016 Consumer Loans/Total Loans and Receivables *$ <= 16.4 AND $2016 Non-Interest Income (Net)/Other Operating Expenses$ <= 161.352849651359 AND $2015 Interest Income/Total Revenues$ > 19.345237038957485 AND $2016 Average Return on Equity$ <= 14.367034148529822 => "Bin 2"
$2014FX Assets/FX Liabilities$ <= 55.03965014196105 AND $2014 Interest Expenses/Total Expenses$ <= 70.70673741221977 AND $2014 Interest Income/Total Revenues$ > 65.60039310568996 AND $2016 Average Return on Equity$ <= 8.441450080924444 AND $2014 Interest Income/Total Assets$ > 2.388168549834992 AND $2016 Consumer Loans/Total Loans and Receivables *$ <= 16.4 AND $2016 Non-Interest Income (Net)/Other Operating Expenses$ <= 161.352849651359 AND $2015 Interest Income/Total Revenues$ > 19.345237038957485 AND $2016 Average Return on Equity$ <= 14.367034148529822 => "Bin 2"
$2014FX Assets/FX Liabilities$ > 55.03965014196105 AND $2014 Interest Expenses/Total Expenses$ <= 70.70673741221977 AND $2014 Interest Income/Total Revenues$ > 65.60039310568996 AND $2016 Average Return on Equity$ <= 8.441450080924444 AND $2014 Interest Income/Total Assets$ > 2.388168549834992 AND $2016 Consumer Loans/Total Loans and Receivables *$ <= 16.4 AND $2016 Non-Interest Income (Net)/Other Operating Expenses$ <= 161.352849651359 AND $2015 Interest Income/Total Revenues$ > 19.345237038957485 AND $2016 Average Return on Equity$ <= 14.367034148529822 => "Bin 1"
$2014 Interest Expenses/Total Expenses$ > 70.70673741221977 AND $2014 Interest Income/ Total Revenues$ > 65.60039310568996 AND $2016 Average Return on Equity$ <= 8.441450080924444 AND $2014 Interest Income/Total Assets$ > 2.388168549834992 AND $2016 Consumer Loans/Total Loans and Receivables *$ <= 16.4 AND $2016 Non-Interest Income (Net)/Other Operating Expenses$ <= 161.352849651359 AND $2015 Interest Income/ Total Revenues$ > 19.345237038957485 AND $2016 Average Return on Equity$ <= 14.367034148529822 => "Bin 2"
$2016 Average Return on Equity$ > 8.441450080924444 AND $2014 Interest Income/Total Assets$ > 2.388168549834992 AND $2016 Consumer Loans/Total Loans and Receivables *$ <= 16.4 AND $2016 Non-Interest Income (Net)/Other Operating Expenses$ <= 161.352849651359 AND $2015 Interest Income/Total Revenues$ > 19.345237038957485 AND $2016 Average Return on Equity$ <= 14.367034148529822 => "Bin 2"
$2016 Consumer Loans/Total Loans and Receivables *$ > 16.4 AND $2016 Non-Interest Income (Net)/Other Operating Expenses$ <= 161.352849651359 AND $2015 Interest Income/

(continued)

Total Revenues$ > 19.345237038957485 AND $2016 Average Return on Equity$ <= 14.367034148529822 => "Bin 3"
$2016 Non-Interest Income (Net)/Other Operating Expenses$ > 161.352849651359 AND $2015 Interest Income/Total Revenues$ > 19.345237038957485 AND $2016 Average Return on Equity$ <= 14.367034148529822 => "Bin 4"
$2016 Average Return on Equity$ > 14.367034148529822 AND TRUE => "Bin 4"

Analysis for 2016

$2014 Average Return on Equity$ <= 7.383781622399939 AND $2014FX Liquid Assets/FX Liabilities$ <= 77.63274459617332 AND $2007 Average Return on Equity$ <= 11.95 AND $2015FX Assets/Total Assets$ <= 60.59754431342453 AND $2015 Average Return on Equity$ <= 14.494905011653533 => "Bin 1"
$2014 Average Return on Equity$ > 7.383781622399939 AND $2014FX Liquid Assets/FX Liabilities$ <= 77.63274459617332 AND $2007 Average Return on Equity$ <= 11.95 AND $2015FX Assets/Total Assets$ <= 60.59754431342453 AND $2015 Average Return on Equity$ <= 14.494905011653533 => "Bin 2"
$2014FX Liquid Assets/FX Liabilities$ > 77.63274459617332 AND $2007 Average Return on Equity$ <= 11.95 AND $2015FX Assets/Total Assets$ <= 60.59754431342453 AND $2015 Average Return on Equity$ <= 14.494905011653533 => "Bin 2"
$2007 Average Return on Equity$ > 11.95 AND $2015FX Assets/Total Assets$ <= 60.59754431342453 AND $2015 Average Return on Equity$ <= 14.494905011653533 => "Bin 3"
$2015FX Assets/Total Assets$ > 60.59754431342453 AND $2015 Average Return on Equity$ <= 14.494905011653533 => "Bin 2"
$2015 Average Return on Equity$ > 14.494905011653533 AND TRUE => "Bin 4"

Analysis for 2015

$2014 Other Operating Expenses/Total Operating Income$ <= 48.38778402624213 AND $2014 Average Return on Equity$ <= 6.772859109446015 => "Bin 2"
$2014 Interest Expenses/Total Expenses$ <= 0.06698594402087821 AND $2014 Other Operating Expenses/Total Operating Income$ > 48.38778402624213 AND $2014 Average Return on Equity$ <= 6.772859109446015 => "Bin 2"
$2014 TL Liquid Assets/Total Assets$ <= 2.791840685802903 AND $2014 Interest Expenses/Total Expenses$ > 0.06698594402087821 AND $2014 Other Operating Expenses/Total Operating Income$ > 48.38778402624213 AND $2014 Average Return on Equity$ <= 6.772859109446015 => "Bin 2"
$2013FX Liabilities/Total Liabilities$ <= 55.5 AND $2014 TL Liquid Assets/Total Assets$ > 2.791840685802903 AND $2014 Interest Expenses/Total Expenses$ > 0.06698594402087821 AND $2014 Other Operating Expenses/Total Operating Income$ > 48.38778402624213 AND $2014 Average Return on Equity$ <= 6.772859109446015 => "Bin 1"
$2013FX Liabilities/Total Liabilities$ > 55.5 AND $2014 TL Liquid Assets/Total Assets$ > 2.791840685802903 AND $2014 Interest Expenses/Total Expenses$ > 0.06698594402087821

(continued)

AND $2014 Other Operating Expenses/Total Operating Income$ > 48.38778402624213 AND $2014 Average Return on Equity$ <= 6.772859109446015 => "Bin 2"
$2014 Liquid Assets/Short Term Liabilities$ <= 32.89545318389918 AND $2014 Average Return on Equity$ > 6.772859109446015 => "Bin 1"
$2011 (Net Balance Sheet Position + Net Off-Balance Sheet Position)/Shareholders' Equity$ <= −5.3 AND $2014 TL Liquid Assets/Total Assets$ <= 33.941827728460524 AND $2014 Interest Expenses/Total Expenses$ <= 67.3570673080648 AND $2014 TL Liquid Assets/Total Assets$ <= 55.16002295728003 AND $2014 Average Return on Equity$ <= 13.94158208020286 AND $2014 Liquid Assets/Short Term Liabilities$ > 32.89545318389918 AND $2014 Average Return on Equity$ > 6.772859109446015 => "Bin 2"
$2007 Interest Income/Total Assets$ <= 9.3 AND $2011 (Net Balance Sheet Position + Net Off-Balance Sheet Position)/Shareholders' Equity$ > −5.3 AND $2014 TL Liquid Assets/Total Assets$ <= 33.941827728460524 AND $2014 Interest Expenses/Total Expenses$ <= 67.3570673080648 AND $2014 TL Liquid Assets/Total Assets$ <= 55.16002295728003 AND $2014 Average Return on Equity$ <= 13.94158208020286 AND $2014 Liquid Assets/Short Term Liabilities$ > 32.89545318389918 AND $2014 Average Return on Equity$ > 6.772859109446015 => "Bin 2"
$2007FX Assets/Total Assets$ <= 37.05 AND $2008 Interest Income/Total Assets_1$ <= 8.15 AND $2007 Interest Income/Total Assets$ > 9.3 AND $2011 (Net Balance Sheet Position + Net Off-Balance Sheet Position)/Shareholders' Equity$ > −5.3 AND $2014 TL Liquid Assets/Total Assets$ <= 33.941827728460524 AND $2014 Interest Expenses/Total Expenses$ <= 67.3570673080648 AND $2014 TL Liquid Assets/Total Assets$ <= 55.16002295728003 AND $2014 Average Return on Equity$ <= 13.94158208020286 AND $2014 Liquid Assets/Short Term Liabilities$ > 32.89545318389918 AND $2014 Average Return on Equity$ > 6.772859109446015 => "Bin 3"
$2007FX Assets/Total Assets$ > 37.05 AND $2008 Interest Income/Total Assets_1$ <= 8.15 AND $2007 Interest Income/Total Assets$ > 9.3 AND $2011 (Net Balance Sheet Position + Net Off-Balance Sheet Position)/Shareholders' Equity$ > −5.3 AND $2014 TL Liquid Assets/Total Assets$ <= 33.941827728460524 AND $2014 Interest Expenses/Total Expenses$ <= 67.3570673080648 AND $2014 TL Liquid Assets/Total Assets$ <= 55.16002295728003 AND $2014 Average Return on Equity$ <= 13.94158208020286 AND $2014 Liquid Assets/Short Term Liabilities$ > 32.89545318389918 AND $2014 Average Return on Equity$ > 6.772859109446015 => "Bin 4"
$2008 Interest Income/Total Assets_1$ > 8.15 AND $2007 Interest Income/Total Assets$ > 9.3 AND $2011 (Net Balance Sheet Position + Net Off-Balance Sheet Position)/Shareholders' Equity $ > −5.3 AND $2014 TL Liquid Assets/Total Assets$ <= 33.941827728460524 AND $2014 Interest Expenses/Total Expenses$ <= 67.3570673080648 AND $2014 TL Liquid Assets/Total Assets$ <= 55.16002295728003 AND $2014 Average Return on Equity$ <= 13.94158208020286 AND $2014 Liquid Assets/Short Term Liabilities$ > 32.89545318389918 AND $2014 Average Return on Equity$ > 6.772859109446015 => "Bin 4"
$2014 TL Liquid Assets/Total Assets$ > 33.941827728460524 AND $2014 Interest Expenses/Total Expenses$ <= 67.3570673080648 AND $2014 TL Liquid Assets/Total Assets$ <= 55.16002295728003 AND $2014 Average Return on Equity$ <= 13.94158208020286 AND $2014 Liquid Assets/Short Term Liabilities$ > 32.89545318389918 AND $2014 Average Return on Equity$ > 6.772859109446015 => "Bin 2"
$2014 Interest Expenses/Total Expenses$ > 67.3570673080648 AND $2014 TL Liquid Assets/Total Assets$ <= 55.16002295728003 AND $2014 Average Return on Equity$ <= 13.94158208020286 AND $2014 Liquid Assets/Short Term Liabilities$ > 32.89545318389918 AND $2014 Average Return on Equity$ > 6.772859109446015 => "Bin 4"
$2014 TL Liquid Assets/Total Assets$ > 55.16002295728003 AND $2014 Average Return on Equity$ <= 13.94158208020286 AND $2014 Liquid Assets/Short Term Liabilities$ >

(continued)

32.89545318389918 AND $2014 Average Return on Equity$ > 6.772859109446015 => "Bin 4"
$2011 Total Revenues/Total Expenses$ <= 130.60000000000002 AND $2014 Average Return on Equity$ > 13.94158208020286 AND $2014 Liquid Assets/Short Term Liabilities$ > 32.89545318389918 AND $2014 Average Return on Equity$ > 6.772859109446015 => "Bin 2"
$2011 Total Revenues/Total Expenses$ > 130.60000000000002 AND $2014 Average Return on Equity$ > 13.94158208020286 AND $2014 Liquid Assets/Short Term Liabilities$ > 32.89545318389918 AND $2014 Average Return on Equity$ > 6.772859109446015 => "Bin 4"

Table 4.8 Pair-wise comparison matrix for all criteria

Criteria	Interest income/Total revenues (C1)			Non-interest income (Net)/Other operating expenses (C2)			Consumer loans/ Total loans (C3)			Interest income/ Total assets (C4)		
Interest income/Total revenues (C1)	1.00	1.00	1.00	0.5	1	1.5	0.5	1	1.5	0.5	1	1.5
Non-interest income (net)/Other operating expenses (C2)	0.67	1.00	2.00	1.00	1.00	1.00	0.5	1	1.5	0.5	1	1.5
Consumer loans/Total loans(C3)	0.67	1.00	2.00	0.67	1.00	2.00	1.00	1.00	1.00	2.5	3	3.5
Interest income/Total assets (C4)	0.67	1.00	2.00	0.67	1.00	2.00	0.29	0.33	0.40	1.00	1.00	1.00
FX liquid assets/FX liabilities (C5)	0.67	1.00	2.00	0.67	1.00	2.00	0.67	1.00	2.00	0.50	0.67	1.00
FX assets/Total assets (C6)	0.67	1.00	2.00	0.67	1.00	2.00	0.67	1.00	2.00	0.67	1.00	2.00
Interest expenses/Total expenses (C7)	0.67	1.00	2.00	0.67	1.00	2.00	0.50	0.67	1.00	0.50	0.67	1.00
TL liquid assets/Total assets (C8)	0.67	1.00	2.00	0.67	1.00	2.00	0.50	0.67	1.00	0.50	0.67	1.00
Criteria	FX liquid assets/FX liabilities (C5)			FX assets/Total assets (C6)			Interest expenses/ Total expenses (C7)			TL liquid assets/ Total assets (C8)		
Interest income/Total revenues (C1)	0.5	1	1.5	0.5	1	1.5	0.5	1	1.5	0.5	1	1.5
Non-interest income (net)/Other operating expenses (C2)	0.5	1	1.5	0.5	1	1.5	0.5	1	1.5	0.5	1	1.5
Consumer loans/Total loans (C3)	0.5	1	1.5	0.5	1	1.5	1	1.5	2	1	1.5	2
Interest income/Total assets (C4)	1	1.5	2	0.5	1	1.5	1	1.5	2	1	1.5	2
FX liquid assets/FX liabilities (C5)	1.00	1.00	1.00	0.5	1	1.5	2.5	3	3.5	2.5	3	3.5
FX assets/Total assets (C6)	0.67	1.00	2.00	1.00	1.00	1.00	2.5	3	3.5	2.5	3	3.5
Interest expenses/Total expenses (C7)	0.29	0.33	0.40	0.29	0.33	0.40	1.00	1.00	1.00	0.5	1	1.5
TL liquid assets/Total assets (C8)	0.29	0.33	0.40	0.29	0.33	0.40	0.67	1.00	2.00	1.00	1.00	1.00

Table 4.9 Inner dependence matrix of the criteria with the respect to criterion 1

Criteria	Non-interest income (Net)/Other operating expenses (C2)			Consumer loans/ Total loans (C3)			Interest income/ Total assets (C4)			FX liquid assets/FX liabilities (C5)		
Non-interest income (Net)/Other operating expenses (C2)	1.00	1.00	1.00	0.5	1	1.5	0.5	1	1.5	0.5	1	1.5
Consumer loans/Total loans (C3)	0.67	1.00	2.00	1.00	1.00	1.00	1	1.5	2	0.5	1	1.5
Interest income/Total assets (C4)	0.67	1.00	2.00	0.50	0.67	1.00	1.00	1.00	1.00	0.5	1	1.5
FX liquid assets/FX liabilities (C5)	0.67	1.00	2.00	0.67	1.00	2.00	0.67	1.00	2.00	1.00	1.00	1.00
FX assets/Total assets (C6)	0.67	1.00	2.00	0.67	1.00	2.00	0.40	0.50	0.67	0.67	1.00	2.00
Interest expenses/Total expenses (C7)	0.67	1.00	2.00	0.50	0.67	1.00	0.67	1.00	2.00	0.33	0.40	0.50
TL liquid assets/Total assets (C8)	0.50	0.67	1.00	0.50	0.67	1.00	0.67	1.00	2.00	0.33	0.40	0.50

Criteria	FX assets/Total assets (C6)			Interest expenses/Total expenses (C7)			TL liquid assets/Total assets (C8)		
Non-interest income (net)/Other operating expenses (C2)	0.5	1	1.5	0.5	1	1.5	1.00	1.50	2.00
Consumer loans/Total loans (C3)	0.5	1	1.5	1	1.5	2	1	1.5	2
Interest income/Total assets (C4)	1.5	2	2.5	0.5	1	1.5	0.5	1	1.5
FX liquid assets/FX liabilities (C5)	0.5	1	1.5	2	2.5	3	2	2.5	3
FX assets/Total assets (C6)	1.00	1.00	1.00	2.5	3	3.5	2.5	3	3.5
Interest expenses/Total expenses (C7)	0.29	0.33	0.40	1.00	1.00	1.00	0.5	1	1.5
TL liquid assets/Total assets (C8)	0.29	0.33	0.40	0.67	1.00	2.00	1.00	1.00	1.00

Table 4.10 Inner dependence matrix of the criteria with the respect to criterion 2

Criteria	Interest income/Total revenues (C1)			Consumer loans/Total loans (C3)			Interest income/Total assets (C4)			FX liquid assets/FX liabilities (C5)		
Interest income/Total revenues (C1)	1.00	1.00	1.00	0.5	1	1.5	0.5	1	1.5	0.5	1	1.5
Consumer loans/Total loans (C3)	0.67	1.00	2.00	1.00	1.00	1.00	0.5	1	1.5	2	2.5	3
Interest income/Total assets (C4)	0.67	1.00	2.00	0.67	1.00	2.00	1.00	1.00	1.00	0.5	1	1.5
FX liquid assets/FX liabilities (C5)	0.67	1.00	2.00	0.33	0.40	0.50	0.67	1.00	2.00	1.00	1.00	1.00
FX assets/Total assets (C6)	0.50	0.67	1.00	0.67	1.00	2.00	0.40	0.50	0.67	0.50	0.67	1.00
Interest expenses/Total expenses (C7)	0.67	1.00	2.00	0.67	1.00	2.00	0.67	1.00	2.00	0.50	0.67	1.00
TL liquid assets/Total assets (C8)	0.50	0.67	1.00	0.67	1.00	2.00	0.67	1.00	2.00	0.33	0.40	0.50

Criteria	FX assets/Total assets (C6)			Interest expenses/Total expenses (C7)			TL liquid assets/Total assets (C8)		
Interest income/Total revenues (C1)	1.00	1.50	2.00	0.5	1	1.5	1.00	1.50	2.00
Consumer loans/Total loans (C3)	0.5	1	1.5	0.5	1	1.5	0.5	1	1.5
Interest income/Total assets (C4)	1.5	2	2.5	0.5	1	1.5	0.5	1	1.5
FX liquid assets/FX liabilities (C5)	1	1.5	2	1	1.5	2	2	2.5	3
FX assets/Total assets (C6)	1.00	1.00	1.00	2.5	3	3.5	2.5	3	3.5
Interest expenses/Total expenses (C7)	0.29	0.33	0.40	1.00	1.00	1.00	0.5	1	1.5
TL liquid assets/Total assets (C8)	0.29	0.33	0.40	0.67	1.00	2.00	1.00	1.00	1.00

Table 4.11 Inner dependence matrix of the criteria with the respect to criterion 3

Criteria	Interest income/ Total revenues (C1)			Non-interest income (Net)/ Other operating expenses (C2)			Interest income/ Total assets (C4)			FX liquid assets/ FX liabilities (C5)		
Interest income/ Total revenues (C1)	1.00	1.00	1.00	1.00	1.50	2.00	1.5	2	2.5	0.5	1	1.5
Non-interest income (net)/ Other operating expenses (C2)	0.50	0.67	1.00	1.00	1.00	1.00	0.5	1	1.5	0.5	1	1.5
Interest income/ Total assets (C4)	0.40	0.50	0.67	0.67	1.00	2.00	1.00	1.00	1.00	0.5	1	1.5
FX liquid assets/FX liabilities (C5)	0.67	1.00	2.00	0.67	1.00	2.00	0.67	1.00	2.00	1.00	1.00	1.00
FX assets/ Total assets (C6)	0.67	1.00	2.00	0.50	0.67	1.00	0.67	1.00	2.00	0.67	1.00	2.00
Interest expenses/ Total expenses (C7)	0.67	1.00	2.00	0.50	0.67	1.00	0.67	1.00	2.00	0.29	0.33	0.40
TL liquid assets/ Total assets (C8)	0.50	0.67	1.00	0.67	1.00	2.00	0.67	1.00	2.00	0.50	0.67	1.00

Criteria	FX assets/Total assets (C6)			Interest expenses/ Total expenses (C7)			TL liquid assets/ Total assets (C8)		
Interest income/Total revenues (C1)	0.5	1	1.5	0.5	1	1.5	1.00	1.50	2.00
Non-interest income (net)/Other operating expenses (C2)	1.00	1.50	2.00	1.00	1.50	2.00	0.5	1	1.5
Interest income/Total assets (C4)	0.5	1	1.5	0.5	1	1.5	0.5	1	1.5
FX liquid assets/FX liabilities (C5)	0.5	1	1.5	2.5	3	3.5	1	1.5	2

(continued)

Table 4.11 (continued)

Criteria	FX assets/Total assets (C6)			Interest expenses/ Total expenses (C7)			TL liquid assets/ Total assets (C8)		
FX assets/Total assets (C6)	1.00	1.00	1.00	2.5	3	3.5	2.5	3	3.5
Interest expenses/Total expenses (C7)	0.29	0.33	0.40	1.00	1.00	1.00	0.5	1	1.5
TL liquid assets/Total assets (C8)	0.29	0.33	0.40	0.67	1.00	2.00	1.00	1.00	1.00

Table 4.12 Inner dependence matrix of the criteria with the respect to criterion 4

Criteria	Interest income/Total revenues (C1)			Non-interest income (Net)/Other operating expenses (C2)			Consumer loans/Total loans(C3)			FX liquid assets/FX liabilities (C5)		
Interest income/Total revenues (C1)	1.00	1.00	1.00	0.5	1	1.5	0.5	1	1.5	1.00	1.50	2.00
Non-interest income (net)/Other operating expenses (C2)	0.67	1.00	2.00	1.00	1.00	1.00	0.5	1	1.5	0.5	1	1.5
Consumer loans/Total loans(C3)	0.67	1.00	2.00	0.67	1.00	2.00	1.00	1.00	1.00	0.5	1	1.5
FX liquid assets/FX liabilities (C5)	0.50	0.67	1.00	0.67	1.00	2.00	0.67	1.00	2.00	1.00	1.00	1.00
FX assets/Total assets (C6)	0.50	0.67	1.00	0.50	0.67	1.00	0.67	1.00	2.00	0.67	1.00	2.00
Interest expenses/Total expenses (C7)	0.67	1.00	2.00	0.50	0.67	1.00	0.40	0.50	0.67	0.33	0.40	0.50
TL liquid assets/Total assets (C8)	0.50	0.67	1.00	0.67	1.00	2.00	0.50	0.67	1.00	0.33	0.40	0.50

Criteria	FX assets/Total assets (C6)			Interest expenses/Total expenses (C7)			TL liquid assets/Total assets (C8)		
Interest income/Total revenues (C1)	1.00	1.50	2.00	0.5	1	1.5	1.00	1.50	2.00
Non-interest income (net)/Other operating expenses (C2)	1.00	1.50	2.00	1.00	1.50	2.00	0.5	1	1.5
Consumer loans/Total loans (C3)	0.5	1	1.5	1.5	2	2.5	1	1.5	2
FX liquid assets/FX liabilities (C5)	0.5	1	1.5	2	2.5	3	2	2.5	3
FX assets/Total assets (C6)	1.00	1.00	1.00	2.5	3	3.5	2.5	3	3.5
Interest expenses/Total expenses (C7)	0.29	0.33	0.40	1.00	1.00	1.00	1.00	1.50	2.00
TL liquid assets/Total assets (C8)	0.29	0.33	0.40	0.50	0.67	1.00	1.00	1.00	1.00

Table 4.13 Inner dependence matrix of the criteria with the respect to criterion 5

Criteria	Interest income/Total revenues (C1)			Non-interest income (Net)/Other operating expenses (C2)			Consumer loans/Total loans (C3)			Interest income/Total assets (C4)		
Interest income/Total revenues (C1)	1.00	1.00	1.00	0.5	1	1.5	0.5	1	1.5	1.00	1.50	2.00
Non-interest income (net)/Other operating expenses (C2)	0.67	1.00	2.00	1.00	1.00	1.00	1.00	1.50	2.00	0.5	1	1.5
Consumer loans/Total loans (C3)	0.67	1.00	2.00	0.50	0.67	1.00	1.00	1.00	1.00	1.5	2	2.5
Interest income/Total assets (C4)	0.50	0.67	1.00	0.67	1.00	2.00	0.40	0.50	0.67	1.00	1.00	1.00
FX assets/Total assets (C6)	0.50	0.67	1.00	0.50	0.67	1.00	0.67	1.00	2.00	0.40	0.50	0.67
Interest expenses/Total expenses (C7)	0.67	1.00	2.00	0.50	0.67	1.00	0.50	0.67	1.00	0.67	1.00	2.00
TL liquid assets/Total assets (C8)	0.50	0.67	1.00	0.67	1.00	2.00	0.40	0.50	0.67	0.67	1.00	2.00

Criteria	FX assets/Total assets (C6)			Interest expenses/Total expenses (C7)			TL liquid assets/Total assets (C8)		
Interest income/Total revenues (C1)	1.00	1.50	2.00	0.5	1	1.5	1.00	1.50	2.00
Non-interest income (net)/Other operating expenses (C2)	1.00	1.50	2.00	1.00	1.50	2.00	0.5	1	1.5
Consumer loans/Total loans (C3)	0.5	1	1.5	1	1.5	2	1.5	2	2.5
Interest income/Total assets (C4)	1.5	2	2.5	0.5	1	1.5	0.5	1	1.5
FX assets/Total assets (C6)	1.00	1.00	1.00	2.5	3	3.5	2.5	3	3.5
Interest expenses/Total expenses (C7)	0.29	0.33	0.40	1.00	1.00	1.00	1.00	1.50	2.00
TL liquid assets/Total assets (C8)	0.29	0.33	0.40	0.50	0.67	1.00	1.00	1.00	1.00

Table 4.14 Inner dependence matrix of the criteria with the respect to criterion 6

Criteria	Interest income/Total revenues (C1)			Non-interest income (Net)/Other operating expenses (C2)			Consumer loans/ Total loans (C3)			Interest income/ Total assets (C4)		
Interest income/Total revenues (C1)	1.00	1.00	1.00	0.5	1	1.5	0.5	1	1.5	0.5	1	1.5
Non-interest income (net)/Other operating expenses (C2)	0.67	1.00	2.00	1.00	1.00	1.00	1.00	1.50	2.00	0.5	1	1.5
Consumer loans/Total loans (C3)	0.67	1.00	2.00	0.50	0.67	1.00	1.00	1.00	1.00	1	1.5	2
Interest income/Total assets (C4)	0.67	1.00	2.00	0.67	1.00	2.00	0.50	0.67	1.00	1.00	1.00	1.00
FX liquid assets/FX liabilities (C5)	0.50	0.67	1.00	0.50	0.67	1.00	0.67	1.00	2.00	0.67	1.00	2.00
Interest expenses/Total expenses (C7)	0.67	1.00	2.00	0.50	0.67	1.00	0.50	0.67	1.00	0.67	1.00	2.00
TL liquid assets/Total assets (C8)	0.50	0.67	1.00	0.67	1.00	2.00	0.33	0.40	0.50	0.67	1.00	2.00

Criteria	FX liquid assets/FX liabilities (C5)			Interest expenses/Total expenses (C7)			TL liquid assets/Total assets (C8)		
Interest income/Total revenues (C1)	1.00	1.50	2.00	0.5	1	1.5	1.00	1.50	2.00
Non-interest income (net)/Other operating expenses (C2)	1.00	1.50	2.00	1.00	1.50	2.00	0.5	1	1.5
Consumer loans/Total loans (C3)	0.5	1	1.5	1	1.5	2	2	2.5	3
Interest income/Total assets (C4)	0.5	1	1.5	0.5	1	1.5	0.5	1	1.5
FX liquid assets/FX liabilities (C5)	1.00	1.00	1.00	2.5	3	3.5	2.5	3	3.5
Interest expenses/Total expenses (C7)	0.29	0.33	0.40	1.00	1.00	1.00	1.00	1.50	2.00
TL liquid assets/Total assets (C8)	0.29	0.33	0.40	0.50	0.67	1.00	1.00	1.00	1.00

Table 4.15 Inner dependence matrix of the criteria with the respect to criterion 7

Criteria	Interest income/Total revenues (C1)			Non-interest income (Net)/Other operating expenses (C2)			Consumer loans/ Total loans (C3)			Interest income/ Total assets (C4)		
Interest income/Total revenues (C1)	1.00	1.00	1.00	1.00	1.50	2.00	0.5	1	1.5	1.00	1.50	2.00
Non-interest income (net)/Other operating expenses (C2)	0.50	0.67	1.00	1.00	1.00	1.00	0.5	1	1.5	0.5	1	1.5
Consumer loans/Total loans (C3)	0.67	1.00	2.00	0.67	1.00	2.00	1.00	1.00	1.00	1	1.5	2
Interest income/Total assets (C4)	0.50	0.67	1.00	0.67	1.00	2.00	0.50	0.67	1.00	1.00	1.00	1.00
FX liquid assets/FX liabilities (C5)	0.67	1.00	2.00	0.67	1.00	2.00	0.67	1.00	2.00	0.67	1.00	2.00
FX assets/Total assets (C6)	0.67	1.00	2.00	0.50	0.67	1.00	0.67	1.00	2.00	0.67	1.00	2.00
TL liquid assets/Total assets (C8)	0.67	1.00	2.00	0.67	1.00	2.00	0.50	0.67	1.00	0.67	1.00	2.00

Criteria	FX liquid assets/FX liabilities (C5)			FX assets/Total assets (C6)			TL liquid assets/Total assets (C8)		
Interest income/Total revenues (C1)	0.5	1	1.5	0.5	1	1.5	0.5	1	1.5
Non-interest income (net)/Other operating expenses (C2)	0.5	1	1.5	1.00	1.50	2.00	0.5	1	1.5
Consumer loans/Total loans (C3)	0.5	1	1.5	0.5	1	1.5	1	1.5	2
Interest income/Total assets (C4)	0.5	1	1.5	0.5	1	1.5	0.5	1	1.5
FX liquid assets/FX liabilities (C5)	1.00	1.00	1.00	0.5	1	1.5	2.00	2.50	3.00
FX assets/Total assets (C6)	0.67	1.00	2.00	1.00	1.00	1.00	2.50	3.00	3.50
TL liquid assets/Total assets (C8)	0.33	0.40	0.50	0.29	0.33	0.40	1.00	1.00	1.00

Table 4.16 Inner dependence matrix of the criteria with the respect to criterion 8

Criteria	Interest income/Total revenues (C1)			Non-interest income (Net)/Other operating expenses (C2)			Consumer loans/ Total loans (C3)			Interest income/ Total assets (C4)		
Interest income/Total revenues (C1)	1.00	1.00	1.00	0.5	1	1.5	0.5	1	1.5	0.5	1	1.5
Non-interest income (net)/Other operating expenses (C2)	0.67	1.00	2.00	1.00	1.00	1.00	0.5	1	1.5	0.5	1	1.5
Consumer loans/Total loans(C3)	0.67	1.00	2.00	0.67	1.00	2.00	1.00	1.00	1.00	1	1.5	2
Interest income/Total assets (C4)	0.67	1.00	2.00	0.67	1.00	2.00	0.50	0.67	1.00	1.00	1.00	1.00
FX liquid assets/FX liabilities (C5)	0.67	1.00	2.00	0.67	1.00	2.00	0.67	1.00	2.00	0.67	1.00	2.00
FX assets/Total assets (C6)	0.67	1.00	2.00	0.50	0.67	1.00	0.67	1.00	2.00	0.67	1.00	2.00
Interest expenses/Total expenses (C7)	0.67	1.00	2.00	0.67	1.00	2.00	0.50	0.67	1.00	0.50	0.67	1.00

Criteria	FX liquid assets/FX liabilities (C5)			FX assets/Total assets (C6)			Interest expenses/Total expenses (C7)		
Interest income/Total revenues (C1)	0.5	1	1.5	0.5	1	1.5	0.5	1	1.5
Non-interest income (net)/Other operating expenses (C2)	0.5	1	1.5	1.00	1.50	2.00	0.5	1	1.5
Consumer loans/Total loans (C3)	0.5	1	1.5	0.5	1	1.5	1	1.5	2
Interest income/Total assets (C4)	0.5	1	1.5	0.5	1	1.5	1.00	1.50	2.00
FX liquid assets/FX liabilities (C5)	1.00	1.00	1.00	0.5	1	1.5	2	2.5	3
FX assets/Total assets (C6)	0.67	1.00	2.00	1.00	1.00	1.00	2.50	3.00	3.50
Interest expenses/Total expenses (C7)	0.33	0.40	0.50	0.29	0.33	0.40	1.00	1.00	1.00

References

Agbeja, O., Adelakun, O. J., & Udi, E. E. (2016). Empirical analysis of counterparty risk and exchange rate risk management on the performance of deposit money banks in Nigeria (2009–2013). *Journal of Accounting & Finance (2158–3625), 16*(2), 106–116.

Agoraki, M. E. K., & Tsamis, A. (2017). Bank profitability and regulation in emerging European markets. *Multinational Finance Journal, 21*(3), 177–210.

Ahamed, M. M. (2017). Asset quality, non-interest income, and bank profitability: Evidence from Indian banks. *Economic Modelling, 63*, 1–14.

Akinkunmi, M. A. (2017). Determinants of banks' profitability in Nigeria: Does relative market power matter. *Journal of Finance, 5*(1), 42–53.

Al Nimer, M., Warrad, L., & Al Omari, R. (2015). The impact of liquidity on Jordanian banks profitability through return on assets. *European Journal of Business and Management, 7*(7), 229–232.

Ali, H., & Shahid, M. A. (2017). The impact of interest rate and exchange rate volatility on banks' stock returns and volatility: Evidence from Pakistan. *International Journal of Commerce and Management, 2*(4), 29–39.

Aliakbari Nouri, F., Khalili Esbouei, S., & Antucheviciene, J. (2015). A hybrid MCDM approach based on fuzzy ANP and fuzzy TOPSIS for technology selection. *Informatica, 26*(3), 369–388.

Alilou, H., Rahmati, O., Singh, V. P., Choubin, B., Pradhan, B., Keesstra, S., … Sadeghi, S. H. (2019). Evaluation of watershed health using fuzzy-ANP approach considering geo-environmental and topo-hydrological criteria. *Journal of Environmental Management, 232*, 22–36.

Aliyu, S., & Yusof, R. M. (2016). Profitability and cost efficiency of Islamic banks: A panel analysis of some selected countries. *International Journal of Economics and Financial Issues, 6* (4), 1736–1743.

Al-Khazali, O. M., & Mirzaei, A. (2017). The impact of oil price movements on bank non-performing loans: Global evidence from oil-exporting countries. *Emerging Markets Review, 31*, 193–208.

Alshatti, A. S. (2015). The effect of the liquidity management on profitability in the Jordanian commercial banks. *International Journal of Business and Management, 10*(1), 62.

Altavilla, C., Boucinha, M., & Peydró, J. L. (2018). Monetary policy and bank profitability in a low interest rate environment. *Economic Policy, 33*(96), 531–586.

Apergis, N., & Lau, C. K. M. (2017). How deviations from FOMC's monetary policy decisions from a benchmark monetary policy rule affect bank profitability: Evidence from US banks. *Journal of Financial Economic Policy, 9*(4), 354–371.

Arteta, C., Kose, M. A., Stocker, M., & Taskin, T. (2018). Implications of negative interest rate policies: An early assessment. *Pacific Economic Review, 23*(1), 8–26.

Ayağ, Z., & Yücekaya, A. (2019). A fuzzy ANP-based GRA approach to evaluate ERP packages. *International Journal of Enterprise Information Systems (IJEIS), 15*(1), 45–68.

Beaton, K. M., & Myrvoda, A. (2016). *Non-performing loans in the Eccu*. International Monetary Fund.

Bech, M. L., & Malkhozov, A. (2016). How have central banks implemented negative policy rates?. *BIS Quarterly Review March*. Bank for International Settlements, March.

Bikker, J. A., & Vervliet, T. M. (2018). Bank profitability and risk-taking under low interest rates. *International Journal of Finance and Economics, 23*(1), 3–18.

Bitar, M., Saad, W., & Benlemlih, M. (2016). Bank risk and performance in the MENA region: The importance of capital requirements. *Economic Systems, 40*(3), 398–421.

Borio, C., Gambacorta, L., & Hofmann, B. (2017). The influence of monetary policy on bank profitability. *International Finance, 20*(1), 48–63.

Bozbura, F. T., Beskese, A., & Kahraman, C. (2007). Prioritization of human capital measurement indicators using fuzzy AHP. *Expert Systems with Applications, 32*(4), 1100–1112.

Brighi, P., & Venturelli, V. (2016). How functional and geographic diversification affect bank profitability during the crisis. *Finance Research Letters, 16*, 1–10.

Chang, D. Y. (1996). Applications of the extent analysis method on fuzzy AHP. *European Journal of Operational Research, 95*(3), 649–655.

Chronopoulos, D. K., Liu, H., McMillan, F. J., & Wilson, J. O. (2015). The dynamics of US bank profitability. *The European Journal of Finance, 21*(5), 426–443.

Claessens, S., Coleman, N., & Donnelly, M. (2018). 'Low-for-long' interest rates and banks' interest margins and profitability: Cross-country evidence. *Journal of Financial Intermediation, 35*, 1–16.

De Jonghe, O., & Öztekin, Ö. (2015). Bank capital management: International evidence. *Journal of Financial Intermediation, 24*(2), 154–177.

Dimitrios, A., Helen, L., & Mike, T. (2016). Determinants of non-performing loans: Evidence from Euro-area countries. *Finance Research Letters, 18*, 116–119.

Dinçer, H., & Yüksel, S. (2018a). Comparative evaluation of BSC-based new service development competencies in Turkish banking sector with the integrated fuzzy hybrid MCDM using content analysis. *International Journal of Fuzzy Systems, 20*(8), 2497–2516.

Dinçer, H., & Yüksel, S. (2018b). Financial sector-based analysis of the G20 economies using the integrated decision-making approach with DEMATEL and TOPSIS. In *Emerging trends in banking and finance* (pp. 210–223). Springer.

Dinçer, H., & Yüksel, S. (2019). An integrated stochastic fuzzy MCDM approach to the balanced scorecard-based service evaluation. *Mathematics and Computers in Simulation, 166*, 93–112. https://doi.org/10.1016/j.matcom.2019.04.008.

Dinçer, H., Hacioglu, U., & Yuksel, S. (2016a). Balanced scorecard-based performance assessment of Turkish banking sector with analytic network process. *International Journal of Decision Sciences & Applications-IJDSA, 1*(1), 1–21.

Dinçer, H., Hacioglu, U., & Yuksel, S. (2016b). Performance assessment of deposit banks with CAMELS analysis using fuzzy ANP-moora approaches and an application on Turkish banking sector. *Asian Journal of Research in Business Economics and Management, 6*(2), 32–56.

Dinçer, H., Hacıoğlu, Ü., & Yüksel, S. (2016c). Managerial and market-based appraisal of agriculture banking using ANP and ELECTRE method. *Management & Organizational Studies, 3*(3), 29–40.

Dinçer, H., Hacıoğlu, Ü., & Yüksel, S. (2017). A strategic approach to global financial crisis in banking sector: A critical appraisal of banking strategies using fuzzy ANP and fuzzy Topsis methods. *International Journal of Sustainable Economies Management (IJSEM), 6*(1), 1–21.

Dinçer, H., Hacıoğlu, Ü., & Yüksel, S. (2018a). Determining influencing factors of currency exchange rate for decision making in global economy using MARS method. In *Geopolitics and strategic management in the global economy* (pp. 261–273). IGI Global.

Dinçer, H., Yuksel, S., & Adalı, Z. (2018b). Relationship between non-performing loans, industry, and economic growth of the African economies and policy recommendations for global growth. In *Globalization and trade integration in developing countries* (pp. 203–228). IGI Global.

Dinçer, H., Yüksel, S., & Şenel, S. (2018c). Analyzing the global risks for the financial crisis after the great depression using comparative hybrid hesitant fuzzy decision-making models: Policy recommendations for sustainable economic growth. *Sustainability, 10*(9), 3126.

Dinçer, H., Yüksel, S., & Adalı, Z. (2019a). Economic effects in Islamic stock development of the European countries: Policy recommendations for ethical behaviors. In *Handbook of research on managerial thinking in global business economics* (pp. 58–78). IGI Global.

Dinçer, H., Yüksel, S., & Çetiner, İ. T. (2019b). Strategy selection for organizational performance of Turkish banking sector with the integrated multi-dimensional decision-making approach. In *Handbook of research on contemporary approaches in management and organizational strategy* (pp. 273–291). IGI Global.

Dinçer, H., Yüksel, S., & Martínez, L. (2019f). Analysis of balanced scorecard-based SERVQUAL criteria based on hesitant decision-making approaches. *Computers & Industrial Engineering, 131*, 1–12.

Dinçer, H., Yüksel, S., & Martínez, L. (2019g). Interval type 2-based hybrid fuzzy evaluation of financial services in E7 economies with DEMATEL-ANP and MOORA methods. *Applied Soft Computing, 79*, 186–202.

Dinçer, H., Yüksel, S., Eti, S., & Tula, A. (2019c). Effects of demographic characteristics on business success: An evidence from Turkish banking sector. In *Handbook of research on business models in modern competitive scenarios* (pp. 304–324). IGI Global.

Dinçer, H., Yüksel, S., Kartal, M. T., & Alpman, G. (2019d). Corporate governance-based evaluation of alternative distribution channels in the Turkish banking sector using quality function deployment with an integrated fuzzy MCDM method. In *Intergenerational governance and leadership in the corporate world: Emerging research and opportunities* (pp. 39–77). IGI Global.

Dinçer, H., Yüksel, S., Yazici, M., & Pınarbaşı, F. (2019e). Assessing corporate social responsibilities in the banking sector: As a tool of strategic communication during the global financial crisis. In *Handbook of research on global issues in financial communication and investment decision making* (pp. 1–27). IGI Global.

Djalilov, K., & Piesse, J. (2016). Determinants of bank profitability in transition countries: What matters most? *Research in International Business and Finance, 38*, 69–82.

Duraj, B., & Moci, E. (2015). Factors influencing the bank profitability-empirical evidence from Albania. *Asian Economic and Financial Review, 5*(3), 483.

Ekanayake, E. M. N. N., & Azeez, A. A. (2015). Determinants of non-performing loans in licensed commercial banks: Evidence from Sri Lanka. *Asian Economic and Financial Review, 5*(6), 868.

Ergeç, E. H., & Ersin, İ. (2018). The relationships between public expenditure and sectorial employment in Turkey. *BİLTÜRK Journal of Economics and Related Studies* e-ISSN 2667-5927, 150.

Ersin, İ. (2018). İhracata Dayalı Büyüme Hipotezinin Test Edilmesi: MINT Ülkeleri Örneği. *Ekonomi, İşletme ve Maliye Araştırmaları Dergisi, 1*(1), 26–38.

Ersin, İ., & Ergeç, E. H. (2018). Harcama Bileşenleri Ve Sektörel İstihdam Arasindaki Nedensellik İlişkisi. *Yönetim ve Ekonomi Araştırmaları Dergisi, 16*(Özel Sayı 1), 161–180.

Ersin, İ., & Yıldırım, C. (2015). İslam Ekonomisi Çerçevesinde Necmettin Erbakan'ın Adil Düzen Söylemi. *Abant İzzet Baysal Üniversitesi Sosyal Bilimler Enstitüsü Dergisi, 15*(1), 143–174.

Eti, S. (2019). The use of quantitative methods in investment decisions: A literature review. In *Handbook of research on global issues in financial communication and investment decision making* (pp. 256–275). IGI Global.

Gambacorta, L., & Shin, H. S. (2018). Why bank capital matters for monetary policy. *Journal of Financial Intermediation, 35*, 17–29.

Garcia, M. T. M., & Guerreiro, J. P. S. M. (2016). Internal and external determinants of banks' profitability: The Portuguese case. *Journal of Economic Studies, 43*(1), 90–107.

Ghosh, A. (2015). Banking-industry specific and regional economic determinants of non-performing loans: Evidence from US states. *Journal of Financial Stability, 20*, 93–104.

Hasanov, F., Bayramli, N., & Al-Musehel, N. (2018). Bank-specific and macroeconomic determinants of Bank profitability: Evidence from an oil-dependent economy. *International Journal of Financial Studies, 6*(3), 78.

Horton, M. M. A., Samiei, H., Epstein, M. N. P., & Ross, M. K. (2016). *Exchange rate developments and policies in the Caucasus and Central Asia*. International Monetary Fund.

Ignatius, J., Rahman, A., Yazdani, M., Šaparauskas, J., & Haron, S. H. (2016). An integrated fuzzy ANP–QFD approach for green building assessment. *Journal of Civil Engineering and Management, 22*(4), 551–563.

Islam, M. A., Sarker, M. N. I., Rahman, M., Sultana, A., & Prodhan, A. S. (2017). Determinants of profitability of commercial banks in Bangladesh. *International Journal of Banking and Financial Law, 1*(1), 1–11.

Jaradat, M. A., & ALkhazaleh, M. H. A. (2018). The effect of liquidity, administrative efficiency and capital adequacy on the profitability of Jordanian banks listed on the Amman Stock Exchange. *International Journal of Academic Research in Accounting, Finance and Management Sciences, 8*(4), 183–194.

Jiang, L., Levine, R., & Lin, C. (2019). Competition and bank liquidity creation. *Journal of Financial and Quantitative Analysis, 54*(2), 1–50.

Jobst, A., & Lin, H. (2016). *Negative interest rate policy (NIRP): Implications for monetary transmission and bank profitability in the Euro Area*. International Monetary Fund.

Kalkavan, H., & Ersin, I. (2019). Determination of factors affecting the south east Asian crisis of 1997 probit-logit panel regression: The south east Asian crisis. In *Handbook of research on global issues in financial communication and investment decision making* (pp. 148–167). IGI Global.

Kassem, N. M., & Sakr, A. (2018). The impact of bank-specific characteristics on the profitability of commercial banks in Egypt. *Journal of Finance, 6*(2), 76–90.

Khan, I., & Ahmad, A. (2017). Assessing banks internal factors as determinants of non-performing loans: Evidence from Pakistani commercial banks. *Journal of Managerial Sciences, 11*(1), 109–125.

Khan, I., Ahmad, A., Khan, M. T., & Ilyas, M. (2018). The impact of GDP, inflation, exchange rate, unemployment and tax rate on the non performing loans of banks: Evidence from Pakistani commercial banks. *Journal of Social Sciences & Humanities (1994–7046), 26*(1), 141–164.

Kumar, V., & Kishore, M. P. (2019). Macroeconomic and bank specific determinants of non-performing loans in UAE conventional bank. *Journal of Banking and Finance, 2*(1), 1–12.

Laryea, E., Ntow-Gyamfi, M., & Alu, A. A. (2016). Nonperforming loans and bank profitability: Evidence from an emerging market. *African Journal of Economic and Management Studies, 7*(4), 462–481.

Lee, C. C., Ning, S. L., & Lee, C. C. (2015). How does bank capital affect bank profitability and risk? Evidence from China's WTO accession. *China & World Economy, 23*(4), 19–39.

Liu, Y., Chen, X., & Ralescu, D. A. (2015). Uncertain currency model and currency option pricing. *International Journal of Intelligent Systems, 30*(1), 40–51.

Madaschi, C., & Pablos Nuevo, I. (2017). *The profitability of banks in a context of negative monetary policy rates: The cases of Sweden and Denmark* (No. 195). ECB Occasional Paper.

Menicucci, E., & Paolucci, G. (2016). The determinants of bank profitability: Empirical evidence from European banking sector. *Journal of Financial Reporting and Accounting, 14*(1), 86–115.

Moussa, M. A. B. (2015). The determinants of bank liquidity: Case of Tunisia. *International Journal of Economics and Financial Issues, 5*(1), 249–259.

Nys, E., Tarazi, A., & Trinugroho, I. (2015). Political connections, bank deposits, and formal deposit insurance. *Journal of Financial Stability, 19*, 83–104.

Oktar, S., & Yüksel, S. (2015). *Bankacılık krizlerinin erken uyarı sinyalleri: Türkiye üzerine bir uygulama*. İstanbul Ticaret Üniversitesi Sosyal Bilimler Dergisi.

Oktar, S., & Yüksel, S. (2016). Bankalarin Türev Ürün Kullanimini Etkileyen Faktörler: Mars Yöntemi ile Bir Inceleme/Determinants of the use derivatives in banking: An analysis with MARS Model. *Finans Politik & Ekonomik Yorumlar, 53*(620), 31.

Osundina, C. K., Ademola, O. J., Olamide, J. O., & Moses, O. I. (2016). Exchange rate volatility and banks performance: Evidence from Nigeria. *IIARD International Journal of Economicsand Business Management, 2*(4), 1–11.

Owusu-Antwi, G., Banerjee, R., & Antwi, J. (2017). Interest rate spread on bank profitability: The case of Ghanaian banks. *Journal of Accounting, Business and Finance Research, 1*(1), 34–45.

Ozgur, O., & Gorus, M. S. (2016). Determinants of deposit bank profitability: Evidence from Turkey. *Journal of Applied Economics and Business Research, 6*(3), 218–231.

Ozili, P. K. (2017). Bank profitability and capital regulation: Evidence from listed and non-listed banks in Africa. *Journal of African Business, 18*(2), 143–168.

Petria, N., Capraru, B., & Ihnatov, I. (2015). Determinants of banks' profitability: Evidence from EU 27 banking systems. *Procedia Economics and Finance, 20*, 518–524.

Rahman, M. M., Hamid, M. K., & Khan, M. A. M. (2015). Determinants of bank profitability: Empirical evidence from Bangladesh. *International Journal of Business and Management, 10* (8), 135.

Ramlan, H., & Adnan, M. S. (2016). The profitability of Islamic and conventional bank: Case study in Malaysia. *Procedia Economics and Finance, 35*, 359–367.

Rani, D. S., & Zergaw, L. N. (2017). Bank specific, industry specific and macroeconomic determinants of bank profitability in Ethiopia. *International Journal of Advanced Research in Management and Social Sciences, 6*(3), 74–96.

Regehr, K., & Sengupta, R. (2016). Has the relationship between bank size and profitability changed?. *Economic Review, (01612387), 101*(2), 49–72.

Riyadi, S. (2017). Financial performance efficiency of Indonesia government banks in improving profitability. *International Journal of Financial Innovation in Banking, 1*(3–4), 239–252.

Said, A. (2018). Effect of the asset quality on the bank profitability: A study of US commercial small banks. *International Research Journal of Applied Finance, 9*(4), 196–204.

Saif-Alyousfi, A. Y., Saha, A., & Md-Rus, R. (2017). Profitability of Saudi commercial banks: A comparative evaluation between domestic and foreign banks using capital adequacy, asset quality, management quality, earning ability and liquidity parameters. *International Journal of Economics and Financial Issues, 7*(2), 477–484.

Samad, A. (2015). Determinants bank profitability: Empirical evidence from Bangladesh commercial banks. *International Journal of Financial Research, 6*(3), 173–179.

Samanlioglu, F., & Ayağ, Z. (2016). Fuzzy ANP-based PROMETHEE II approach for evaluation of machine tool alternatives. *Journal of Intelligent Fuzzy Systems, 30*(4), 2223–2235.

Saunders, A., Schmid, M., & Walter, I. (2016). *Non-interest income and bank performance: Does ring-fencing reduce bank risk*. Working Papers on Finance (2014/17), 1417–1477.

Scheiber, T., Silgoner, M., & Stern, C. (2016). The development of bank profitability in Denmark, Sweden and Switzerland during a period of ultra-low and negative interest rates. *Focus on European Economic Integration, 3*, 8–28.

Tan, Y. (2016). The impacts of risk and competition on bank profitability in China. *Journal of International Financial Markets, Institutions and Money, 40*, 85–110.

Thornton, J., & Vasilakis, C. (2019). Negative policy interest rates and exchange rate behavior: Further results. *Finance Research Letters*. Elsevier, Vol. 29(*C*), pp. 61–67.

Topak, M. S., & Talu, N. H. (2017). Bank specific and macroeconomic determinants of bank profitability: Evidence from Turkey. *International Journal of Economics and Financial Issues, 7*(2), 574–584.

Trad, N., Trabelsi, M. A., & Goux, J. F. (2017). Risk and profitability of Islamic banks: A religious deception or an alternative solution? *European Research on Management and Business Economics, 23*(1), 40–45.

Tran, V. T., Lin, C. T., & Nguyen, H. (2016). Liquidity creation, regulatory capital, and bank profitability. *International Review of Financial Analysis, 48*, 98–109.

Tunay, K. B., & Yüksel, S. (2017). The relationship between corporate governance and foreign ownership of the banks in developing countries. *Contaduría y administración, 62*(5), 1627–1642.

Tunay, N., Yüksel, S., & Tunay, K. B. (2019). The effects of technology on Bank performance in advanced and emerging economies: An empirical analysis. In *Handbook of research on managerial thinking in global business economics* (pp. 263–280). IGI Global.

Uygun, Ö., Kaçamak, H., & Kahraman, Ü. A. (2015). An integrated DEMATEL and fuzzy ANP techniques for evaluation and selection of outsourcing provider for a telecommunication company. *Computers & Industrial Engineering, 86*, 137–146.

Vinodh, S., Balagi, T. S., & Patil, A. (2016). A hybrid MCDM approach for agile concept selection using fuzzy DEMATEL, fuzzy ANP and fuzzy TOPSIS. *The International Journal of Advanced Manufacturing Technology, 83*(9–12), 1979–1987.

Vithessonthi, C. (2016). Deflation, bank credit growth, and non-performing loans: Evidence from Japan. *International Review of Financial Analysis, 45*, 295–305.

Winarso, E., & Salim, I. A. (2017). The influence of risk management to the return on asset (ROA) banking sector (case study of bank in Indonesia listed in Indonesia Stock Exchange). *Advances in Economics and Business, 5*(7), 382–393.
Xu, Z., Elomri, A., Pokharel, S., & Ming, X. G. (2017). Product-service supplier pre-evaluation with modified fuzzy ANP reducing decision information distortion. *International Journal of Computer Integrated Manufacturing, 30*(7), 738–754.
Yüksel, S. (2017a). Determinants of the credit risk in developing countries after economic crisis: A case of Turkish banking sector. In *Global financial crisis and its ramifications on capital markets* (pp. 401–415). Springer.
Yüksel, S. (2017b). Strategies out of global recession in emerging markets: An application for 2008 global crisis. In *Global business strategies in crisis* (pp. 57–75). Springer.
Yüksel, S., & Kavak, P. T. (2019). Do financial investment decisions affect economic development?: An analysis on mortgage loans in Turkey. In *Handbook of research on global issues in financial communication and investment decision making* (pp. 168–191). IGI Global.
Yüksel, S., & Özsarı, M. (2016). Impact of consumer loans on inflation and current account deficit: A Toda Yamamoto causality test for Turkey. *World Journal of Applied Economics, 2*(2), 3–14.
Yüksel, S., & Özsari, M. (2017). Identifying the factors influence Turkish deposit banks to join corporate social responsibility activities by using panel Probit method. *International Journal of Finance & Banking Studies, 6*(1), 39.
Yüksel, S., & Zengin, S. (2016a). Identifying the determinants of interest rate risk of the banks: A case of Turkish banking sector. *International Journal of Research in Business and Social Science, 5*(6), 12–28.
Yüksel, S., & Zengin, S. (2016b). Leading indicators of 2008 global crisis: An analysis with logit and mars methods. *Finansal Araştırmalar ve Çalışmalar Dergisi, 8*(15), 495–518.
Yuksel, S., & Zengin, S. (2017). Influencing factors of net interest margin in Turkish banking sector. *International Journal of Economics and Financial Issues, 7*(1), 178–191.
Yüksel, S., Mukhtarov, S., & Mammadov, E. (2016a). Comparing the efficiency of Turkish and Azerbaijani banks: An application with data envelopment analysis. *International Journal of Economics and Financial Issues, 6*(3), 1059–1067.
Yüksel, S., Özsarı, M., & Canöz, İ. (2016b). Influencing factors of currency risk of deposit banks in Turkey by using probit method. *International Journal of Commerce and Finance, 2*(Full Issue), 85–95.
Yüksel, S., Zengin, S., & Kartal, M. T. (2016c). Identifying the macroeconomic factors influencing credit card usage in Turkey by using MARS method. *China-USA Business Review, 15*(12), 611–615.
Yüksel, S., Canöz, İ., & Adalı, Z. (2017a). Türkiye'deki Mevduat Bankalarının Fiyat-Kazanç Oranını Etkileyen Değişkenlerin Mars Yöntemi İle Belirlenmesi. *Fiscaoeconomia, 3*, 40–55.
Yüksel, S., Canöz, İ., & Özsarı, M. (2017b). Causality relationship between interest rate of deposit banks and profit share rate of islamic banks in Turkey. *Ikonomika, 2*(2), 131–148.
Zarrouk, H., Ben Jedidia, K., & Moualhi, M. (2016). Is Islamic bank profitability driven by same forces as conventional banks? *International Journal of Islamic and Middle Eastern Finance and Management, 9*(1), 46–66.
Zengin, S., & Yüksel, S. (2016a). A comparison of the views of internal controllers/auditors and branch/call center personnel of the banks for operational risk: A case for Turkish banking sector. *International Journal of Finance & Banking Studies, 5*(4), 10.
Zengin, S., & Yüksel, S. (2016b). Likidite riskini etkileyen faktörler: Türk bankacılık sektörü üzerine bir inceleme. *İstanbul Ticaret Üniversitesi Sosyal Bilimler Dergisi, 15*(29), 77–95.
Zheng, C., Rahman, M., Begum, M., & Ashraf, B. (2017). Capital regulation, the cost of financial intermediation and bank profitability: Evidence from Bangladesh. *Journal of Risk and Financial Management, 10*(2), 9.

Chapter 5
The Influence of the Politicians on Macroeconomic Performance: An Analysis of Donald Trump's Tweets

Abstract The aim of this study is to understand the role of the politicians on the macroeconomic situation of the countries. For this purpose, the tweets of Donald Trump are taken into consideration. Text mining approach is used to evaluate these tweets and most used words are identified. Next, all-important keywords are matched with significant topics and 4 different classes are identified for this condition, which are financial, social, military, and political issues. After that, these keywords are ranked with the help of fuzzy VIKOR approach according to their impacts on macroeconomic performance. In this context, five different factors are also defined, which represent macroeconomic performance that are economic growth, unemployment, inflation, international trade, and industrial development. The findings show that political and economic factors are the most important items which affect macroeconomic situation of the country. It is recommended that politicians should not make negative explanations about political and financial conditions in order not to have unfavorable results in the economic activities.

Keywords Politic intervention · Stock exchanges · Text mining · Fuzzy VIKOR

5.1 Introduction

Economic performance is crucial for countries. Therefore, all countries make significant efforts to improve their macroeconomic situation. However, there are several important issues affecting the macroeconomic performance of countries. Therefore, countries need to pay attention to all of these different issues in order to have a continuous economic growth. For example, in order for the countries to improve their economic situation, investments in the country need to be increased. To this end, countries support some national and international investors. In addition to this, these investments also offer new employment opportunities to people. This contributes to the reduction of the unemployment rate.

On the other hand, some factors negatively affect the economic performance of countries. In this context, it is accepted that the high inflation rate has a negative

G. Silahtaroğlu et al., *Data Science and Multiple Criteria Decision Making Approaches in Finance*, Multiple Criteria Decision Making,
https://doi.org/10.1007/978-3-030-74176-1_5

impact on the country's economy. The main reason for this is that high inflation increases the uncertainty in the market. In an environment with high uncertainty, investors will be reluctant to invest. This situation will negatively affect the economic activity in the country. In addition to high inflation, the high interest rate also reduces the economic performance of the country. In an environment where interest rates are high, new investments are decreasing as investors' costs will increase. As a result, these companies prefer to employ fewer people.

In addition, the statements of politicians are considered to have a significant impact on the economy of the country. Politicians frequently comment on political, economic, social, and cultural issues. These statements may have a positive effect on the economy of the country at times, but in some cases this effect is seen as negative. In the event of economic uncertainty in the country, government officials can make an explanation and aim to give confidence to the market. However, in some cases it is understood that the statements of these officials had a negative impact on the country's economy. For example, as a result of political tension between the two countries, it is likely that one of the state officials would have a harsh and negative statement that could harm the country's economy.

Especially with the effect of globalization, the economic negativities of the big countries will have a very negative effect on other countries. In parallel, a statement by the state authorities of these big countries is affecting other countries as well. The most important example of this can be seen in 2013 when the president of the Federal Reserve Bank made explanations about the country's new economic policies. After this statement on monetary tightening, the economy of many countries was adversely affected. Today, the statements made by US President Donald Trump are followed by many countries around the world. President Trump's statements on Twitter are thought to have an impact on many countries' economies.

In this study, it is aimed to analyze the role of the politicians on the macroeconomic performance of the countries. For this purpose, Donald Trump's tweets are considered in the analysis process. These tweets are evaluated by using text mining approach. After that, the main classes are determined according to the results. On the other hand, fuzzy VIKOR methodology is used to rank these items according to their importance. Moreover, for macroeconomic factors, 5 different variables are selected, which are economic growth, unemployment, inflation, international trade, and industrial development.

This study has main novelties which contribute to the literature. First of all, text mining and fuzzy VIKOR approach are firstly considered in this study with the aim of understanding the role of the politicians on the macroeconomic performance. Additionally, politicians' explanations are firstly categorized according to their effects on the economy. Moreover, using the tweets of Donald Trump also increases the originality of this study because nowadays it is very popular.

This study has four different sections. This first section gives the main significance of the topic. In this context, the importance of the politicians' explanations and using fuzzy logic are explained. In addition to this situation, literature is reviewed in the second section. Hence, the missing part can be underlined in this process. The third part gives information about both methodology and analysis results. In the last part, recommendations are given based on these analysis results.

5.2 Literature Review

The impact of state policies and politicians on the economy is very popular in the literature. In the analyzes, it is seen that the studies focus on very different areas. Many authors have focused on the positive aspects of this relationship. Touchton (2016) stated that the effective implementation of government policies would increase investments in the country. Kryszczuk and Wenzel (2016) mentioned the positive effect of this issue on technological development in the country. Stated that there are successful state policies behind the rapid growth of the Chinese economy. On the other hand, Cao et al. (2018), Torfing and Ansell (2017), Sørensen (2016), Douglas (2016), and Schnitzer et al. (2017) are other researchers who think that effective state policies will contribute to stable economic development in the country.

On the other hand, some of the studies emphasized the negative effects of wrong state policies on economic development in the country. As an example, Kideghesho (2016) conducted research on the results of state policies in Tanzania. In this study, it was determined that the wrong and incomplete government policies increased the crime rate in the country. This situation negatively affects the economic development of the country. Kozlov et al. (2018) carried out a similar study for Russia and underlined the same issues. According to Christensen et al. (2017), it is inevitable that economic problems have occurred if state policies cannot manage the problem of foreign migration. Khan and Krishnan (2019), Pellegata and Memoli (2018), and Krishnan and Khan (2018) defined that corruption by the state authorities caused economic damage in the country.

In addition to them, it is also underlined that when there is high bureaucracy, it will cause economic activities of the countries negatively. Im (2017) emphasized this situation for South Korea. He defined that bureaucratic dysfunction causes some problems for democratization. It is also determined that this situation has a negative influence on free market operations. Similarly, Shafiq et al. (2017) stated this issue for Pakistan in their study. Moreover, Yan and Wooi (2016) tried to analyze the impact of the election on stock market returns. In this study, government-owned banks of Indonesia, Malaysia, and Thailand are taken into consideration. They identified that inefficient governmental policies during the election periods decreased the performance of the stock markets for these countries. Also, Tang and Huhe (2019) and Prato and Strulovici (2017) are other important studies that focused on this issue for different regions.

Furthermore, some studies also stated that politicians may have negative effects on the economic performance of the countries while having too much debt. In this framework, Falagiarda and Gregori (2015) made a study for Italian economy. They identified that because of the high debt, the Italian government had to increase tax rate and this situation decreased the macroeconomic activities in the country. Parallel to this study, Cohen and Karatzimas (2018) also focused on Greek economy. They reached the conclusion that Greek economy suffered from the financial crisis due to high debt amount. In addition to these studies, Borriello (2017) and Cellini and Cuccia (2016) also made an analysis for Spanish and Italian economies for the same scope. They identified that having high amount of uncontrolled debt by the governments led to important financial problems for these countries. On the other side, the role of the political economy was also evaluated for different sectors, such as agriculture (David, 2018) and banking (Wang et al., 2019). Moreover, Ridge et al. (2018), Fu et al. (2017), and Wong (2015) also determined that political connections of the companies have a direct effect on their profitability.

This subject was also considered for the local government level by many researchers. For instance, Reitan et al. (2015) evaluated this subject and concluded that the success of the local politicians has a significant positive effect on the economy of these regions. Chapple and Montero (2018) made a similar analysis for Latin American countries. They also identified that effective local government makes a contribution to the macroeconomic performance. Also, Olausson and Wihlborg (2018) evaluated the local development projects in Swedish municipalities and underlined the same issue. This subject was also assessed by many different researchers (Sancino & Budd, 2017; Mu et al., 2019; Romolini et al., 2015). This literature review gives information that a new study for this subject with an original methodology makes an important contribution to the literature.

5.3 An Application on Donald Trump's Tweets

5.3.1 Fuzzy VIKOR

VIKOR methodology is a type of multicriteria decision-making method. It aims to rank different alternatives with respect to their significance. On the other side, in fuzzy VIKOR approach, expert opinions are taken into consideration. This method mainly includes five different steps. Firstly, linguistic evaluations are obtained for decision makers' evaluations (Opricovic & Tzeng, 2004). In this circumstance, Eq. (5.1) is used.

$$\widetilde{x}_{ij} = \frac{1}{k}\left[\sum\nolimits_{e=1}^{n} \widetilde{x}_{ij}^{\,e}\right]_{,i=1,2,3,\ldots,m} \tag{5.1}$$

Secondly, the fuzzy best and worst values ($\widetilde{f}_j^{\,*}$ and $\widetilde{f}_j^{\,-}$) are computed as in the Eq. (5.2).

$$\widetilde{f}_J^* = \max_i \widetilde{x}_{ij}, \text{and } \widetilde{f}_j^- = \min_i \widetilde{x}_{ij} \quad (5.2)$$

In the third aspect, thirdly, the mean group utility and maximal regret are identified by using the Eqs. (5.3) and (5.4) (Mardani et al., 2016).

$$\widetilde{S}_i = \sum_{i=1}^{n} \widetilde{w}_j \frac{\left(\left|\widetilde{f}_j^* - \widetilde{x}_{ij}\right|\right)}{\left(\left|\widetilde{f}_j^* - \widetilde{f}_j^-\right|\right)} \quad (5.3)$$

$$\widetilde{R}_i = \max{}_j \left[\widetilde{w}_j \frac{\left(\left|\widetilde{f}_j^* - \widetilde{x}_{ij}\right|\right)}{\left(\left|\widetilde{f}_j^* - \widetilde{f}_j^-\right|\right)} \right] \quad (5.4)$$

In addition to them, the value of $\widetilde{Q}_i$ is computed with the help of the Eq. (5.5).

$$\widetilde{Q}_i = v\left(\widetilde{S}_i - \widetilde{S}^*\right)/\left(\widetilde{S}^- - \widetilde{S}^*\right) + (1 - v)\left(\widetilde{R}_i - \widetilde{R}^*\right)/\left(\widetilde{R}^- - \widetilde{R}^*\right) \quad (5.5)$$

In the Eq. (5.5), v represents the weight of the strategy of maximum group utility whereas 1—v shows the weight of the individual regret. Finally, values of S, R, and Q are ranked for the criteria. Fuzzy VIKOR approach was used in many different purposes in the literature, such as supplier selection (Awasthi & Kannan, 2016; Awasthi et al., 2018; You et al., 2015), green supply chain management (Rostamzadeh et al., 2015; Akman, 2015), risk analysis (Safari et al., 2016; Dinçer and Hacıoğlu, 2015; Dinçer et al., 2018), service quality assessment (Gupta, 2018; Dinçer, 2018; Dinçer & Yüksel, 2019), waste management (Mir et al., 2016), stock selection (Dinçer & Hacıoğlu, 2014), and performance management (Dinçer & Hacıoğlu, 2013; Dinçer & Görener, 2011; Dinçer et al., 2013; Dinçer & Yüksel, 2018; Dinçer et al., 2019a, 2019b).

5.3.2 Analysis Results

Firstly, the most frequent terms are extracted and then clustered together using the pointwise mutual information and distance between their co-occurrence probability distributions. A term can be considered as member of a cluster if it is similar to all the terms inside it according to one of the similarity measures. If more than one cluster meets this condition, the one with the highest average score is used. If no cluster is similar, a new one is created. After this is completed, each term is ranked in decreasing order of the deviation between their expected cluster co-occurrence and the actual observed co-occurrence value. The terms with the highest divergence are returned as keywords.

Steps to prepare text data for machine learning model are listed below:

- Merge all posts into a single file.
- Eliminate irrelevant numbers and dates.
- Eliminate punctuation marks.
- Convert each word into small letters.
- Apply N-Char filter to eliminate words less than 3 letters.
- Apply tokenization.
- Grammatically label each word according to its usage in the speech (Part of Speech Tagging).
- Eliminate all unwanted words (stop words) such as in, on, it, this, none.
- Eliminate some parts of speech such as linkage words, definite, and indefinite articles.
- Pivot the keywords by dates they have been used in posts by Mr. Trump.

Moreover, we used twenty keywords extracted from tweets. They are:

- Witch
- Wall
- Trade
- Time
- Strong
- Crime
- Senate
- Security
- Russia
- People
- North
- Money
- Military
- Media
- Korea
- Job
- Country
- Honor
- FBI
- Fake

While considering these twenty mostly used keywords, the important criteria based on the politicians' tweets are defined. These factors are demonstrated in Table 5.1. In this table, supported literature is also given.

Table 5.1 gives information that mainly four different factors are identified based on Trump's tweets which are financial, social, military, and political. In this study, fuzzy VIKOR methodology is also considered to rank these four different criteria according to their importance. In this context, four different macroeconomic variables are taken into consideration as criteria that are economic growth (C1), unemployment (C2), inflation (C3), international trade (C4), and industrial development

Table 5.1 Criteria based on Donald Trump's tweets

Factors	Keywords	References
Financial	Trade	Costello (2019), Carbo-Valverde et al. (2016), Manova and Yu (2016), Rajapakse et al. (2018)
	Money	Ma and Liu (2018), Trejos and Wright (2016), Trelewicz (2017), Sawai et al. (2018)
	Job	Puni et al. (2016), Diakomihalis and Bolovinou (2018), McIsaac et al. (2019), Bouwhuis et al. (2017)
Social	Crime	Delgado et al. (2015), Zehr (2019), Suglia et al. (2016), Fennelly and Perry (2018)
	Security	Aldawood and Skinner (2019), Frolova et al. (2016), Kittinger et al. (2015), Soomro et al. (2016)
	Media	Ngai et al. (2015), Cheng et al. (2017), Andreassen et al. (2016), Alalwan et al. (2017)
Military	Military	Kwan et al. (2017), Gribble et al. (2018)
	FBI	Rudolph (2018), Kaussler and Hastedt (2017)
Political	Wall	Wolhuter et al. (2019), Hernández and Cannon (2017)
	Senate	Underhill and Rimmer (2017), Bilotkach (2018)
	Russia	Baradat and Phillips (2016), Mikhaylov (2019)
	Korea	Lee (2019), Song et al. (2018)

Table 5.2 Linguistic and fuzzy evaluations

Definition	Triangular fuzzy numbers		
Worst (W)	0	0	2.5
Poor (P)	0	2.5	5
Fair (F)	2.5	5	7.5
Good (G)	5	7.5	10
Best (B)	7.5	10	10

Source: Dinçer et al. (2016)

(C5). For this purpose, 5 different experts made evaluations and the weights of each criteria are accepted as the same. Additionally, triangular fuzzy numbers are used in this process which are stated in Table 5.2.

Table 5.3 also gives information about the linguistic evaluations of 5 different decision makers.

In addition to them, fuzzy decision matrixes of these 5 different decision makers are demonstrated on Tables 5.4–5.7. Moreover, fuzzy decision matrix of 4 different alternatives based on 5 different criteria is given on Table 5.8. After that, some mathematical computations are made, and the alternatives are ranked. The details of this process are given in Tables 5.9–5.11. Table 5.11 gives information that financial factors are the most important alternatives. Similarly, political and military factors also have the second and third places. On the other side, social factors take the last place. This situation explains that financial and political statements of the politicians have highest effect on the macroeconomic situation of the country.

Table 5.3 Linguistic evaluations for decision matrix

	Alternative 1 (Financial)					Alternative 2 (Social)					Alternative 3 (Military)					Alternative 4 (Political)				
	DM1	DM2	DM3	DM4	DM5	DM1	DM2	DM3	DM4	DM5	DM1	DM2	DM3	DM4	DM5	DM1	DM2	DM3	DM4	DM5
C1	B	G	G	F	G	F	F	G	G	G	G	G	G	G	G	G	B	G	F	F
C2	B	B	G	G	G	F	F	F	G	G	F	P	F	G	F	G	G	F	F	F
C3	B	G	G	G	F	F	F	F	G	G	F	F	G	G	F	F	F	F	F	F
C4	G	G	B	G	F	G	F	F	G	F	G	F	G	F	F	G	G	F	G	F
C5	G	B	G	G	F	G	G	G	F	F	G	G	F	F	G	G	G	G	G	F

5.4 Conclusion

Countries make significant efforts in order to increase their economic performance. For example, they try to attract the attentions of the investors to enter their countries. The main reason is that new job opportunities can be created so that unemployment rate can be decreased. In this framework, they give tax incentive or necessary locations to these investors. In this process, the explanations of the politicians are also important. Because they are the main authority of the government, investors always follow their statement. These explanations can sometimes be very beneficial to attract these investors. However, in some situations, they may cause some problems that have negative effects on the macroeconomic performance of the countries.

In this study, it is aimed to understand the role of the politicians on the macroeconomic situation of the countries. Within this framework, the tweets of Donald Trump are taken into consideration. These tweets are analyzed with the help of text mining approach. In this process, the most important words are defined as a result of this analysis. After that these words are evaluated and all-important keywords are matched with significant topics. As a result, 4 different classes are identified for this condition which are financial, social, military, and political issues.

In the next process, these keywords are ranked with the help of fuzzy VIKOR approach according to their impacts on macroeconomic performance. For this situation, 5 different factors are also defined which represent macroeconomic performance that are economic growth, unemployment, inflation, international trade, and industrial development. In this analysis process, it is accepted that all these factors have the same weights (20%). The finding show that political and economic factors are the most important items, which affect macroeconomic situation of the country. On the other side, social and military factors are on the last ranks.

According to these findings, it is understood that when Trump has tweets related to the financial and political factors, it affects macroeconomic performance of the country. Because of this situation, it is recommended that politicians should not make negative explanations about political and financial conditions. The main reason is that any negative words related to these items have an unfavorable result in the economic activities. Hence, they should be very careful to select the words related to these issues.

The results show that Donald Trump has tweets mainly for 4 different categories, such as financial, social, military, and political issues. It is concluded that financial and political factors are more important for the macroeconomic performance of the countries. This situation indicates that when Trump has tweets for these factors, it has a significant influence on the macroeconomic issues. Therefore, it is recommended that politicians should not make negative explanations about political and financial conditions. Otherwise, there is a risk of having volatility in the economy of this country. This situation can be prohibited by making necessary adjustments to the legal issues.

This study aims to make evaluations about the role of the politicians on the macroeconomic performance of the countries. In order to reach more appropriate results, tweets of Donald Trump are analyzed with the help of text mining approach. After that, important factors in these tweets are defined. In the next process, these factors are ranked by using fuzzy VIKOR approach. Nevertheless, in the future studies, a new analysis can be performed with different methodology, such as interval type-2 fuzzy TOPSIS. In addition to this aspect, different politicians can be taken into consideration as well.

Appendix 1

Key Terms and Definitions

TOPSIS: Technique for Order Preference by Similarity to Ideal Solution
US: United States
VIKOR: VIseKriterijumska Optimizacija I Kompromisno Resenje

Appendix 2

Table 5.4 Fuzzy decision matrix of decision makers for Alternative 1

Criteria	DM1			DM2			DM3			DM4			DM5		
C1	7.5	10	10	5	7.5	10	5	7.5	10	2.5	5	7.5	5	7.5	10
C2	7.5	10	10	7.5	10	10	5	7.5	10	5	7.5	10	5	7.5	10
C3	7.5	10	10	5	7.5	10	5	7.5	10	5	7.5	10	2.5	5	7.5
C4	5	7.5	10	5	7.5	10	7.5	10	10	5	7.5	10	2.5	5	7.5
C5	5	7.5	10	7.5	10	10	5	7.5	10	5	7.5	10	2.5	5	7.5

Table 5.5 Fuzzy decision matrix of decision makers for Alternative 2

Criteria	DM1			DM2			DM3			DM4			DM5		
C1	2.5	5	7.5	2.5	5	7.5	5	7.5	10	5	7.5	10	5	7.5	10
C2	2.5	5	7.5	2.5	5	7.5	2.5	5	7.5	5	7.5	10	5	7.5	10
C3	2.5	5	7.5	2.5	5	7.5	2.5	5	7.5	5	7.5	10	5	7.5	10
C4	5	7.5	10	2.5	5	7.5	2.5	5	7.5	5	7.5	10	2.5	5	7.5
C5	5	7.5	10	5	7.5	10	5	7.5	10	2.5	5	7.5	2.5	5	7.5

Table 5.6 Fuzzy decision matrix of decision makers for Alternative 3

Criteria	DM1			DM2			DM3			DM4			DM5		
C1	5	7.5	10	5	7.5	10	5	7.5	10	5	7.5	10	5	7.5	10
C2	2.5	5	7.5	0	2.5	5	2.5	5	7.5	5	7.5	10	2.5	5	7.5
C3	2.5	5	7.5	2.5	5	7.5	5	7.5	10	5	7.5	10	2.5	5	7.5
C4	5	7.5	10	2.5	5	7.5	5	7.5	10	2.5	5	7.5	2.5	5	7.5
C5	5	7.5	10	5	7.5	10	2.5	5	7.5	2.5	5	7.5	5	7.5	10

Table 5.7 Fuzzy decision matrix of decision makers for Alternative 4

Criteria	DM1			DM2			DM3			DM4			DM5		
C1	5	7.5	10	7.5	10	10	5	7.5	10	2.5	5	7.5	2.5	5	7.5
C2	5	7.5	10	5	7.5	10	2.5	5	7.5	2.5	5	7.5	2.5	5	7.5
C3	2.5	5	7.5	2.5	5	7.5	2.5	5	7.5	2.5	5	7.5	2.5	5	7.5
C4	5	7.5	10	5	7.5	10	2.5	5	7.5	5	7.5	10	2.5	5	7.5
C5	5	7.5	10	5	7.5	10	5	7.5	10	5	7.5	10	2.5	5	7.5

Table 5.8 Fuzzy decision matrix

	Alternative 1 (Financial)			Alternative 2 (Social)			Alternative 3 (Military)			Alternative 4 (Political)		
Criterion 1	5.00	7.50	9.50	4.00	6.50	9.00	5.00	7.50	10.00	4.50	7.00	9.00
Criterion 2	6.00	8.50	10.00	3.50	6.00	8.50	2.50	5.00	7.50	3.50	6.00	8.50
Criterion 3	5.00	7.50	9.50	3.50	6.00	8.50	3.50	6.00	8.50	2.50	5.00	7.50
Criterion 4	5.00	7.50	9.50	3.50	6.00	8.50	3.50	6.00	8.50	4.00	6.50	9.00
Criterion 5	5.00	7.50	9.50	4.00	6.50	9.00	4.00	6.50	9.00	4.50	7.00	9.50

Table 5.9 The values of $\tilde{f}_j^*$ and $\tilde{f}_j^-$

	$\tilde{f}_j^*$			$\tilde{f}_j^-$		
C1	5.00	7.50	10.00	4.00	6.50	9.00
C2	6.00	8.50	10.00	2.50	5.00	7.50
C3	5.00	7.50	9.50	2.50	5.00	7.50
C4	5.00	7.50	9.50	3.50	6.00	8.50
C5	5.00	7.50	9.50	4.00	6.50	9.00

Table 5.10 The values of Si, Ri, and Qi for final ranking (v:0.5)

Alternatives	Si	Ri	Qi	Ranking
Alternative 1 (Financial)	0.033	0.033	0.000	1
Alternative 2 (Social)	0.849	0.200	1.000	4
Alternative 3 (Military)	0.713	0.200	0.917	3
Alternative 4 (Political)	0.657	0.200	0.882	2

Table 5.11 Qi and ranking results for several v values

	v:0		v:0.1		v:0.2		v:0.3		v:0.4		v:0.5	
Alternatives	Qi	Ranking	Qi	Ranking	Qi	Ranking	Qi	Ranking	Qi	Ranking	Qi	Ranking
A1	0.000	1	0.000	1	0.000	1	0.000	1	0.000	1	0.000	1
A2	1.000	2	1.000	4	1.000	4	1.000	4	1.000	4	1.000	4
A3	1.000	2	0.983	3	0.967	3	0.950	3	0.934	3	0.917	3
A4	1.000	2	0.976	2	0.953	2	0.929	2	0.905	2	0.882	2

	v:0.6		v:0.7		v:0.8		v:0.9		v:1	
Alternatives	Qi	Ranking	Qi	Ranking	Qi	Ranking	Qi	Ranking	Qi	Ranking
A1	0.000	1	0.000	1	0.000	1	0.000	1	0.000	1
A2	1.000	4	1.000	4	1.000	4	1.000	4	1.000	4
A3	0.900	3	0.884	3	0.867	3	0.851	3	0.834	3
A4	0.858	2	0.834	2	0.811	2	0.787	2	0.763	2

References

Akman, G. (2015). Evaluating suppliers to include green supplier development programs via fuzzy C-means and VIKOR methods. *Computers & Industrial Engineering, 86*, 69–82.

Alalwan, A. A., Rana, N. P., Dwivedi, Y. K., & Algharabat, R. (2017). Social media in marketing: A review and analysis of the existing literature. *Telematics and Informatics, 34*(7), 1177–1190.

Aldawood, H., & Skinner, G. (2019). Reviewing cyber security social engineering training and awareness programs—Pitfalls and ongoing issues. *Future Internet, 11*(3), 73.

Andreassen, C. S., Billieux, J., Griffiths, M. D., Kuss, D. J., Demetrovics, Z., Mazzoni, E., & Pallesen, S. (2016). The relationship between addictive use of social media and video games and symptoms of psychiatric disorders: A large-scale cross-sectional study. *Psychology of Addictive Behaviors, 30*(2), 252.

Awasthi, A., & Kannan, G. (2016). Green supplier development program selection using NGT and VIKOR under fuzzy environment. *Computers & Industrial Engineering, 91*, 100–108.

Awasthi, A., Govindan, K., & Gold, S. (2018). Multi-tier sustainable global supplier selection using a fuzzy AHP-VIKOR based approach. *International Journal of Production Economics, 195*, 106–117.

Baradat, L. P., & Phillips, J. A. (2016). *Political ideologies: Their origins and impact*. Routledge.

Bilotkach, V. (2018). Political economy of infrastructure investment: Evidence from the economic stimulus airport grants. *Economics of Transportation, 13*, 27–35.

Borriello, A. (2017). 'There is no alternative': How Italian and Spanish leaders' discourse obscured the political nature of austerity. *Discourse & Society, 28*(3), 241–261.

Bouwhuis, S., Geuskens, G. A., Boot, C. R., Bongers, P. M., & van der Beek, A. J. (2017). Predictors of transitions from single to multiple job holding: Results of a longitudinal study among employees aged 45–64 in the Netherlands. *American Journal of Industrial Medicine, 60* (8), 696–710.

Cao, C., Cheng, C. S., Xia, C., & Zeng, C. (2018). *Corporate tax benefits from politicians' hometown*. Changyuan and Zeng, Cheng, Corporate Tax Benefits from Politicians' Hometown (September 18, 2018).

Carbo-Valverde, S., Rodriguez-Fernandez, F., & Udell, G. F. (2016). Trade credit, the financial crisis, and SME access to finance. *Journal of Money, Credit and Banking, 48*(1), 113–143.

Cellini, R., & Cuccia, T. (2016). The public spending for culture in the face of decentralization processes and economic recession: The case of Italy. In *The artful economist* (pp. 89–109). Springer.

Chapple, K., & Montero, S. (2018). Governing local economic development in Latin America: Situating the debate. In *Fragile governance and local economic development* (pp. 31–44). Routledge.

Cheng, X., Fu, S., & de Vreede, G. J. (2017). Understanding trust influencing factors in social media communication: A qualitative study. *International Journal of Information Management, 37*(2), 25–35.

Christensen, T., Lægreid, P., & Norman, R. (2017). Organizing immigration—A comparison of New Zealand and Norway. In *Transcending new public management* (pp. 123–146). Routledge.

Cohen, S., & Karatzimas, S. (2018). The role of the Troika on the Greek central government accounting reforms: The reprioritization riddle. *International Journal of Public Sector Management, 31*(3), 316–330.

Costello, A. M. (2019). The value of collateral in trade finance. *Journal of Financial Economics, 134*(1), 70–90.

David, M. (2018). Review of the role of political economy with respect to agricultural policymaking in Africa. *International Journal of Scientific Research and Management, 6*(06). https://doi.org/10.18535/ijsrm/v6i6.sh03

Delgado, R., Wing, A. K., & Stefancic, J. (2015). Rodrigo's eighth chronicle: Black crime, white fears—On the social construction of threat. In *Law unbound!* (pp. 129–148). Routledge.

Diakomihalis, M., & Bolovinou, E. (2018). Job satisfaction of transference teachers to administration/finance positions. *International Journal of Academic Research in Business and Social Sciences, 8*(5), 102–122.

Dinçer, H. (2018). HHI-based evaluation of the European banking sector using an integrated fuzzy approach. *Kybernetes, 48*(6), 1195–1215.

Dinçer, H., & Görener, A. (2011). Performans değerlendirmesinde AHP-VIKOR ve AHP-TOPSIS yaklaşımları: hizmet sektöründe bir uygulama. *Sigma: Mühendislik ve Fen Bilimleri Dergisi, 29*, 244–260.

Dinçer, H., & Hacıoğlu, U. (2013). Performance evaluation with fuzzy VIKOR and AHP method based on customer satisfaction in Turkish banking sector. *Kybernetes, 42*(7), 1072–1085.

Dinçer, H., & Hacıoğlu, Ü. (2014). A comparative hybrid method in technical analysis for stock selection process in banking sector by fuzzy AHP-TOPSIS and VIKOR method. In *Global strategies in banking and finance* (pp. 187–204). IGI Global.

Dinçer, H., & Hacıoğlu, U. (2015). A comparative performance evaluation on bipolar risks in emerging capital markets using fuzzy AHP-TOPSIS and VIKOR approaches. *Engineering Economics, 26*(2), 118–129.

Dinçer, H., & Yüksel, S. (2018). Comparative evaluation of BSC-based new service development competencies in Turkish banking sector with the integrated fuzzy hybrid MCDM using content analysis. *International Journal of Fuzzy Systems, 20*(8), 2497–2516.

Dinçer, H., & Yüksel, S. (2019). An integrated stochastic fuzzy MCDM approach to the balanced scorecard-based service evaluation. *Mathematics and Computers in Simulation (MATCOM).* Elsevier, vol. 166(C), pp. 93–112.

Dinçer, H., Hacıoğlu, U., & Yilmaz, R. (2013). The effect of integrated marketing communication competencies on banking performance: Analysis with fuzzy VIKOR method. *Actual Problems of Economics, 143*(5), 247–260.

Dinçer, H., Hacıoğlu, U., Tatoglu, E., & Delen, D. (2016). A fuzzy-hybrid analytic model to assess investors' perceptions for industry selection. *Decision Support Systems, 86*, 24–34.

Dinçer, H., Yüksel, S., & Şenel, S. (2018). Analyzing the global risks for the financial crisis after the great depression using comparative hybrid hesitant fuzzy decision-making models: Policy recommendations for sustainable economic growth. *Sustainability, 10*(9), 3126.

Dinçer, H., Yüksel, S., Korsakienė, R., Raišienė, A. G., & Bilan, Y. (2019a). IT2 hybrid decision-making approach to performance measurement of internationalized firms in the Baltic States. *Sustainability, 11*(1), 296.

Dinçer, H., Yüksel, S., & Pınarbaşı, F. (2019b). Technology acceptance model-based website evaluation of service industry: An application on the companies listed in BIST via hybrid MCDM. In *Multi-criteria decision-making models for website evaluation* (pp. 1–28). IGI Global.

Douglas, S. (2016). Value-oriented public management in vulnerable societies: Assessing the impact of public value management practices in three Caribbean countries. *Commonwealth & Comparative Politics, 54*(4), 536–556.

Falagiarda, M., & Gregori, W. D. (2015). The impact of fiscal policy announcements by the Italian government on the sovereign spread: A comparative analysis. *European Journal of Political Economy, 39*, 288–304.

Fennelly, L. J., & Perry, M. A. (2018). Milan: Crime prevention through Urban Design 1. In *CPTED and traditional security countermeasures* (pp. 153–155). CRC Press.

Frolova, E. V., Vinichenko, M. V., Kirillov, A. V., Rogach, O. V., & Kabanova, E. E. (2016). Development of social infrastructure in the management practices of local authorities: Trends and factors. *International Journal of Environmental and Science Education, 11*(15), 7421–7430.

Fu, J., Shimamoto, D., & Todo, Y. (2017). Can firms with political connections borrow more than those without? Evidence from firm-level data for Indonesia. *Journal of Asian Economics, 52*, 45–55.

Gribble, R., Thandi, G. K., Goodwin, L., & Fear, N. T. (2018). Hazardous alcohol consumption among spouses or partners of military service personnel: A systematic review of the literature. *Journal of the Royal Army Medical Corps, 164*(5), 380–388.

Gupta, H. (2018). Evaluating service quality of airline industry using hybrid best worst method and VIKOR. *Journal of Air Transport Management, 68*, 35–47.

Hernández, R., & Cannon, J. (2017). Intellectuals, civil society, and political power in Cuba. *Social Research: An International Quarterly, 84*(2), 407–428.

Im, T. (2017). Revisiting bureaucratic dysfunction: The role of bureaucracy in democratization. In *The experience of democracy and bureaucracy in South Korea* (pp. 1–21). Emerald Publishing Limited.

Kaussler, B., & Hastedt, G. P. (2017). *US foreign policy towards the Middle East: The realpolitik of deceit*. Routledge.

Khan, A., & Krishnan, S. (2019). Conceptualizing the impact of corruption in national institutions and national stakeholder service systems on e-government maturity. *International Journal of Information Management, 46*, 23–36.

Kideghesho, J. R. (2016). Reversing the trend of wildlife crime in Tanzania: Challenges and opportunities. *Biodiversity and Conservation, 25*(3), 427–449.

Kittinger, J. N., Teneva, L. T., Koike, H., Stamoulis, K. A., Kittinger, D. S., Oleson, K. L., … Friedlander, A. M. (2015). From reef to table: Social and ecological factors affecting coral reef fisheries, artisanal seafood supply chains, and seafood security. *PLoS One, 10*(8), e0123856.

Kozlov, V., Libman, A., & Schultz, A. (2018). Testosterone and repression in non-democracies: Evidence from a sample of Russian governors. *Kyklos, 71*(2), 244–278.

Krishnan, S., & Khan, A. (2018, June). Theorizing the relationship of corruption in national institutions with E-government maturity. In *International working conference on transfer and diffusion of IT* (pp. 177–193). Springer.

Kryszczuk, M. D., & Wenzel, M. (2016). Trade unions and the impact of technological changes on the labour market. *Myśl Ekonomiczna i Polityczna, 3*(54), 59–84.

Kwan, J., Jones, M., Hull, L., Wessely, S., Fear, N., & MacManus, D. (2017). Violent behavior among military reservists. *Aggressive Behavior, 43*(3), 273–280.

Lee, Y. (2019). Political viability of the Russia-North Korea-South Korea gas pipeline project: An analysis of the role of the US. *Energies, 12*(10), 1895.

Ma, D., & Liu, C. (2018). Money, finance and commerce in Chinese history: An introduction with reference to the special issue. *Frontiers of Economics in China, 13*(3), 313–321.

Manova, K., & Yu, Z. (2016). How firms export: Processing vs. ordinary trade with financial frictions. *Journal of International Economics, 100*, 120–137.

Mardani, A., Zavadskas, E., Govindan, K., Amat Senin, A., & Jusoh, A. (2016). VIKOR technique: A systematic review of the state of the art literature on methodologies and applications. *Sustainability, 8*(1), 37.

McIsaac, M., Scott, A., & Kalb, G. (2019). The role of financial factors in the mobility and location choices of general practitioners in Australia. *Human Resources for Health, 17*(1), 34.

Mikhaylov, A. (2019). Oil and gas budget revenues in Russia after crisis in 2015. *International Journal of Energy Economics and Policy, 9*(2), 375–380.

Mir, M. A., Ghazvinei, P. T., Sulaiman, N. M. N., Basri, N. E. A., Saheri, S., Mahmood, N. Z., … Aghamohammadi, N. (2016). Application of TOPSIS and VIKOR improved versions in a multi criteria decision analysis to develop an optimized municipal solid waste management model. *Journal of Environmental Management, 166*, 109–115.

Mu, R., de Jong, M., & Koppenjan, J. (2019). Assessing and explaining interagency collaboration performance: A comparative case study of local governments in China. *Public Management Review, 21*(4), 581–605.

Ngai, E. W., Tao, S. S., & Moon, K. K. (2015). Social media research: Theories, constructs, and conceptual frameworks. *International Journal of Information Management, 35*(1), 33–44.

Olausson, A., & Wihlborg, E. (2018). 11. The legitimacy of political entrepreneurs in networks: Lessons from local development projects in Swedish municipalities. In *Governance and political entrepreneurship in Europe: Promoting growth and welfare in times of crisis*, 229. Edward Elgar Publishing.

Opricovic, S., & Tzeng, G. H. (2004). Compromise solution by MCDM methods: A comparative analysis of VIKOR and TOPSIS. *European Journal of Operational Research, 156*(2), 445–455.

Pellegata, A., & Memoli, V. (2018). Corruption and satisfaction with democracy: The conditional role of electoral disproportionality and ballot control. *European Political Science Review, 10*(3), 393–416.

Prato, C., & Strulovici, B. (2017). The hidden cost of direct democracy: How ballot initiatives affect politicians' selection and incentives. *Journal of Theoretical Politics, 29*(3), 440–466.

Puni, A., Agyemang, C. B., & Asamoah, E. S. (2016). Religiosity, job status and whistle-blowing: Evidence from micro-finance companies in the Ga-East District of the Greater Accra region of Ghana. *Global Journal of Human Resource Management, 4*(1), 52–64.

Rajapakse, S., Morin, F., Ostbye, T., & De Silva, V. (2018). Healthcare seeking behaviour among female garment workers in Koggala Free Trade Zone, Sri Lanka. *Journal of the College of Community Physicians of Sri Lanka, 24*(4), 149–155.

Reitan, M., Gustafsson, K., & Blekesaune, A. (2015). Do local government reforms result in higher levels of trust in local politicians? *Local Government Studies, 41*(1), 156–179.

Ridge, J. W., Hill, A. D., & Ingram, A. (2018). The signaling role of politician stock ownership: Effects on lobbying intensity. *Journal of Management, 44*(5), 2116–2141.

Romolini, A., Gori, E., & Fissi, S. (2015). Public corporate governance and performance information in local utilities: The different perceptions of politicians and managers. *Administratie si Management Public, 25*, 55.

Rostamzadeh, R., Govindan, K., Esmaeili, A., & Sabaghi, M. (2015). Application of fuzzy VIKOR for evaluation of green supply chain management practices. *Ecological Indicators, 49*, 188–203.

Rudolph, R. M. (2018). Framing Sino-American military relations: The power and problem of perception in preventing geostrategic security cooperation between China and the United States. *Asia & The Pacific Policy Studies, 5*(2), 182–195.

Safari, H., Faraji, Z., & Majidian, S. (2016). Identifying and evaluating enterprise architecture risks using FMEA and fuzzy VIKOR. *Journal of Intelligent Manufacturing, 27*(2), 475–486.

Sancino, A., & Budd, L. (2017). The potential of community leadership and the new roles for public managers and politicians. In S. Sacchetti, A. Christoforou, & M. Mosca (Eds.), *Social regeneration and local development: Cooperation, social economy and public participation*, 175–185. Routledge.

Sawai, J. P., Juhari, R., Kahar, R., Ismail, Z., & Sawai, R. P. (2018). Financial strain, financial management practices, marital satisfaction and marital stability among newlyweds. *Management & Accounting Review, 17*(3), 1–16.

Schnitzer, M., Scheiber, S., Kornexl, E., & Thöni, E. (2017). Politicians' perspective on the community-related impacts of major sports events—A case study for Innsbruck-Tyrol. *Sport in Society, 20*(7), 880–904.

Shafiq, M., Sultana, R., & Munir, M. (2017). Political rhetoric; Slogan politics in Pakistan and role of parliament. *FWU Journal of Social Sciences, 11*(2), 26–38.

Song, M., Park, H. J., & Jung, K. (2018). Do political similarities facilitate interlocal collaboration? *Public Administration Review, 78*(2), 261–269.

Soomro, Z. A., Shah, M. H., & Ahmed, J. (2016). Information security management needs more holistic approach: A literature review. *International Journal of Information Management, 36*(2), 215–225.

Sørensen, E. (2016). The role of elected politicians in collaborative policy innovation. In *Enhancing public innovation by transforming public governance* (pp. 178–196). Cambridge University Press.

Suglia, S. F., Shelton, R. C., Hsiao, A., Wang, Y. C., Rundle, A., & Link, B. G. (2016). Why the neighborhood social environment is critical in obesity prevention. *Journal of Urban Health, 93* (1), 206–212.

Tang, M., & Huhe, N. (2019). Contextualizing the economic basis of political support: Government economic engagement, economic perceptions, and democratic satisfaction. *Political Research Quarterly, 1065912919831774.*

Torfing, J., & Ansell, C. (2017). Strengthening political leadership and policy innovation through the expansion of collaborative forms of governance. *Public Management Review, 19*(1), 37–54.

Touchton, M. (2016). The benefits of balance: Credibility, the rule of law, and investment in Latin America. *Latin American Research Review, 51*(2), 195–216.

Trejos, A., & Wright, R. (2016). Search-based models of money and finance: An integrated approach. *Journal of Economic Theory, 164*, 10–31.

Trelewicz, J. Q. (2017). Big data and big money: The role of data in the financial sector. *IT Professional, 19*(3), 8–10.

Underhill, E., & Rimmer, M. (2017). Private governance, state regulation and employment standards: How political factors shape their nexus in Australian horticulture. *Relations Industrielles/ Industrial Relations, 72*(1), 33–55.

Wang, L., Menkhoff, L., Schröder, M., & Xu, X. (2019). Politicians' promotion incentives and bank risk exposure in China. *Journal of Banking & Finance, 99*, 63–94.

Wolhuter, C., Nel, M., Želvys, R., & Alisauskiene, S. (2019). Part 7: Thirty years since the fall of the Berlin Wall: Educational reforms worldwide. *Glocal Education in Practice: Teaching, Researching, and Citizenship*, BCES Conference Books, Volume17. Sofia: Bulgarian Comparative Education Society, p. 216.

Wong, W. (2015). Public managers must also be leaders: The hollowing-out of leadership and public management reform in Hong Kong. In *Asian leadership in policy and governance* (pp. 261–285). Emerald Group Publishing Limited.

Yan, W. W., & Wooi, H. C. (2016). The impact of election on stock market returns of government-owned banks: The case of Indonesia, Malaysia and Thailand. *Asian Journal of Business and Accounting, 9*(1), 31–58.

You, X. Y., You, J. X., Liu, H. C., & Zhen, L. (2015). Group multi-criteria supplier selection using an extended VIKOR method with interval 2-tuple linguistic information. *Expert Systems with Applications, 42*(4), 1906–1916.

Zehr, H. (2019). *Crime and the development of modern society: Patterns of criminality in nineteenth century Germany and France*. Routledge.

Chapter 6
How Is the Stock Exchange Index Affected by the Disclosures of Politicians?

Abstract The main purpose of this study is to understand the main influence of the politicians' disclosure on the stock exchange index. In this context, a machine learning model is built in order to understand the hidden patterns behind the daily changes (rises and falls) of Dow Johns index. In the fourth chapter of this book, Donald Trump's personal tweets are obtained to make evaluations. Similarly, in the analysis process of this chapter, these tweets and four-day time series Dow Johns industrial average values are taken into consideration. The findings show that when Mr. Trump uses the word witch at least once, it is certain that the index will rise. On the other side, when he uses both the word military and witch on the same day, the index gets a steep high. These results give an idea that when politicians use negative words, it increases the volatility in the stock market. Similar to this situation, if their disclosures are related to military issues, the stock exchange will also be influenced. Therefore, it is strongly recommended that politicians should choose their words carefully in order not to increase the volatility in the stock market.

Keywords Politicians' disclosures · Stock exchanges · Machine learning

6.1 Introduction

The stock market is an important platform affecting a country's economy. Companies have access to investors through the stock exchange. In this way, they can easily access this fund they need for their new investments. On the other hand, the stock market is also an important opportunity for investors who own funds. These investors have the chance to earn income by evaluating their savings through the stock market (Dinçer, Yüksel, & Adalı, 2019a; Patel et al., 2015).

Based on the above-mentioned information, it is possible to say that the stock market has a serious impact on the economic performance of a country. If there is a problem in the stock market, this situation will have a negative impact on the national economy. This problem will prevent firms from accessing the funds they

G. Silahtaroğlu et al., *Data Science and Multiple Criteria Decision Making Approaches in Finance*, Multiple Criteria Decision Making,
https://doi.org/10.1007/978-3-030-74176-1_6

need. As a result, firms whose profitability has fallen will have to remove workers (Dinçer & Yüksel, 2018; Moura & Norden, 2018).

Therefore, the performance of the stock market should be high. In this context, it is important to determine the factors that affect the performance of the stock market. As a result of determining these factors, it will be possible to avoid a possible problem early. Otherwise, the related problem will grow further and start to damage the country's economy (Emir et al., 2015; Oliveira et al., 2016).

It is possible to talk about many factors that can affect the performance of the stock market. For example, high inflation in a country increases the uncertainty in the market. This situation negatively affects the performance of the stock market. In parallel, the decline in the country's economic growth will have a negative impact. On the other hand, external factors, such as oil prices and gold prices, are considered to influence the stock market's performance (Amit et al., 2018).

The statements made by the politicians are another factor affecting the stock market index in the country. Especially with the effect of globalization, there is a serious technological development in the world (Dinçer, Yüksel, Pınarbaşı, & Çetiner, 2019c). Therefore, the statements made by the politicians are rapidly reaching a very large audience. Recently, a significant number of politicians are actively using social media. In this context, the statements made by the politicians on social media have a significant impact on the stock market's performance. Even a word used in this platform can be very important (Qiu et al., 2016). Hence, it is obvious that in any problematic conditions, cash flow can be transferred immediately from one country to another.

In this study, it is aimed to evaluate whether politicians' disclosures have an influence on the stock market index. In this framework, Donald Trump's tweets, which were provided and used in the fourth chapter, are taken into consideration. In the analysis process, a machine learning model is generated to see the hidden patterns behind the daily changes of Dow Johns index. The data used in this study is provided from two different sources. The first source is related to Dow Johns industrial averages whereas the other is the tweets posted by the President of the USA, Donald Trump's. With the help of this analysis, it can be possible to understand how politicians affect stock exchange index.

6.2 Literature Review

Stock exchange of the countries can be affected by many different factors. This situation was also underlined in various studies. Some of them focused on the relationship between exchange rate volatility and stock exchange. For example, Jain and Biswal (2016) made an assessment on the stock market in India and concluded that when local currency depreciates, stock exchange is affected by this situation negatively. Gay (2016) also made a similar analysis for five different countries and reached the same conclusion. Moreover, Mitra (2017), Iqbal (2017) and Gong and Dai (2017) also underlined the importance of this issue. In addition,

Ramírez et al. (2017) aimed to make evaluation on the Mexican stock exchange and defined that in case of exchange rate volatility, there is a decrease in the stock market. This situation was also discussed by Arthur (2018) and Moghaddam et al. (2016).

In addition to the exchange rate, the relationship between industrial production and stock market was also assessed by many different researchers. Jacobsen et al. (2018) tried to predict stock market index and reached the conclusion that there is a positive correlation between industrial production and stock market index. Parallel to this study, Huang and Startz (2018), Jareño and Negrut (2016), and Hanif (2019) also underlined the importance of this situation for the stock market in the United States. On the other side, Peiro (2016) made assessment for the stock market in Europe and concluded that stock market volatility was mainly caused because of the problems in industrial development. Chiang and Chen (2017) also identified this situation for Asian countries. Additionally, Ciner (2019) made a similar analysis for various countries with Granger causality approach and identified this issue. Choudhry et al. (2016), Li, Cheng, and Yang (2017a), Lütkepohl and Netšunajev (2018), and (Ding et al., 2017) stated that industries of the countries should be improved in order to develop stock market.

Inflation is accepted as another factor that may affect stock exchange index. Because inflation represents the increase in the price levels of the goods, there will be uncertainty in the market in case of high inflation. This situation has a negative influence on the investment amount because the countries become unwilling to make new investments. Hence, the stock market will be affected in a negative manner. Iqbal (2017) made an econometric analysis to understand the determinant of the stock exchange and defined that inflation rate plays a key role. Jareño et al. (2016), Pradhan et al. (2015), Ghazali et al. (2018), and Ghosh and Kanjilal (2016) also determined that inflation rate is a key indicator of the stock exchange. This situation was also underlined by many different researchers in the literature (Rachael & Moses, 2017; Otieno et al., 2019; Schmidt-Hebbel & Carrasco, 2016; Uwubanmwen & Eghosa, 2015; Bouri et al., 2017).

According to the literature analysis, it is defined that another important variable of the stock exchange is interest rate. Interest rate mainly affects investment amount in the country. When there is high interest rate in the economy, companies will decrease investment amount because the cost becomes higher. Lower investment amount decreases the profitability of the companies which has a negative influence on the stock prices (Yüksel & Zengin, 2016). Within this framework, Babajide et al. (2016) made an analysis for Nigeria and concluded that high interest rate decreases the performance of the stock exchange. Jammazi et al. (2017), Rachael and Moses (2017), Galí and Gambetti (2015), and Adam et al. (2016) also underlined the significance of this issue. On the other side, Valera et al. (2017) used GARCH method and identified that stock market uncertainty is mainly caused by interest rate volatility. Furthermore, Blanchard et al. (2018), Moya-Martínez et al. (2015), Hajilee and Al Nasser (2017), Dinçer, Yüksel, and Kartal (2019b), Jain and Biswal (2016), Amarasinghe (2015), and Ferrer et al. (2016) also determined that stock exchange performance is decreased in case of high interest rate.

On the other side, according to some other researchers, it is defined that foreign direct investment is a significant issue to improve stock market in the countries. Foreign direct investment has a very positive contribution to the economy by increasing the trade volume. With the help of this condition, stock exchange index can increase. In this context, Paramati et al. (2016) made a study related to the stock markets of emerging economies. They underlined that stock market is affected by the foreign direct investment amount. Apergis et al. (2016) and Kariuki (2015) identified the same issues for African countries. This result was also defined for different regions, such as ASEAN countries (Pradhan et al., 2019), Sri Lanka (Rajapakse, 2019), and emerging economies (Nguyen et al., 2018).

Because economic growth is an important indicator of the economic performance of the countries, some studies accepted this variable as the determinant of the stock market performance (Azam et al., 2016; Dinçer, Hacıoğlu, & Yüksel, 2018a; Nyasha & Odhiambo, 2017). For instance, Li, Zhang, and Xiao (2017b), Giannetti and Wang (2016), Mamun et al. (2018), and Babajide et al. (2016) determined that stock market performance is better for the countries where economic growth is high. Parallel to the economic growth, it is also defined that banking performance of the countries has a direct impact on the stock market index (Dinçer, Yüksel, & Kartal, 2019b). As an example, Cave et al. (2019), Tang and Ho (2017), Levine et al. (2016), Zafar et al. (2019), and Rjoub et al. (2017) concluded that banking sector has a contribution to the stock market performance.

In addition to these studies, it is claimed that there is a relationship between gold price and stock market. In this framework, when gold price increases, there is a decrease in the demand of the gold (Dinçer, Yüksel, & Şenel, 2018b). This situation has an increasing role in the demands of stocks (Gokmenoglu & Fazlollahi, 2015; Sakphoowadon et al., 2018). Jain and Biswal (2016), Bams et al. (2017), Bouri et al. (Bouri et al., 2017), and Dyhrberg (2016) showed that gold price directly affects the performance of stock market. Furthermore, some studies also underlined the significance of the oil prices on stock market. For instance, Ghosh and Kanjilal (2016), Jain and Biswal (2016), Kang et al. (2015), and Zhu et al. (2016) made a study about the determinants of the stock market. They determined that stock market is mainly affected by the oil price. Similar to them, Huang et al. (2017), Ding et al. (2017), and Salisu and Isah (2017) defined that oil price volatility is the main factor of the stock market performance.

According to the results of the literature review, it is understood that stock market performance is very popular among the researchers. A lot of studies were generated in order to understand what affects the performance of the stock market. In these studies, different methodologies are taken into consideration, such as GARCH, regression, and decision tree approaches. Therefore, it can be said that a new study can contribute to the literature which focuses on this subject by using an original method like machine learning.

6.3 The Analysis of the Impacts of Donald Trump's Tweets on Dow Jones Index

The objective of this study is to build a machine learning model to extract hidden patterns behind the daily changes (rises and falls) of Dow Johns index. In order to achieve this objective, Donald Trump's personal tweets and four-day time series Dow Johns industrial average values have been used. The model has been trained to predict next day's index closing value.

The data to train model has been gathered from two different sources. One is Dow Johns industrial averages, the other is the tweets posted by the President of the USA, Donald Trump's. In order to extract tweets, a special API (Application Programme Interface) served by Twitter inc. has been used. The API and Tweeter allow a limited time range to extract old tweets. So, in the study, tweets between 04/15/2018 and 02/06/2019 have been extracted. In 205 days, Mr. Trump posted 3.192 tweets. All of the posts have been used in the study. Some of the posts are given in Table 6.1 to give an idea to the reader.

All posts merged in one text file to be input for pre-processing text mining model. On the other hand, Dow Johns industrial averages between the same dates have been collected. Both datasets have been merged into a single data set to be used in the machine learning model. In the text mining model, all text data cleaned, tokenized, and turned into a bag of words (BoW). After that weighted keywords have been extracted from all tweets. For this purpose, chi-square keyword extracting model has been used. This model extracts relevant keywords using co-occurrence statistics as described in (Matsuo & Ishizuka, 2004). After pivoting process, data looked like as it is in Table 6.2. If a word was not used in a post in one day, its value is zero, otherwise the number of times it appeared in posts that day is the value of the word.

On the other hand, Dow Johns averages have been organized in time series format with a four-day lag. In this, model instead of using the averages directly, difference between previous day and the current day has been used as the value for each day. They are given in Table 6.3.

The class variable both acts as the supervisor in the machine learning process and also represents the parameter to be predicted by the machine. Since the objective of the study is to predict how much and in what way (negative or positive) Dow Johns average will change, "change between values today and yesterday" should be attained as class. Most of the supervised learning algorithms need class variable in nominal format. So, it was necessary to change the type of the variable from float to nominal. For this purpose, Fuzzy C-Means unsupervised machine learning algorithm has been used. The algorithm suggested five nominal values to be used as class. Table 6.4 shows the statistics produced by Fuzzy C-Means algorithm and Table 6.5 indicates the nominal value ranges.

A snapshot of the dataset ready for machine learning is depicted in Table 6.6. As it is seen, on some days Mr. Trump did not post any tweets. These cells have been kept as #N/A in order to see the effect of silence over Down Johns Index.

Table 6.1 Some of Donald Trump's tweets

Melania and I send our greetings to those celebrating the Lunar New Year. Today, people across the United States and around the world mark the beginning of the Lunar New Year with spectacular fireworks displays, joyful festivals, and family gatherings... https://t.co/yM6qZng5m0	2/5/19 20:08
Tremendous numbers of people are coming up through Mexico in the hopes of flooding our southern border. We have sent additional military. We will build a Human Wall if necessary. If we had a real wall, this would be a non-event!	2/5/19 17:10
With caravans marching through Mexico and toward our country, republicans must be prepared to do whatever is necessary for STRONG border security. Dems do nothing. If there is no wall, there is no security. Human trafficking, drugs and criminals of all dimensions—KEEP OUT!	2/4/19 1:03
Thank you to brit. This is a very big deal in Europe. Fake news is the enemy of the people! https://t.co/WX0o8gaiMC	1/27/19 18:27
We are not even into February and the cost of illegal immigration so far this year is $18,959,495,168. Cost Friday was $603,331,392. There are at least 25,772,342 illegal aliens, not the 11,000,000 that have been reported for years, in our country. So ridiculous! DHS	1/27/19 16:44
WITCH HUNT!	1/27/19 4:51
Thank you to the republican National Committee, (the RNC), who voted UNANIMOUSLY yesterday to support me in the upcoming 2020 election. Considering that we have done more than any administration in the first two years, this should be easy. More great things now in the works!	1/26/19 17:23
Thank you to Amy Kremer, women for trump co-founder, for doing such a great interview with Martha MacCallum ... And by the way, women have the lowest unemployment numbers in many decades—at the highest pay ever. Proud of that!	1/18/19 4:36
We lose 300 Americans a week, 90% of which comes through the southern border. These numbers will be DRASTICALLY REDUCED if we have a wall!	1/11/19 5:42
Great tweet today by Tyler Q. Houlton @SpoxDHS on the #FakeNews being put out by @CNN, a proud member of the opposition party. @TSA is doing a great job!	1/5/19 19:13

In the study, we have used Random Forest Decision Tree Learning. Random forest decision tree learning exploits multiple numbers of decision tree algorithms. Each algorithm is trained on different rows or records which are chosen randomly. Although decision trees are thought to be weak learners, this handicap is eliminated by using multiple tree algorithms like GINI index, gain ratio by running them on different sets of records. On other hand, decision trees generate IF-ELSE-THEN rules which can be understood, reviewed, and applied by humans easily. This is the main reason that we have chosen a decision tree model for analysis. We used accuracy, recall, specificity, and error rate for the evaluation of the models.

$$Accuracy = \frac{TP + TN}{TP + TN + FP + FN}$$

Table 6.2 Data obtained from the tweets

Date	Witch	Wall	Trade	Time	Strong	Crime	Senate	Security	Russia	People	North	Money	Military	Media	Korea	Job	Country	Honor	FBI	Fake
#	0	0	0	0	0	0	1	0	0	1	0	0	0	1	0	0	0	0	0	0
#	0	2	0	0	1	0	0	1	0	1	0	0	1	0	0	1	0	1	0	0
#	2	0	0	1	2	0	0	0	0	2	0	1	0	1	0	3	0	0	1	0
#	0	6	1	1	1	1	1	1	0	1	1	1	0	1	1	0	0	1	0	0
#	0	1	0	2	0	0	0	1	0	2	2	0	0	0	2	0	0	1	0	0
#	0	0	0	0	0	0	1	0	0	1	0	0	0	0	0	0	0	0	0	0
#	0	1	1	0	0	0	0	0	0	1	0	0	1	1	0	1	0	0	0	0
#	1	1	0	1	0	0	0	0	0	1	0	0	0	0	0	0	0	0	0	1
#	0	2	0	2	0	2	0	1	0	2	2	0	0	3	2	1	0	1	1	2
#	0	4	0	1	0	4	0	1	0	0	0	0	0	0	0	0	0	1	0	0
#	0	5	0	1	1	3	2	4	2	3	0	0	0	2	0	0	0	4	2	4
#	1	2	1	1	0	1	0	1	0	2	0	0	0	0	0	0	0	1	0	1
#	0	0	0	1	0	0	0	0	0	0	0	0	0	0	0	0	0	0	0	0
#	0	0	0	0	0	1	0	0	0	0	0	0	0	0	0	0	0	0	0	0
#	0	2	1	3	0	2	0	1	1	3	1	0	0	1	0	1	0	1	3	0
#	0	1	0	1	0	1	0	1	3	3	0	0	0	1	0	0	0	1	1	1
#	0	4	1	2	1	0	0	0	0	1	0	0	0	1	0	0	0	0	0	1

Table 6.3 Data obtained from the tweets

Date	Change between values today and yesterday	Change between values 1 and 2 days ago	Change between values 2 and 3 days ago	Change between values 3 and 4 days ago
2/5/19	−170.26	−175.48	−64.22	15.19
2/4/19	−175.48	−64.22	15.19	−434.9
2/1/19	−64.22	15.19	−434.9	−51.74
1/31/19	15.19	−434.9	−51.74	208.98
1/30/19	−434.9	−51.74	208.98	−183.96
1/29/19	−51.74	208.98	−183.96	22.38
1/28/19	208.98	−183.96	22.38	−171.14
1/25/19	−183.96	22.38	−171.14	301.87
1/24/19	22.38	−171.14	301.87	−336.25
1/23/19	−171.14	301.87	−336.25	−162.94
1/22/19	301.87	−336.25	−162.94	−141.57
1/18/19	−336.25	−162.94	−141.57	−155.75
1/17/19	−162.94	−141.57	−155.75	86.11
1/16/19	−141.57	−155.75	86.11	5.97
1/15/19	−155.75	86.11	5.97	−122.8
1/14/19	86.11	5.97	−122.8	−91.67
1/11/19	5.97	−122.8	−91.67	−256.1

Table 6.4 Statistics produced by Fuzzy C-Means algorithm

Statistics	Value
Variation among nominals	2705522.64
Partition coefficient	0.75
Partition entropy	−0.47
XieBeni index	0.46

Table 6.5 Statistics produced by Fuzzy C-Means algorithm

Label	Average diversion from previous day
3	> = 112
2	(−100) – 112
1	(−400) – (−100)
−1	(−24.000) – (−400)
−2	<(−24.000)

$$Error\ Rate = \frac{FP + FN}{TP + TN + FP + FN}$$

$$Specificity = \frac{TN}{TN + FP}$$

$$Recall = \frac{TP}{TP + FN}$$

Table 6.6 Analysis of Donald Trump's tweets

Date	Class	Change between values today and yesterday	Change between values 1 and 2 days ago	Change between values 2 and 3 days ago	Change between values 3 and 4 days ago	Witch	Wall	Trade	Time	....	FBI	Fake
2/5/19	1	−170.26	−175.48	−64.22	15.19	0	0	0	0	0	0	0
2/4/19	2	−175.48	−64.22	15.19	−434.9	0	2	0	0	1	0	0
2/1/19	2	−64.22	15.19	−434.9	−51.74	2	0	0	1	0	1	0
1/31/19	−1	15.19	−434.9	−51.74	208.98	0	6	1	1	1	0	0
1/30/19	2	−434.9	−51.74	208.98	−183.96	0	1	0	2	1	0	0
1/29/19	3	−51.74	208.98	−183.96	22.38	0	0	0	0	0	0	0
1/28/19	1	208.98	−183.96	22.38	−171.14	0	1	1	0	0	0	0
1/25/19	2	−183.96	22.38	−171.14	301.87	1	1	0	1	0	0	1
1/24/19	1	22.38	−171.14	301.87	−336.25	0	2	0	2	1	1	2
1/23/19	3	−171.14	301.87	−336.25	−162.94	0	4	0	1	1	0	0
1/22/19	1	301.87	−336.25	−162.94	−141.57	0	5	0	1	4	2	4
1/18/19	1	−336.25	−162.94	−141.57	−155.75	1	2	1	1	1	0	1
1/17/19	1	−162.94	−141.57	−155.75	86.11	0	0	0	1	0	0	0
1/16/19	1	−141.57	−155.75	86.11	5.97	0	0	0	0	0	0	0
1/15/19	2	−155.75	86.11	5.97	−122.8	0	2	1	3	1	3	0
1/14/19	2	86.11	5.97	−122.8	−91.67	0	1	0	1	1	1	1
1/11/19	1	5.97	−122.8	−91.67	−256.1	0	4	1	2	0	0	1
1/10/19	2	−122.8	−91.67	−256.1	−98.19	0	2	0	0	5	0	1
1/9/19	1	−91.67	−256.1	−98.19	−746.94	0	1	1	1	1	0	1
1/8/19	2	−256.1	−98.19	−746.94	660.02	0	0	1	1	0	0	0
1/7/19	−1	−98.19	−746.94	660.02	−18.78	0	0	0	2	1	0	3
1/4/19	3	−746.94	660.02	−18.78	−265.06	0	0	0	3	0	0	1
1/3/19	2	660.02	−18.78	−265.06	76.42	0	2	1	1	2	0	0
1/2/19	1	−18.78	−265.06	76.42	−260.37	0	1	1	1	3	0	0

(continued)

Table 6.6 (continued)

Date	Class	Change between values today and yesterday	Change between values 1 and 2 days ago	Change between values 2 and 3 days ago	Change between values 3 and 4 days ago	Witch	Wall	Trade	Time	....	FBI	Fake
12/31/18	2	−265.06	76.42	−260.37	−1086.25	0	4	0	1	2	0	2
12/28/18	1	76.42	−260.37	−1086.25	653.17	1	4	1	1	1	1	1
12/27/18	−1	−260.37	−1086.25	653.17	414.23	0	5	0	1	2	0	0
12/26/18	3	−1086.25	653.17	414.23	464.06	0	0	0	0	0	0	0
12/24/18	3	653.17	414.23	464.06	351.98	0	4	3	1	3	0	1
12/21/18	3	414.23	464.06	351.98	−82.66	#N/A	#N/A	#N/A	#N/A	#N/A	#N/A	#N/A
12/20/18	3	464.06	351.98	−82.66	507.53	#N/A	#N/A	#N/A	#N/A	#N/A	#N/A	#N/A
12/19/18	2	351.98	−82.66	507.53	496.87	#N/A	#N/A	#N/A	#N/A	#N/A	#N/A	#N/A
12/18/18	3	−82.66	507.53	496.87	−70.11	2	1	0	0	0	1	0
12/17/18	3	507.53	496.87	−70.11	−157.03	0	1	1	1	1	0	0
12/14/18	2	496.87	−70.11	−157.03	53.02	0	0	1	0	0	0	0
12/13/18	1	−70.11	−157.03	53.02	−34.31	1	1	0	0	0	1	0

Table 6.7 Accuracy statistics

True positives rate	False positives rate	True negatives rate	False negatives rate
0.887096774			
Recall	Precision	Sensitivity	Specificity
0.56	0.88	0.56	0.97
	F-measure	Accuracy	Cohen's kappa
	0.90	0.89	0.83

Table 6.8 Confusion matrix

	True positive	False positive	True negative	False negative
1	17.00	3.00	42.00	0.00
2	25.00	2.00	33.00	2.00
3	13.00	2.00	45.00	2.00
−1	0	0	60	2
−2	0	0	61	1
Overall	11.00	1.40	48.20	1.40

As it can be seen in Accuracy Statistics table, Dow Johns average can be predicted with an accuracy of 89%. 90% F-measure d-suggests that the model can be used for predictions. Random forest algorithm generated 10 different models to achieve this success. In order to give an idea to the reader, we have presented one of the models and its parameters. The chosen model reveals that the most important parameter to predict Dow Johns index is whether Mr. Trump uses the word witch or not. If he uses the word witch at least once it is certain that the index will rise. If he uses both the word military and witch on the same day, the index gets a steep high. Other rules generated by the algorithm can be read from the tree. The details are given in Tables 6.7 and 6.8.

6.4 Conclusion

Stock exchange has a great importance for the sustainability of the economies because of many different ways. Firstly, it is a platform where lots of countries reach the funds they need. Moreover, a lot of investors can also make investment by using this platform. In many different countries, stock market reached a significant amount. Therefore, some actions should be taken to prevent volatility in this market. In this context, government prepares some legal regulations for this purpose. Otherwise, there is a significant possibility for the investors and companies to make high amount of losses.

The main objective of this study is to evaluate whether politicians' disclosures affect stock market index. For this purpose, Donald Trump's tweets, which were provided and used in the fourth chapter, are taken into consideration. Additionally, a machine learning model is generated to see the hidden patterns behind the daily changes of Dow Johns index. The data to train model has been gathered from two different sources. The first source is related to Dow Johns industrial averages whereas the other is the tweets posted by the President of the USA, Donald Trump's. In order to extract tweets, a special API (Application Programme Interface) served by Twitter inc. has been used.

The chosen model reveals that the most important parameters to predict Dow Johns index. According to the results, it is found that Dow Johns index increases when Mr. Trump uses the word witch at least once. In addition to this situation, when he uses both the word military and witch on the same day, this index gets a steep high. While considering these factors, it is mainly concluded that there is a correlation about the disclosure of the politicians and stock market index. In other words, it is determined that politicians have a strong influence on the volatility of the stock market.

These results give an idea that when politicians use negative words, it increases the volatility in the stock market. Similar to this situation, if their disclosures are related to the military issues, the stock exchange will also be influenced. Therefore, it is strongly recommended that politicians should choose their words carefully in order not to increase the volatility in the stock market. Otherwise, there is a great risk that both investors and companies can suffer from the significant amount of the losses.

In this study, the influence of the politicians' disclosures on the stock market index is evaluated. Within this framework, Donald Trump's tweets are considered by using random forest decision tree learning. In the future studies, a different methodology can be implemented for this purpose, such as interval type-2 fuzzy logic.

Appendix

Key Terms and Definitions

API:	Application Programme Interface
ASEAN:	Association of Southeast Asian Nations
R&D:	Research and Development
US:	United States

References

Adam, K., Marcet, A., & Nicolini, J. P. (2016). Stock market volatility and learning. *The Journal of Finance, 71*(1), 33–82.

Amarasinghe, A. (2015). Dynamic relationship between interest rate and stock price: Empirical evidence from Colombo stock exchange. *International Journal of Business and Social Science, 6*(4), 92–97.

Amit, R., Feldman, E., & Villalonga, B. (2018). *Family firms and the stock market performance of acquisitions and divestitures*. Available at SSRN 3303061.

Apergis, N., Paramati, S. R., & Ummalla, M. (2016). The effect of foreign direct investment and stock market growth on clean energy use across a panel of emerging market economies. *Energy Economics, 56*, 29–41.

Arthur, W. B. (2018). Asset pricing under endogenous expectations in an artificial stock market. In *The economy as an evolving complex system II* (pp. 31–60). CRC Press.

Azam, M., Haseeb, M., Samsi, A. B., & Raji, J. O. (2016). Stock market development and economic growth: Evidences from Asia-4 countries. *International Journal of Economics and Financial Issues, 6*(3), 1200–1208.

Babajide, A., Isola, L., & Somoye, R. O. (2016). Stock market response to economic growth and interest rate volatility: Evidence from Nigeria. *International Journal of Economics and Financial Issues, 6*(1), 354–360.

Bams, D., Blanchard, G., Honarvar, I., & Lehnert, T. (2017). Does oil and gold price uncertainty matter for the stock market? *Journal of Empirical Finance, 44*, 270–285.

Blanchard, O., Collins, C. G., Jahan-Parvar, M. R., Pellet, T., & Wilson, B. A. (2018). A year of rising dangerously? The US stock market performance in the aftermath of the presidential election. *Journal of Policy Modeling, 40*(3), 489–502.

Bouri, E., Jain, A., Biswal, P. C., & Roubaud, D. (2017). Cointegration and nonlinear causality amongst gold, oil, and the Indian stock market: Evidence from implied volatility indices. *Resources Policy, 52*, 201–206.

Cave, J., Chaudhuri, K., & Kumbhakar, S. C. (2019). Do banking sector and stock market development matter for economic growth? *Empirical Economics*, 1–23. https://doi.org/10.1007/s00181-019-01692-7.

Chiang, T. C., & Chen, X. (2017). Stock market activities and industrial production growth: Evidence from 20 international markets. In *Advances in Pacific Basin business economics and finance* (pp. 39–75). Emerald Publishing Limited.

Choudhry, T., Papadimitriou, F. I., & Shabi, S. (2016). Stock market volatility and business cycle: Evidence from linear and nonlinear causality tests. *Journal of Banking & Finance, 66*, 89–101.

Ciner, C. (2019). Does the stock market contain information about economic growth? Time-varying out of sample causality tests. *Applied Economics Letters, 26*(13), 1138–1142.

Dinçer, H., & Yüksel, S. (2018). Financial sector-based analysis of the G20 economies using the integrated decision-making approach with DEMATEL and TOPSIS. In *Emerging trends in banking and finance* (pp. 210–223). Springer.

Dinçer, H., Hacıoğlu, Ü., & Yüksel, S. (2018a). Evaluating the effects of economic imbalances on gold Price in Turkey with MARS method and discussions on microfinance. In *Microfinance and its impact on entrepreneurial development, sustainability, and inclusive growth* (pp. 115–137). IGI Global.

Dinçer, H., Yüksel, S., & Şenel, S. (2018b). Analyzing the global risks for the financial crisis after the great depression using comparative hybrid hesitant fuzzy decision-making models: Policy recommendations for sustainable economic growth. *Sustainability, 10*(9), 3126.

Dinçer, H., Yüksel, S., & Adalı, Z. (2019a). Economic effects in Islamic stock development of the European countries: Policy recommendations for ethical behaviors. In *Handbook of research on managerial thinking in global business economics* (pp. 58–78). IGI Global.

Dinçer, H., Yüksel, S., & Kartal, M. T. (2019b). The role of bank interest rate in the competitive emerging markets to provide financial and economic stability. *Ekonomi, İşletme ve Maliye Araştırmaları Dergisi, 1*(2). https://ssrn.com/abstract=3355939

Dinçer, H., Yüksel, S., Pınarbaşı, F., & Çetiner, İ. T. (2019c). Measurement of economic and banking stability in emerging markets by considering income inequality and nonperforming loans. In *Maintaining financial stability in times of risk and uncertainty* (pp. 49–68). IGI Global.

Ding, Z., Liu, Z., Zhang, Y., & Long, R. (2017). The contagion effect of international crude oil price fluctuations on Chinese stock market investor sentiment. *Applied Energy, 187*, 27–36.

Dyhrberg, A. H. (2016). Bitcoin, gold and the dollar—A GARCH volatility analysis. *Finance Research Letters, 16*, 85–92.

Emir, S., Dincer, H., Hacioglu, U., & Yuksel, S. (2015). Comparative study of outlier detection algorithms via fundamental analysis variables. *International Journal of Research in Business and Social Science (2147–4478), 4*(4), 45–60.

Ferrer, R., Bolós, V. J., & Benítez, R. (2016). Interest rate changes and stock returns: A European multi-country study with wavelets. *International Review of Economics & Finance, 44*, 1–12.

Galí, J., & Gambetti, L. (2015). The effects of monetary policy on stock market bubbles: Some evidence. *American Economic Journal: Macroeconomics, 7*(1), 233–257.

Gay, R. D. (2016). Effect of macroeconomic variables on stock market returns for four emerging economies: Brazil, Russia, India, and China. *The International Business & Economics Research Journal (Online), 15*(3), 119.

Ghazali, M. F., Lean, H. H., & Bahari, Z. (2018). Gold investment in Malaysia: Refuge from stock market turmoil or inflation-protector? *The Journal of Social Sciences Research, 2*, 214–224.

Ghosh, S., & Kanjilal, K. (2016). Co-movement of international crude oil price and Indian stock market: Evidences from nonlinear cointegration tests. *Energy Economics, 53*, 111–117.

Giannetti, M., & Wang, T. Y. (2016). Corporate scandals and household stock market participation. *The Journal of Finance, 71*(6), 2591–2636.

Gokmenoglu, K. K., & Fazlollahi, N. (2015). The interactions among gold, oil, and stock market: Evidence from S&P500. *Procedia Economics and Finance, 25*, 478–488.

Gong, P., & Dai, J. (2017). Monetary policy, exchange rate fluctuation, and herding behavior in the stock market. *Journal of Business Research, 76*, 34–43.

Hajilee, M., & Al Nasser, O. M. (2017). The impact of interest rate volatility on stock market development: Evidence from emerging markets. *The Journal of Developing Areas, 51*(2), 301–313.

Hanif, M. (2019). *Integration of macroeconomic variables and stock market—A comparison of conventional and Islamic indexes*. AMRC (Conference) 2019, UAE University, Alain, United Arab Emirates [March 24–26].

Huang, Y. F., & Startz, R. (2018). *Improved recession forecasts considering stock market volatility*. Available at SSRN 3297949.

Huang, S., An, H., Gao, X., & Sun, X. (2017). Do oil price asymmetric effects on the stock market persist in multiple time horizons? *Applied Energy, 185*, 1799–1808.

Iqbal, J. (2017). Does gold hedge stock market, inflation and exchange rate risks? An econometric investigation. *International Review of Economics & Finance, 48*, 1–17.

Jacobsen, B., Marshall, B. R., & Visaltanachoti, N. (2018). Stock market predictability and industrial metal returns. *Management Science*. https://doi.org/10.1287/mnsc.2017.2933.

Jain, A., & Biswal, P. C. (2016). Dynamic linkages among oil price, gold price, exchange rate, and stock market in India. *Resources Policy, 49*, 179–185.

Jammazi, R., Ferrer, R., Jareño, F., & Hammoudeh, S. M. (2017). Main driving factors of the interest rate-stock market Granger causality. *International Review of Financial Analysis, 52*, 260–280.

Jareño, F., & Negrut, L. (2016). US stock market and macroeconomic factors. *Journal of Applied Business Research, 32*(1), 325.

Jareño, F., Ferrer, R., & Miroslavova, S. (2016). US stock market sensitivity to interest and inflation rates: A quantile regression approach. *Applied Economics, 48*(26), 2469–2481.

Kang, W., Ratti, R. A., & Yoon, K. H. (2015). The impact of oil price shocks on the stock market return and volatility relationship. *Journal of International Financial Markets, Institutions and Money, 34*, 41–54.

Kariuki, C. (2015). The determinants of foreign direct investment in the African union. *Journal of Economics, Business and Management, 3*(3), 346–351.

Levine, R., Lin, C., & Xie, W. (2016). Spare tire? Stock markets, banking crises, and economic recoveries. *Journal of Financial Economics, 120*(1), 81–101.

Li, Q., Cheng, K., & Yang, X. (2017a). Response pattern of stock returns to international oil price shocks: From the perspective of China's oil industrial chain. *Applied Energy, 185*, 1821–1831.

Li, X., Zhang, J., & Xiao, Z. (2017b). Accounting earnings, market valuation and economic growth. *Journal of Accounting and Economics, 5*, 4.

Lütkepohl, H., & Netšunajev, A. (2018). The relation between monetary policy and the stock market in Europe. *Econometrics, 6*(3), 36.

Mamun, A., Ali, M. H., Hoque, N., Mowla, M. M., & Basher, S. (2018). The causality between stock market development and economic growth: Econometric evidence from Bangladesh. *International Journal of Economics and Finance, 10*(5), 212–220.

Matsuo, Y., & Ishizuka, M. (2004). Keyword extraction from a single document using word co-occurrence statistical information. *International Journal on Artificial Intelligence Tools, 13* (01), 157–169.

Mitra, P. K. (2017). Dynamics of volatility spillover between the Indian stock market and foreign exchange market return. *Academy of Accounting and Financial studies Journal, 21*(2), 1–11.

Moghaddam, A. H., Moghaddam, M. H., & Esfandyari, M. (2016). Stock market index prediction using artificial neural network. *Journal of Economics, Finance and Administrative Science, 21* (41), 89–93.

Moura, L., & Norden, L. (2018). *Does transparency pay off in the long-run? Evidence from stock market segment switches in Brazil.* Evidence from Stock Market Segment Switches in Brazil (September 1, 2018).

Moya-Martínez, P., Ferrer-Lapeña, R., & Escribano-Sotos, F. (2015). Interest rate changes and stock returns in Spain: A wavelet analysis. *BRQ Business Research Quarterly, 18*(2), 95–110.

Nguyen, C. P., Schinckus, C., Su, T. D., & Chong, F. (2018). Institutions, inward foreign direct investment, trade openness and credit level in emerging market economies. *Review of Development Finance, 8*(2), 75–88.

Nyasha, S., & Odhiambo, N. M. (2017). Banks, stock market development and economic growth in Kenya: An empirical investigation. *Journal of African Business, 18*(1), 1–23.

Oliveira, N., Cortez, P., & Areal, N. (2016). Stock market sentiment lexicon acquisition using microblogging data and statistical measures. *Decision Support Systems, 85*, 62–73.

Otieno, D. A., Ngugi, R. W., & Muriu, P. W. (2019). The impact of inflation rate on stock market returns: Evidence from Kenya. *Journal of Economics and Finance, 43*(1), 73–90.

Paramati, S. R., Ummalla, M., & Apergis, N. (2016). The effect of foreign direct investment and stock market growth on clean energy use across a panel of emerging market economies. *Energy Economics, 56*, 29–41.

Patel, J., Shah, S., Thakkar, P., & Kotecha, K. (2015). Predicting stock market index using fusion of machine learning techniques. *Expert Systems with Applications, 42*(4), 2162–2172.

Peiro, A. (2016). Stock prices and macroeconomic factors: Some European evidence. *International Review of Economics & Finance, 41*, 287–294.

Pradhan, R. P., Arvin, M. B., & Bahmani, S. (2015). Causal nexus between economic growth, inflation, and stock market development: The case of OECD countries. *Global Finance Journal, 27*, 98–111.

Pradhan, R. P., Arvin, M. B., & Hall, J. H. (2019). The nexus between economic growth, stock market depth, trade openness, and foreign direct investment: The case of ASEAN countries. *The Singapore Economic Review, 64*(03), 461–493.

Qiu, M., Song, Y., & Akagi, F. (2016). Application of artificial neural network for the prediction of stock market returns: The case of the Japanese stock market. *Chaos, Solitons & Fractals, 85*, 1–7.

Rachael, N., & Moses, W. (2017). The effect of interest rate control on the stock market performance, a case of Nairobi securities exchange market. *International Journal of Current Aspects in Finance (IJCAF), 4*(1), 48–54.

Rajapakse, C. R. (2019). Stock market performance, exchange rate volatility and foreign direct investment to Sri Lanka. *Asia Proceedings of Social Sciences, 4*(3), 20–22.

Ramírez, S. L. C., Meza, R. R., & Martinez, F. V. (2017). Non-linear multivariate dependence between the Mexican stock market index and the exchange rate: Efficiency hypothesis and political cycle in Mexico (1994–2012). *Revista Mexicana de Economía y Finanzas (REMEF): nueva época, 12*(1), 91–102.

Rjoub, H., Civcir, I., & Resatoglu, N. G. (2017). Micro and macroeconomic determinants of stock prices: The case of Turkish banking sector. *Romanian Journal of Economic Forecasting, 20*(1), 150–166.

Sakphoowadon, S., Wisitpongphan, N., & Haruechaiyasak, C. (2018, September). Probabilistic lexicon-based approach for stock market prediction: A case study of the Stock Exchange of Thailand (SET). In *2018 18th International symposium on communications and information technologies (ISCIT)* (pp. 383–388). IEEE.

Salisu, A. A., & Isah, K. O. (2017). Revisiting the oil price and stock market nexus: A nonlinear panel ARDL approach. *Economic Modelling, 66*, 258–271.

Schmidt-Hebbel, K., & Carrasco, M. (2016). The past and future of inflation targeting: Implications for emerging-market and developing economies. In *Monetary policy in India* (pp. 583–622). Springer.

Tang, H. M., & Ho, C. M. (2017). Banking, stock market and economic growth in four ASEAN countries: Evidence from linear and nonlinear methods. *IUP Journal of Applied Finance, 23*(2), 5.

Uwubanmwen, A., & Eghosa, I. L. (2015). Inflation rate and stock returns: Evidence from the Nigerian stock market. *International Journal of Business and Social Science, 6*(11), 155–167.

Valera, H. G. A., Holmes, M. J., & Hassan, G. (2017). Stock market uncertainty and interest rate behaviour: A panel GARCH approach. *Applied Economics Letters, 24*(11), 732–735.

Yüksel, S., & Zengin, S. (2016). Identifying the determinants of interest rate risk of the banks: A case of Turkish banking sector. *International Journal of Research in Business and Social Science, 5*(6), 12–28.

Zafar, M. W., Zaidi, S. A. H., Sinha, A., Gedikli, A., & Hou, F. (2019). The role of stock market and banking sector development, and renewable energy consumption in carbon emissions: Insights from G-7 and N-11 countries. *Resources Policy, 62*, 427–436.

Zhu, H., Guo, Y., You, W., & Xu, Y. (2016). The heterogeneity dependence between crude oil price changes and industry stock market returns in China: Evidence from a quantile regression approach. *Energy Economics, 55*, 30–41.

Chapter 7
Defining the Significant Factors of Currency Exchange Rate Risk by Considering Text Mining and Fuzzy AHP

Abstract This study aims to determine the factors affecting the exchange rate risk of companies. In this context, firstly, articles in the ScienceDirect database that contain exchange rate risk in their titles, abstracts, and keywords are provided. Single, double, and triple words were identified in 152 different studies that were published after 2018, which met the relevant criteria. As a result of the analysis of these words, 4 different criteria that could affect the exchange rate risk were determined. The relevant criteria were then weighted with fuzzy AHP. The findings indicate that the macroeconomic performance of countries is the most important determinant of exchange rate risk. In addition, wrong risk management practices of companies play also an important role for this risk. Thus, it is recommended that the government should design necessary regulations for the companies not to take too much currency exchange risk.

Keywords Currency exchange rate risk · Fuzzy AHP · Text mining

7.1 Introduction

The main purpose of companies is to achieve profitability. In this context, companies try to reduce their costs while increasing their revenues. In order to increase revenues, companies develop many different strategies (Brogi & Lagasio, 2019). Developing new products and services, entering different sectors, and increasing sales volume are among the most common examples of such strategies (Li et al., 2017). In addition, companies are taking some measures to reduce their costs. Reducing the benefits, dismissing some of the personnel, and finding suppliers with cheaper products are among the exemplary practices in this context (Lado-Sestayo et al., 2016).

It is also important that the profitability of companies is continuous as well as the profitability of the companies. If companies focus only on their short-term profitability, some measures that are not taken can lead to bankruptcy in the long run (Lloret, 2016). In this context, it is very necessary for the company to establish its

G. Silahtaroğlu et al., *Data Science and Multiple Criteria Decision Making Approaches in Finance*, Multiple Criteria Decision Making,
https://doi.org/10.1007/978-3-030-74176-1_7

policies on a long-term basis. To this end, companies need to establish long-term strategies. In addition, it is very important that they keep up with their competitors by following current developments in the market (Reichardt & Rogge, 2016). In addition, companies' products and services must meet customer expectations. Therefore, as a long-term practice, companies need to periodically analyze customer expectations (Uvarova et al., 2016). In this way, it will be possible to change strategies for customer expectations that change according to market conditions.

Risk management is one of the issues that companies should take into consideration when making long-term planning. Companies face many risks due to their activities. One of the biggest risks of a company is that although it sells a good, it cannot obtain its money from the other party. This is expressed in the literature as credit risk (Mukhtarov et al., 2018; Yüksel, 2016, 2017). In addition, operational risk is another important risk for companies. Examples of the type of operational risk include natural disasters, terrorist attacks, and problems arising from company personnel (Mignola et al., 2016; Zengin & Yüksel, 2016). On the other hand, companies may suffer losses due to instability in the market. The most important example of this type of risk, which is defined as market risk in the literature, is the extraordinary change in interest rate (Drechsler et al., 2018; Esposito et al., 2015; Yüksel & Zengin, 2016).

Exchange rate risk is also a very important type of risk for companies. In general terms, it can be defined as the loss of companies as a result of the extraordinary increase or decrease in the exchange rate (Beckmann & Stix, 2015; Ito et al., 2016). In this context, the foreign exchange position of the companies' balance sheets should be controlled. If the company's foreign currency debt exceeds its foreign currency receivable, it is defined as open position (Dinçer et al., 2018a; Omar et al., 2017; Yüksel et al., 2016). In this case, a possible increase in the exchange rate will cause serious damage to the company (Gadanecz et al., 2018). The main reason for this is that as the exchange rate increases, the company's debts increase automatically.

Similar to the sudden increase in the exchange rate, the unusual decrease of the exchange rate may cause significant losses to the companies (Gadanecz et al., 2018). If the foreign exchange debt of the companies is much higher, the decrease in the exchange rate will be negative for the company (Lan et al., 2015; Papaioannou, 2015). The main reason for this is that as a result of the decreasing exchange rate, the assets of the company are decreasing. This situation will negatively affect the profitability of the company. Taking these issues into consideration, it is understood that effective management of exchange rate risk is very important (Mukhtarov et al., 2019; Tunc et al., 2018). In this context, measures should be taken to control the balance sheet position periodically and to manage the risk by using derivative products (Oktar & Yüksel, 2016).

The purpose of this study is to determine the factors that increase the companies' exchange rate risk. In this context, firstly, articles published after 2018 were obtained from the ScienceDirect database. In the selection of the articles in question, the inclusion of the exchange rate risk in the title, abstract and keywords has been determined as the criterion. In this context, a summary of the maximum number of single, double, and triple words is provided in the abstracts of 252 articles reached. As a result of the analysis on these words, 4 different criteria that affect the exchange rate risk of companies have been determined. In the second part of the analysis part of the study, these criteria were weighted with fuzzy AHP method.

It is possible to mention many differences of this study compared to others. Firstly, as a result of a very large article review, the factors affecting exchange rate risk are grouped. On the other hand, these criteria were weighted according to their severity. This list of criteria will guide both academicians and company executives. In addition, text mining and fuzzy logic approach has been taken into consideration for the first time in this study on exchange rate risk. Therefore, this study aims to provide an important contribution to the literature.

7.2 Literature Review

Exchange rate risk is vital for companies. Many companies had to go bankrupt because their operations were progressing smoothly, as they could not manage exchange rate risk effectively (Eichler & Roevekamp, 2018). In other words, even if a company has a high profitability, it may become unable to continue its activities if it does not take the necessary measures for exchange rate risk. This issue, which is very important for companies, attracts the attention of researchers. As a result, a large literature on exchange rate risk has emerged. A significant part of the studies focused on the measurement of exchange rate risk. The first condition for effective risk management is the identification of this risk (Balduzzi et al., 2018). However, this situation requires serious technical knowledge (Fratzscher et al., 2018; Mantzura & Schreiber, 2019). There are many different approaches for measuring the exchange rate risks of companies (Kim & Chance, 2018). In order to use these approaches correctly, companies need qualified personnel (Nurrahmat et al., 2017). In this context, it would be appropriate for the company to either employ personnel who are familiar with these issues or to develop existing personnel for this purpose.

Measures to be taken to manage exchange rate risk have been emphasized in a certain section of the studies. As mentioned earlier, exchange rate risk is very important for companies. Therefore, this risk needs to be managed effectively (Santillán-Salgado et al., 2016; Vohra & Fabozzi, 2019). In this framework, Díaz and Vaquero (2017) and Álvarez Espinoza and Hansen (2017) indicated that in order to manage the exchange rate risk successfully, measures should be taken to prevent this risk after correctly defined risk. It is possible to take these measures in two different ways. First, companies should monitor the foreign exchange positions on their balance sheets periodically and ensure that there are not many open positions (Chakravorty & Awasthi, 2018). In addition, according to Du et al. (2018) and Prakash and Gopal (2019), it is possible to close the deficits in the foreign exchange position by using financial derivative products.

It is emphasized by many researchers that macroeconomic factors of a country also affect the exchange rate risk of companies in that country (Colacito et al., 2018;

Mimouni, 2017; Mitchener & Weidenmier, 2015). In this context, the most underlined factor is the high debt of the state. Ersal-Kiziler and Nguyen (2016) and Beckmann and Stix (2015) concluded that in countries with high government debt, the demand for exchange rates will increase. As a result, there will be significant increases in the exchange rate. This situation will adversely affect companies with high foreign currency debt. In addition, exchange rate risk increases in countries with high inflation. Basri et al. (2019), Ito et al. (2018), and Karolyi and Wu (2017) underlined that since high inflation will increase uncertainty in the country, foreign investors will not want to stay in the country. In this case, foreign exchange will become more valuable than domestic currency. On the other hand, Du et al. (2016) and Gadanecz et al. (2018) indicated that the statements made by the state authorities are considered to have an impact on the exchange rate risk. In addition to the macroeconomic factors, Chernov et al. (2018), Kamau et al. (2015), Du and Schreger (2016), and Richmond (2019) demonstrated that financial performance of the companies is directly related to the currency risks they are taking.

According to some researchers, another factor determining the exchange rate risk of companies is global economic conditions. Particularly with the effect of globalization, an event in one country has an impact on the economic issues in another country (Hakim & Al Wahili, 2017). For example, a significant majority of the financial crises, especially in recent years, have not only been limited in the country where the crisis began, but have spread to many other countries (Dinçer et al., 2018b; Helísek, 2019; Husted et al., 2018). Because globalization has increased trade between countries, a significant majority of companies trade in foreign currencies. This increases the exchange rate risk of companies (Hua et al., 2018). On the other hand, even today, the statements made by the managers of the big countries cause the economic conditions in other countries to be affected (Rattanapanurak, 2017).

In the majority of studies conducted in the literature on exchange rate risk, this type of crisis is analyzed for different purposes. Some researchers have focused on measuring exchange rate risk. Methods such as ARCH, GARCH, Monte Carlo simulation, and ARIMA were preferred in these studies. In addition to these studies, how to manage exchange rate risk, the relationship between exchange rate risk and financial performance, and the impact of government policies on exchange rate risk are other topics covered. In a new study, it is thought that how to reduce the exchange rate risk should be handled with a different method. In parallel to this, the subject mentioned in this study is handled with text mining and fuzzy AHP approaches and it is aimed to complete this deficiency in the literature.

7.3 Fuzzy AHP

Saaty (1977) developed an analytic hierarchy process mainly with the aim of evaluating different items. In this process, pair-wise comparison is performed to reach this objective. This method is very helpful to make decision under complex environment and there are many different alternatives. This approach is considered with fuzzy logic in this study by using the method of Chang (1996). In the first step, a pair-wise comparison matrix is created as in the Eq. (7.1).

$$\widetilde{A} = \begin{bmatrix} 1 & \widetilde{a}_{12} & \widetilde{a}_{13} & & \cdots & \widetilde{a}_{1m} \\ \widetilde{a}_{21} & 1 & \widetilde{a}_{23} & & \cdots & \widetilde{a}_{2m} \\ \widetilde{a}_{31} & \widetilde{a}_{32} & 1 & & \cdots & \widetilde{a}_{3m} \\ \vdots & \vdots & \vdots & \ddots & & \vdots \\ \widetilde{a}_{n1} & \widetilde{a}_{n2} & \widetilde{a}_{n3} & & \cdots & 1 \end{bmatrix} \tag{7.1}$$

On the other side, the second step is related to the calculation of the fuzzy synthetic extent (Si) that is given in the Eqs. (7.2)–(7.5).

$$S_j = \sum\nolimits_{j=1}^{m} M_{gi}^{j} \otimes \left(\sum\nolimits_{i=1}^{n} \sum\nolimits_{j=1}^{m} M_{gi}^{j}\right)^{-1} \tag{7.2}$$

$$\sum\nolimits_{j=1}^{m} M_{gi}^{j} = \left(\sum\nolimits_{j=1}^{m} l_j, \sum\nolimits_{j=1}^{m} m_j, \sum\nolimits_{j=1}^{m} u_j\right) \tag{7.3}$$

$$\sum\nolimits_{i=1}^{n} \sum\nolimits_{j=1}^{m} M_{gi}^{j} = \left(\sum\nolimits_{j=1}^{m} l_i, \sum\nolimits_{j=1}^{m} m_i, \sum\nolimits_{j=1}^{m} u_i\right) \tag{7.4}$$

$$\left[\sum\nolimits_{i=1}^{n} \sum\nolimits_{j=1}^{m} M_{gi}^{j}\right]^{-1} = \left(\frac{1}{\sum_{i=1}^{n} u_i}, \frac{1}{\sum_{i=1}^{n} m_i}, \frac{1}{\sum_{i=1}^{n} l_i}\right) \tag{7.5}$$

In these equations, l, m, and u represent a set of triangle fuzzy numbers. The third step includes the calculation of the degree of possibility. In this process, Eqs. (7.6)–(7.8) are taken into consideration.

$$V(M_2 \geq M_1) = sup\left[min\left(\mu_{M_1}(x), \mu_{M_2}(y)\right)\right] \tag{7.6}$$

$$V(M_2 \geq M_1) = hgt(M_1 \cap M_2) = \mu_{M_2}(d) \tag{7.7}$$

$$= \begin{cases} 1, & if \quad m_2 \geq m_1, \\ 0, & if \quad l_1 \geq u_2, \\ \dfrac{l_1 - u_2}{(m_2 - u_2) - (m_1 - l_1)} & otherwise \end{cases} \tag{7.8}$$

Moreover, the fourth step gives information about the computation of the following degree of possibility.

$$\begin{aligned} \mathrm{V}(\mathrm{M} \geq \mathrm{M}_1, \mathrm{M}_2, \ldots \mathrm{M}_k) &= \mathrm{V}[(\mathrm{M} \geq \mathrm{M}_1) \text{ and } (\mathrm{M} \geq \mathrm{M}_2) \text{ and} \ldots (\mathrm{M} \geq \mathrm{M}_k)] \\ &= \min\ \mathrm{V}(\mathrm{M} \geq \mathrm{M}_i) \end{aligned}$$

In the final stage, factors are normalized with the Eq. (7.9).

$$w = (d(A_1), d(A_2), \ldots, d(A_n))^T \tag{7.9}$$

Fuzzy AHP approach was considered by many researchers for different purposes, such as energy investment (Kaya & Kahraman, 2010; Dincer et al., 2019; Heo et al., 2010), banking industry (Haghighi et al., 2010; Dinçer & Yüksel, 2018; Mandic et al., 2014; Dincer & Hacioglu, 2013; Dincer, 2015), service quality (Dinçer & Gorener, 2011; Büyüközkan et al., 2011).

7.4 The Analysis on the Journals Reviewed in Sciencedirect

In this study, it is aimed to determine the factors affecting the exchange rate risk of companies. In this context, the analysis process of the study consists of two different stages. In the first part of the analysis, a total of 152 different articles were provided in the ScienceDirect database with a currency exchange in the keyword or title. After that, the most commonly used single, double, and triple words in the abstract sections of the articles were determined by the text mining method. The lists of these words are given in the abstract section of the study. By considering these words, 4 different factors are identified which can affect the currency exchange rate risk.

Table 7.1 indicates 4 different indicators of currency exchange risk. These are derived from the keywords obtained from the articles. The first indicator is the volatility in other factors in the market. In this framework, extraordinary increase in other rates, such as interest rate and federal reserve amount can affect currency exchanges. The second factor is related to the macroeconomic performance of the country. When there is a problem in the economy of the country like low GDP, stock market and financial crisis period, and currency exchange rate tends to be more volatile. Ineffective risk management of the companies can be another reason for currency exchange rate risk. Hence, appropriate methodologies should be taken into consideration in order to estimate and manage this risk in an effective manner. On

Table 7.1 Criteria generated from the keywords

Criteria	Related keywords
Volatility in other factors in the market	Market, price, return, rates, dollar, financial, deviation, Japanese yen, federal reserve, British pound, Swiss franc, Korean won, foreign currency exchange, foreign exchange rates
Macroeconomic performance of the country	Economic, stock, bank, finance, demand, right reserve, central bank, financial market, reserve bank, stock market, financial crisis, federal reserve bank, gross domestic product
Ineffective risk management of the companies	Estimate, parameter, approach, measure, consider, cost, predict, calculate, forecast, assumption, strategy, derive, Monte Carlo, artificial neural network, exchange rate prediction
Problems of global trade condition	Trade, produce, raw material, purchase power, raw material cost

Table 7.2 The fuzzy scale of the pair-wise comparison

Definition	Triangular fuzzy numbers		
Equally important (EI)	0.5	1	1.5
Weakly more important (WI)	1	1.5	2
Strongly more important (SI)	1.5	2	2.5
Very strongly more important (VI)	2	2.5	3
Absolutely more important (AI)	2.5	3	3.5

Source: Chang (1996)

the other side, there can be some problems of global trade conditions, such as low trade and high raw material cost. This situation has a direct influence on the currency exchange rate risk.

In the second stage of the analysis, these 4 different factors are weighted by using fuzzy AHP approach. In this process, fuzzy scales for the pair-wise comparison, stated in Table 7.2, are taken into consideration.

Next, the linguistic evaluations are obtained from the decision makers. They are given in Table 7.3.

After that, these linguistic evaluations are converted into fuzzy numbers. The fuzzy pair-wise comparison matrix for each decision makers is demonstrated in Tables 7.9–7.12. By considering these tables, averaged fuzzy pair-wise comparison matrix is created. This matrix is indicated in Table 7.4.

In the last stage, the weights and ranking results of the criteria are calculated. These results are detailed in Table 7.5.

Table 7.5 gives information that macroeconomic performance of the country is the most significant determinant of the currency exchange rate risk. Additionally, ineffective risk management of the companies is also accepted as another important indicator for this risk. On the other hand, volatility in other factors in the market and problems of global trade conditions are less important to explain the currency exchange rate risk.

7.5 Conclusion

In this study, the factors affecting the exchange rate risk of companies are examined. In this context, first of all, by using the ScienceDirect database, the articles included the word exchange rate risk in the title, abstract, or keywords are taken into consideration. In the examinations conducted, articles published after 2018 were examined. In the abstracts of these articles, the most common single, double, and triple words were determined. Using these words, 4 different indicators that could affect the exchange rate risk were identified. These factors were weighted according to their significance using fuzzy AHP method.

As a result, it is concluded that the macroeconomic performance of countries is the most important determinant of exchange rate risk. In addition, wrong risk

Table 7.3 Linguistic evaluations for pair-wise comparison matrix

Criteria/	Volatility in other factors in the market (C1)				Macroeconomic performance of the country (C2)				Ineffective risk management of the companies (C3)				Problems of global trade condition (C4)			
decision makers	DM1	DM2	DM3	DM4	DM1	DM2	DM3	DM4	DM1	DM2	DM3	DM4	DM1	DM2	DM3	DM4
C1					EI	EI	EI	EI	EI	EI	EI	EI	EI	EI	WI	EI
C2									SI	SI	WI	WI	VI	SI	SI	WI
C3													EI	WI	SI	SI
C4																

Table 7.4 Averaged fuzzy pair-wise comparison matrix

Criteria	Volatility in other factors in the market (C1)			Macroeconomic performance of the country (C2)			Ineffective risk management of the companies (C3)			Problems of global trade condition (C4)		
Volatility in other factors in the market (C1)	1.00	1.00	1.00	0.50	1.00	1.50	0.50	1.00	1.50	0.63	1.13	1.75
Macroeconomic performance of the country (C2)	0.67	1.00	2.00	1.00	1.00	1.00	1.25	1.75	2.38	1.50	2.00	2.50
Ineffective risk management of the companies (C3)	0.67	1.00	2.00	0.43	0.58	0.83	1.00	1.00	1.00	1.13	1.63	2.13
Problems of global trade condition (C4)	0.60	0.92	1.75	0.41	0.52	0.71	0.49	0.67	1.08	1.00	1.00	1.00

Table 7.5 Weights and ranking results of the criteria

Criteria	Weights	Ranks
Volatility in other factors in the market (C1)	0.244	3
Macroeconomic performance of the country (C2)	0.330	1
Ineffective risk management of the companies (C3)	0.251	2
Problems of global trade condition (C4)	0.175	4

management practices of companies are also important determinants of this type of risk. On the other hand, the riskiness of other factors in the market and the negativities experienced in global trade are less important than other criteria. From this point of view, it is understood that the most duties fall to the government in order to minimize the exchange rate risk of the companies. In this context, the exchange rate risk of companies will be easier to be managed with effective regulations. This situation can eliminate a very important threat to the national economy.

It is identified that macroeconomic performance of the country is the most important indicator of currency exchange rate risk. Additionally, it is also concluded that ineffective risk management of the companies also plays a very important role in this risk. This situation indicates that companies are taking higher currency risks when there is a problem in the economy. Hence, the government should design necessary regulations for the companies not to take too much currency exchange risk. In this framework, it should be prohibited for the countries to have high open balance sheet position and these companies should be guided by the government to manage exchange rate risks using derivative products.

Fuzzy AHP approach is taken into consideration in this study to reach the objective. In a future study, these criteria can also be weighted by different methods, such as fuzzy ANP. This situation provides a chance to make a comparative analysis. In addition to this issue, fuzzy DEMATEL model can also be considered in the analysis process so that impact relation map between the criteria can be created. On the other side, different risk types like interest rate risk and liquidity risk can be evaluated in new analysis. It is thought that these new studies make also contribution to the literature.

Appendix 1

Key Terms and Definitions

AHP:	Analytical Hierarchy Process
ANP:	Analytical Network Process
ARCH:	Autoregressive Conditional Heteroskedasticity
ARIMA:	Autoregressive Integrated Moving Average
DEMATEL:	Decision-Making Trial and Evaluation Laboratory
GARCH:	Generalized Autoregressive Conditional Heteroskedasticity

Appendix 2

Table 7.6 List of top single words in abstracts

Study	Determine	Cost	Country	Select	Observation	Coefficient	Natural	Reason	Size
Increase	Suggest	Condition	Accord	Weight	Reserve	Economy	Assumption	Finance	Variable
Represent	Set	Close	Improve	List	e-mail	Strong	Establish	Science	Online
Currency	Approach	Perform	Introduce	Bank	Theory	Control	Decision	Prese	Company
Include	Support	Produce	Introduction	Obtain	Compute	Sery	Probability	Cause	Alternative
Market	Paper	Apply	Significant	Stock	Found	Equation	Strategy	Global	Deviation
Model	Trade	Particular	Tion	Process	Standard	Component	Linear	Extend	Discuss
Test	Base	Application	Elsevier	Equal	Property	Journal	Accept	Move	Achieve
Provide	Measure	Rate	Develop	Research	Empirical	Example	Pattern	Interval	Additional
Economic	Follow	Account	Data	Statistical	Common	Regard	Independent	Local	Vector
Compare	Assume	Relative	Average	Dynamic	Changes	Concern	Design	Construct	Wide
Estimate	Similar	Factor	Conclusion	Identify	Vary	Consist	Index	Trend	Conclude
Term	Effect	Predict	Relate	Unit	Information	Positive	Satisfy	Initial	Denote
Correspond	Level	Recent	Value	Scale	Allow	Start	Constant	Imply	Amount
Day	Consider	Calculate	Error	Decrease	Impact	Correlation	Policy	Variation	Derive
Method	Exist	Forecast	Note	Statistic	Random	Http	Future	Associate	Literature
Function	Fig	Indicate	Analysis	Keyword	Comparison	Observe	Development	Occur	Address
Form	Time	Distribution	Dollar	Consider	Reflect	Lower	Department	Demand	Individual
Report	Define	Use	Current	Process	Risk	Require	Model	Appear	Simulation
Mean	Affect	Generate	Receive	Values	Foreign	Prices	Characteristic	Review	Power
Price	Depend	Final	Financial	Direct	Shown	Real	Matter	Behavior	Business
Period	Main	Section	Expect	References	Evaluate	Product	Various	Potential	Adjust
System	Return	Rates	Available	International	Step	Relationship	Low	Obtain	Asset
Parameter	Exchange	Respective	Analyze	Table	Hold	Structure	Approximate	Negative	Maximum
Author	Describe	University	Examine	Propose	Change	Month	Network	Fix	Relation
Follow	Reduce	Previous	Lead	Right	Due	Total	Variables	Effective	Solution

Table 7.7 List of top double words in abstracts

Right reserv	Follow section	Standard deviation	British pound	Estimate	Helpful comment	Positive negative	Form February	Maximum minimum	Comment suggestion
Correspond author	Japanese yen	Journal homepage	Financial market	Swiss franc	Foreign currency	Different	Important	Monte Carlo	Ourna homepage
Currency exchange	e-mail address	Neural network	Rest organize	Sciverse ScienceDirect	Cambridge pres	Anonymous referees	Between	Purchase power	Trade partner
Front matter	Organize follow	Elsevier science	John Wiley	Doi org101016j	Identical distribute	Science ltd	Abstract paper	Short run	Variables
List available	Available online	Publish Elsevier	Increase decrease	Move average	German mark	Interna tional	Market	Take account	Significant
e-mail address	Time sery	History receive	Conclude remark	Inc right	Probability density	Radial basis	Science engineer	Environment	Stock market
Elsevier right	Currency	Tel fax	Fore- cast	Online www	Computer science	Department physic	Current account	Acknowledgement author	Department economic
Exchange rates	Fax e-mail	Matter Elsevier	Available sciverse	Null hypothesis	Receive December	Support grant	Upper bound	Middle east	Financial crisis
Revise form	Reserv keyword	ScienceDirect homepage	Elsevier inc	Indepen- dent	Economic	Dollar usd	Tarticle history	Receive revise	Direct investment
Author tel	Random walk	Brownian motion	Performance	Partial support	Receive ju	North American	Wwwelsevier comlocate	Form October	Standard
Available ScienceDirect	Federal reserve	Raw material	Data set	By-nc-nd license	January December	Complex system	Short term	Power law	Acad sci
Http doi	Ltd right	Matter pii	Technical report	Reserve bank	Develope	Author fax	Article by-nc-nd	University technology	Institute technology
Exchange rate	ScienceDirect journal	Maximum likelihood	Foreign exchange	ScienceDirect journal	Foreign	School business	Creativecommon orglicensesby-nc-nd40	Information	Support vector
Content list	Jel classification	Central bank	los generality	Shown fig	Oper res	Journal economic	Absolute percentage	Top bottom	Previous study

Article history	Play role	Mean square	Wiley son	Section brief	Algorithm	Artificial neural	Std dev	Korean won	Wall street
Author e-mail	Hong Kong	Vice versa	Com locate	Mod el	Repre sent	Skewness kurtosis	Error term	King saud	License http
Reserv introduction	Elsevier ltd	Accept online	Correspond	Homepage wwwelsevier	Http creativecommon	Section describes	System	Acknowledgement thank	Wide range
Usa receive	Gradient descent	Ieee Tran	Science technology	Currency rates	Average	Receive October			

Table 7.8 List of top triple words in abstracts

Elsevier right reserv	Science right reserv	Homepage wwwelsevier comlocate	wwwe lsev com	Elsevier right reserv
List available ScienceDirect	Rest organize follow	Article history receive	Lsev com locate	List available ScienceDirect
Content list available	Fax e-mail address	Access article by-nc-nd	Receive November revise	Content list available
Currency exchange rates	Inc right reserv	Article by-nc-nd license	Fax e-mail address	Currency exchange rates
Correspond author tel	Elsevier science right	Elsevier science ltd	Artificial neural network	Correspond author tel
Right reserv introduction	Author tel fax	Science ltd right	By-nc-nd license http	Right reserv introduction
Correspond author e-mail	List available sciverse	Author tel e-mail	Publish Elsevier ltd	Correspond author e-mail
Currency exchange rate	Online www sciencedirectcom	Revise form october	Financial time sery	Currency exchange rate
ScienceDirect journal homepage	Right reserv pac	Revise form February	Sciverse ScienceDirect journal	ScienceDirect journal homepage
Organize follow section	Elsevier ltd right	ScienceDirect ourna homepage	Acknowledgement author grateful	Organize follow section
Right reserv keyword	Journal homepage wwwelseviercomlocatephysa	Ourna homepage wwwe	e-mail addr 0378–4371	Right reserv keyword
Ltd right reserv	Available sciverse ScienceDirect	Tarticle history receive	Addr 0378–4371 doi101016jphphysica	Ltd right reserv
Available ScienceDirect journal	Elsevier inc right	License http creativecommon	Probability density function	Available sciencedirect journal
Author e-mail address	John Wiley son	Http creativecommon orglicensesby-nc-nd40	Foreign exchange rates	Author e-mail address
Front matter Elsevier	Federal reserve bank	Chao soliton fractal	Research partial support	Front matter Elsevier
Front matter pii	Http doi org101016j	Independent identical distribute	Author publish Elsevier	Front matter pii
Tel fax e-mail	Foreign currency exchange	Receive revise form	Receive December revise	Tel fax e-mail
Available online www	Right reserv jel	Www sciencedirectcom DcienceDirect	December revise form	Available online www

Available ScienceDirect homepage	Homepage wwwelsev	Follow section describes	Exchange rate prediction	Available ScienceDirect homepage
Author e-mail address	Reserv jel classification	Available ScienceDirect ourna	Correspond author fax	Author e-mail address
History receive November	Journal homepage wwwelsevier	Raw material cost	Fractional Brownian motion	History receive November
Form February accept	References mantegna Stanley	Online jel classification	Non-gaussian chapman hall	Form February accept
Central limit theorem	Britain pound gbp	Currency exchange data	Referees helpful comment	Central limit theorem
Jel classification f31	Tsonis heller takayasu	Receive ju revise	Revise form accept	Jel classification f31
Front matter doi101016j	Heller takayasu marumo	Ju revise form	Publish Elsevier inc	Front matter doi101016j
ScienceDirect homepage wwwelsevier	Corp lakeside avenue	Revise form April	Mathematical computer model	ScienceDirect homepage wwwelsevier
Journal operational research	Receive January abstract	Japanese yen jpy	Department mathematic university	Journal operational research
Maximum likelihood estimation	Pac 0250-r keyword	Author fax e-mail	Journal king saud	Maximum likelihood estimation
Japanese yen British	Schwarz morgenegg bank	Oarticle history accept	Saud university computer	Japanese yen British
Yen British pound	Galluccio caldarelli marsili	Structure follow section	University computer information	Yen British pound
Generalization revisit communication	Caldarelli marsili y-c	5u1t 6u2t 7u3t	Computer information sciences	Generalization revisit communication
Kluwer academic publisher	Marsili y-c zhang	Revise form January	Proceed follow section	Kluwer academic publisher
Production host elsevier	Time sery data	Exchange rates use	Median maximum minimum	Production host Elsevier
Autoregressive move average	Paper organize follow	University Nevada Reno	Wiley son ltd	
Tel e-mail address	Akaike criterion aic	Nevada Reno Usa	Approximate continuous function	

(continued)

Table 7.8 (continued)

Elsevier right reserv	Science right reserv	Homepage wwwelsevier comlocate	wwwe lsev com	Elsevier right reserv
Radial basis function	Figure legend reader	Gros domestic product	Usa article history	
King saud university	Legend reader referr	South African rand	Play vital role	
Particle swarm optimization	Reader referr web	Sciverse ScienceDirect ourna	Gradient descent method	
Matter Elsevier ltd	Article presscorrespond e-mail	Siksha ëoí anusandhan	History receive revise	
Revise form November	Presscorrespond e-mail addr	Absolute percentage mape	Revise form ju	

Table 7.9 Fuzzy pair-wise comparison matrix for DM1

Criteria	Volatility in other factors in the market (C1)			Macroeconomic performance of the country (C2)			Ineffective risk management of the companies (C3)			Problems of global trade condition (C4)		
Volatility in other factors in the market (C1)	1.00	1.00	1.00	0.50	1.00	1.50	0.50	1.00	1.50	0.50	1.00	1.50
Macroeconomic performance of the country (C2)	0.67	1.00	2.00	1.00	1.00	1.00	1.50	2.00	2.50	2.00	2.50	3.00
Ineffective risk management of the companies (C3)	0.67	1.00	2.00	0.40	0.50	0.67	1.00	1.00	1.00	0.50	1.00	1.50
Problems of global trade condition (C4)	0.67	1.00	2.00	0.33	0.40	0.50	0.67	1.00	2.00	1.00	1.00	1.00

Table 7.10 Fuzzy pair-wise comparison matrix for DM2

Criteria	Volatility in other factors in the market (C1)			Macroeconomic performance of the country (C2)			Ineffective risk management of the companies (C3)			Problems of global trade condition (C4)		
Volatility in other factors in the market (C1)	1.00	1.00	1.00	0.50	1.00	1.50	0.50	1.00	1.50	0.50	1.00	1.50
Macroeconomic performance of the country (C2)	0.67	1.00	2.00	1.00	1.00	1.00	1.50	2.00	2.50	1.50	2.00	2.50
Ineffective risk management of the companies (C3)	0.67	1.00	2.00	0.40	0.50	0.67	1.00	1.00	1.00	1.00	1.50	2.00
Problems of global trade condition (C4)	0.67	1.00	2.00	0.40	0.50	0.67	0.50	0.67	1.00	1.00	1.00	1.00

Table 7.11 Fuzzy pair-wise comparison matrix for DM3

Criteria	Volatility in other factors in the market (C1)			Macroeconomic performance of the country (C2)			Ineffective risk management of the companies (C3)			Problems of global trade condition (C4)		
Volatility in other factors in the market (C1)	1.00	1.00	1.00	0.50	1.00	1.50	0.50	1.00	1.50	1.00	1.50	2.50
Macroeconomic performance of the country (C2)	0.67	1.00	2.00	1.00	1.00	1.00	1.00	1.50	2.50	1.50	2.00	2.50
Ineffective risk management of the companies (C3)	0.67	1.00	2.00	0.40	0.67	1.00	1.00	1.00	1.00	1.50	2.00	2.50
Problems of global trade condition (C4)	0.40	0.67	1.00	0.40	0.50	0.67	0.40	0.50	0.67	1.00	1.00	1.00

Table 7.12 Fuzzy pair-wise comparison matrix for DM4

Criteria	Volatility in other factors in the market (C1)			Macroeconomic performance of the country (C2)			Ineffective risk management of the companies (C3)			Problems of global trade condition (C4)		
Volatility in other factors in the market (C1)	1.00	1.00	1.00	0.50	1.00	1.50	0.50	1.00	1.50	0.50	1.00	1.50
Macroeconomic performance of the country (C2)	0.67	1.00	2.00	1.00	1.00	1.00	1.00	1.50	2.00	1.00	1.50	2.00
Ineffective risk management of the companies (C3)	0.67	1.00	2.00	0.50	0.67	1.00	1.00	1.00	1.00	1.50	2.00	2.50
Problems of global trade condition (C4)	0.67	1.00	2.00	0.50	0.67	1.00	0.40	0.50	0.67	1.00	1.00	1.00

References

Álvarez Espinoza, R., & Hansen, E. (2017). *Corporate currency risk and hedging in Chile: Real and financial effects* (No. IDB-WP-769). IDB Working Paper Series.

Balduzzi, P., Chiang, I., & Ethan, H. (2018). Real exchange rates and currency risk premiums. *The Review of Asset Pricing Studies, 10*(1), 94–121. https://doi.org/10.1093/rapstu/raz002

Basri, B., Harnaji, B., & Kartinah, K. (2019, July). The effect of inflation rate and rupiah currency exchange rate fluctuation toward stock risk at Indonesia capital market. In *International Conference on Banking, Accounting, Management, and Economics (ICOBAME 2018)*. Atlantis Press.

Beckmann, E., & Stix, H. (2015). Foreign currency borrowing and knowledge about exchange rate risk. *Journal of Economic Behavior & Organization, 112*, 1–16.

Brogi, M., & Lagasio, V. (2019). Environmental, social, and governance and company profitability: Are financial intermediaries different? *Corporate Social Responsibility and Environmental Management, 26*(3), 576–587.

Büyüközkan, G., Çifçi, G., & Güleryüz, S. (2011). Strategic analysis of healthcare service quality using fuzzy AHP methodology. *Expert Systems with Applications, 38*(8), 9407–9424.

Chakravorty, G., & Awasthi, A. (2018). *Dynamic hedging of currency risk in investment strategies*. Available at SSRN 3289292.

Chang, D. Y. (1996). Applications of the extent analysis method on fuzzy AHP. *European Journal of Operational Research, 95*(3), 649–655.

Chernov, M., Graveline, J., & Zviadadze, I. (2018). Crash risk in currency returns. *Journal of Financial and Quantitative Analysis, 53*(1), 137–170.

Colacito, R., Croce, M. M., Gavazzoni, F., & Ready, R. (2018). Currency risk factors in a recursive multicountry economy. *The Journal of Finance, 73*(6), 2719–2756.

Díaz, J. M., & Vaquero, D. D. (2017). Foreign currency risk management practices in Spanish companies: An empirical analysis. *Aestimatio: The IEB International Journal of Finance, 14*, 132–163.

Dinçer, H., Hacıoğlu, Ü., & Yüksel, S. (2018a). Evaluating the effects of economic imbalances on gold Price in Turkey with MARS method and discussions on microfinance. In *Microfinance and its impact on entrepreneurial development, sustainability, and inclusive growth* (pp. 115–137). IGI Global.

Dincer, H. (2015). Profit-based stock selection approach in banking sector using fuzzy AHP and MOORA method. *Global Business and Economics Research Journal, 4*(2), 1–26.

Dinçer, H., Hacıoğlu, Ü., & Yüksel, S. (2018b). Determining influencing factors of currency exchange rate for decision making in global economy using MARS method. In *Geopolitics and strategic management in the global economy* (pp. 261–273). IGI Global.

Dinçer, H., & Gorener, A. (2011). Performance evaluation using AHP-VIKOR and AHPTOPSIS approaches: The case of service sector. *Sigma Journal of Engineering and Natural Sciences, 29* (3), 244–260.

Dincer, H., & Hacioglu, U. (2013). Performance evaluation with fuzzy VIKOR and AHP method based on customer satisfaction in Turkish banking sector. *Kybernetes, 42*(7), 1072–1085.

Dinçer, H., & Yüksel, S. (2018). Comparative evaluation of BSC-based new service development competencies in Turkish banking sector with the integrated fuzzy hybrid MCDM using content analysis. *International Journal of Fuzzy Systems, 20*(8), 2497–2516.

Dincer, H., Yüksel, S., & Martinez, L. (2019). Balanced scorecard-based analysis about European energy investment policies: A hybrid hesitant fuzzy decision-making approach with quality function deployment. *Expert Systems with Applications, 115*, 152–171.

Drechsler, I., Savov, A., & Schnabl, P. (2018). *Banking on deposits: Maturity transformation without interest rate risk* (No. w24582). National Bureau of Economic Research.

Du, D., Hu, O., & Zhao, X. (2016). Currency risk premium and US macroeconomic announcement. *Journal of Financial Research, 39*(4), 359–388.

Du, J., Wang, J. N., Hsu, Y. T., & Lai, K. K. (2018). The importance of hedging currency risk: Evidence from CNY and CNH. *Economic Modelling, 75*, 81–92.

Du, W., & Schreger, J. (2016). *Sovereign risk, currency risk, and corporate balance sheets*. Harvard Business School BGIE Unit Working Paper (17-024).

Eichler, S., & Roevekamp, I. (2018). A market-based measure for currency risk in managed exchange rate regimes. *Journal of International Financial Markets, Institutions and Money, 57*, 141–159.

Ersal-Kiziler, E., & Nguyen, H. (2016). *Euro currency risk and the geography of debt flows to peripheral European monetary union members*. The World Bank.

Esposito, L., Nobili, A., & Ropele, T. (2015). The management of interest rate risk during the crisis: Evidence from Italian banks. *Journal of Banking & Finance, 59*, 486–504.

Fratzscher, M., Menkhoff, L., Sarno, L., Schmeling, M., & Stoehr, T. (2018). *Systematic intervention and currency risk Premia*. Available at SSRN 3119907.

Gadanecz, B., Miyajima, K., & Shu, C. (2018). Emerging market local currency sovereign bond yields: The role of exchange rate risk. *International Review of Economics & Finance, 57*, 371–401.

Haghighi, M., Divandari, A., & Keimasi, M. (2010). The impact of 3D e-readiness on e-banking development in Iran: A fuzzy AHP analysis. *Expert Systems with Applications, 37*(6), 4084–4093.

Hakim, H. T. A., & Al Wahili, S. M. S. (2017). Effect of the outlet of sale of foreign currency in the exchange rate risk. *Iraqi Administrative Sciences Journal, 1*(4), 47–82.

Helísek, M. (2019). Exchange rate Mechanism II and the risk of currency crisis-empiricism and theory. *Journal of International Studies, 12*(1), 297–312.

Heo, E., Kim, J., & Boo, K. J. (2010). Analysis of the assessment factors for renewable energy dissemination program evaluation using fuzzy AHP. *Renewable and Sustainable Energy Reviews, 14*(8), 2214–2220.

Hua, X., Huang, W., & Jiang, Y. (2018). Controlled currency regime and pricing of exchange rate risk: Evidence from China. *Journal of Accounting, Auditing & Finance*, 0148558X18781144.

Husted, L., Rogers, J., & Sun, B. (2018). Uncertainty, currency excess returns, and risk reversals. *Journal of International Money and Finance, 88*, 228–241.

Ito, T., Koibuchi, S., Sato, K., & Shimizu, J. (2016). Exchange rate exposure and risk management: The case of Japanese exporting firms. *Journal of the Japanese and International Economies, 41*, 17–29.

Ito, T., Koibuchi, S., Sato, K., & Shimizu, J. (2018). *Choice of invoice currency and exchange rate risk management: 2017 questionnaire survey with Japanese headquarters*. RIETI Discussion Paper Series 18-J-025 (in Japanese).

Kamau, P., Inanga, E. L., & Rwegasira, K. (2015). Currency risk impact on the financial performance of multilateral banks. *Journal of Financial Reporting and Accounting, 13*(1), 91–118.

Karolyi, G. A., & Wu, Y. (2017). *Another look at currency risk in international stock returns*. Available at SSRN 3056845.

Kaya, T., & Kahraman, C. (2010). Multicriteria renewable energy planning using an integrated fuzzy VIKOR & AHP methodology: The case of Istanbul. *Energy, 35*(6), 2517–2527.

Kim, S. F., & Chance, D. M. (2018). An empirical analysis of corporate currency risk management policies and practices. *Pacific-Basin Finance Journal, 47*, 109–128.

Lado-Sestayo, R., Otero-González, L., Vivel-Búa, M., & Martorell-Cunill, O. (2016). Impact of location on profitability in the Spanish hotel sector. *Tourism Management, 52*, 405–415.

Lan, L. H., Chen, C. C., & Chuang, S. S. (2015). Exchange rate risk management: What can we learn from financial crises? *Economic Modelling, 45*, 187–192.

Li, D., Zheng, M., Cao, C., Chen, X., Ren, S., & Huang, M. (2017). The impact of legitimacy pressure and corporate profitability on green innovation: Evidence from China top 100. *Journal of Cleaner Production, 141*, 41–49.

Lloret, A. (2016). Modeling corporate sustainability strategy. *Journal of Business Research, 69*(2), 418–425.

Mandic, K., Delibasic, B., Knezevic, S., & Benkovic, S. (2014). Analysis of the financial parameters of Serbian banks through the application of the fuzzy AHP and TOPSIS methods. *Economic Modelling, 43*, 30–37.

Mantzura, A., & Schreiber, B. Z. (2019). Predicting foreign investors' carry trade activity in the Israeli FX market using a time-varying currency risk premium approach. *International Review of Economics & Finance, 59*, 438–457.

Mignola, G., Ugoccioni, R., & Cope, E. (2016). Comments on the Basel Committee on Banking Supervision proposal for a new standardized approach for operational risk. *Journal of Operational Risk, 11*(3), 1–20.

Mimouni, K. (2017). Currency risk and microcredit interest rates. *Emerging Markets Review, 31*, 80–95.

Mitchener, K. J., & Weidenmier, M. D. (2015). Was the classical gold standard credible on the periphery? Evidence from currency risk. *The Journal of Economic History, 75*(2), 479–511.

Mukhtarov, S., Yüksel, S., & Mammadov, E. (2018). Factors that increase credit risk of Azerbaijani banks. *Journal of International Studies, 11*(2), 63–75.

Mukhtarov, S., Yüksel, S., Ibadov, E., & Hamidov, H. (2019). The effectiveness of exchange rate channel in Azerbaijan: An empirical analysis. *Banks and Bank Systems, 14*(1), 111.

Nurrahmat, M. H., Noviyanti, L., & Bachrudin, A. (2017, March). Estimation of value at risk in currency exchange rate portfolio using asymmetric GJR-GARCH copula. In *AIP Conference Proceedings* (Vol. 1827, no. 1, p. 020006). AIP Publishing.

Oktar, S., & Yüksel, S. (2016). Bankalarin Türev Ürün Kullanimini Etkileyen Faktörler: Mars Yöntemi ile Bir Inceleme/Determinants of the use derivatives in banking: An analysis with MARS model. *Finans Politik & Ekonomik Yorumlar, 53*(620), 31.

Omar, A. B., Mohammad, K. N. B. T., & Ahmad, N. B. (2017). Exposure to foreign exchange rate risk: A review of empirical evidences. *Journal of Insurance and Financial Management, 2*(5), 17–34.

Papaioannou, M. (2015). Exchange rate risk measurement and management: Issues and approaches for public debt managers. *South-Eastern Europe Journal of Economics, 7*(1), 7–34.

Prakash, K. B., & Gopal, C. V. (2019). *Pareto currency risk management strategy—A passive hedge*. Currency Risk Management: Selected Research Papers, 43.

Rattanapanurak, J. (2017). *Effect of exchange rate volatility on currency carry trade and risk factor compensation of currency carry trade in G10 and emerging market* (Doctoral dissertation, Chulalongkorn University).

Reichardt, K., & Rogge, K. (2016). How the policy mix impacts innovation: Findings from company case studies on offshore wind in Germany. *Environmental Innovation and Societal Transitions, 18*, 62–81.

Richmond, R. J. (2019). Trade network centrality and currency risk premia. *The Journal of Finance, 74*(3), 1315–1361.

Saaty, T. L. (1977). A scaling method for priorities in hierarchical structures. *Journal of Mathematical Psychology, 15*(3), 234–281.

Santillán-Salgado, R. J., Ulin-Lastra, M. G., & López-Herrera, F. (2016). Currency exchange rate risk hedging strategies using MXN/USD MexDer futures contracts. *International Journal of Bonds and Derivatives, 2*(3), 186–210.

Tunc, C., Solakoglu, M. N., Babuscu, S., & Hazar, A. (2018). Exchange rate risk and international trade: The role of third country effect. *Economics Letters, 167*, 152–155.

Uvarova, S., Belyaeva, S., Kankhva, V., & Vlasenko, V. (2016). Implementation of innovative strategy in underground construction as a basis for sustainable economic development of a construction enterprise. *Procedia Engineering, 165*, 1317–1322.

Vohra, S., & Fabozzi, F. J. (2019). Effectiveness of developed and emerging market FX options in active currency risk management. *Journal of International Money and Finance, 96*, 130–146.
Yüksel, S. (2016). Bankaların Takipteki Krediler Oranını Belirleyen Faktörler: Türkiye İçin Bir Model Önerisi. *Bankacılar Dergisi, 98*, 41–56.
Yüksel, S. (2017). Determinants of the credit risk in developing countries after economic crisis: A case of Turkish banking sector. In *Global financial crisis and its ramifications on capital markets* (pp. 401–415). Springer.
Yüksel, S., & Zengin, S. (2016). Identifying the determinants of interest rate risk of the banks: A case of Turkish banking sector. *International Journal of Research in Business and Social Science, 5*(6), 12–28.
Yüksel, S., Özsarı, M., & Canöz, İ. (2016). Influencing factors of currency risk of deposit banks in Turkey by using probit method. *International Journal of Commerce and Finance, 2*(2), 85–95.
Zengin, S., & Yüksel, S. (2016). A comparison of the views of internal controllers/auditors and branch/call center personnel of the banks for operational risk: A case for Turkish banking sector. *International Journal of Finance & Banking Studies, 5*(4), 10.

Chapter 8
Emerging Applications and the Future of Data Science

Abstract In this part of the book, current approaches to data science will be evaluated. In this context, what kind of applications the data science may have in the future will be evaluated. For this purpose, it is thought that companies will first have a new data analysis department. Thanks to this team, it is emphasized that companies will constantly analyze data and produce strategies based on these analysis results. On the other hand, it is concluded that social media will be more important in the future in data analysis. Moreover, these applications are expected to provide a very significant database for companies. In addition to these issues, companies are expected to use new data programs in the future. In this context, it is clear that companies that quickly adapt to these new applications will have a serious competitive advantage compared to others.

Keywords Data science · Future applications · Emerging trends

8.1 Building an Effective Data Science Team

Data science has become very popular, especially in recent years. This popularity has attracted the attention of academics. As a result, in the literature, this issue has been analyzed by researchers for different purposes, especially in recent years. In addition to this aforementioned issue, the subject of data science is also on the agenda of companies. In this context, companies have started to give importance to this issue very seriously. Companies have started to collect customer data primarily for this purpose. In this framework, previous expenditures of customers, surveys with customers, and social media accounts of customers were taken into account as data sources. Then, these data are analyzed by companies and future strategies are produced.

On the other hand, another issue that is important in this process is the quality of the staff performing data analysis. These analyzes are not applications that every staff can do. Therefore, the personnel to be selected by the companies must have certain knowledge and equipment. For this purpose, companies need to pay attention

G. Silahtaroğlu et al., *Data Science and Multiple Criteria Decision Making Approaches in Finance*, Multiple Criteria Decision Making,
https://doi.org/10.1007/978-3-030-74176-1_8

to staff selection. It is important for the personnel to be selected to have the necessary information about management information systems. In addition, existing personnel should follow current developments. In this context, necessary training should be provided to company personnel on current issues.

In this context, every company is expected to have an effective data science department within the scope of future data science practices. It is thought that a large number of staff will work in this department. Basically, the staff working in this department will be responsible for the supply and analysis of the data of the company's customers. As a result of the analysis made by the personnel of this department, consultancy will be made to the senior management of the company. This will contribute to companies to produce strategies. Thanks to such a department, it will be possible for the company to perform data analysis continuously.

8.2 Examining Social Media

Social media has become very popular, especially in recent years. The vast majority of people use social media apps like Facebook, Twitter, and Instagram. Another important issue in this process is that people often share information in their social media accounts. This information may also be related to the consumption habits of the customers. This means an important data regarding the future strategies of the companies. For the future of data science, social media accounts are considered to be more important in the future. In this context, it is estimated that some members of the data analysis team created by the companies will only analyze social media accounts.

8.3 Data Program

Data analysis can be done by many different computer programs today. As an example, many data can be analyzed thanks to the Microsoft Excel program. The formulas in the mentioned program serve this purpose. On the other hand, the Microsoft Word program can be preferred for the analysis of many data. In this context, it is possible to determine the most frequently mentioned words in the data set obtained. Another important application in this process is the KNIME program. Thanks to this program, many different analyzes such as artificial neural networks, decision trees, and data mining can be done.

One of the biggest expectations for the future is the production of data from new sources. New programs are expected to be used in the analysis of these data. In other words, companies are expected to use new data programs in the future. Within this framework, it is obvious that companies, which quickly adapt to these new applications, will have an important competitive advantage in comparison with their rivals. Otherwise, it will be impossible for these companies to survive in these competitive industries.

8.4 Conclusion

All countries aim at economic development and thus improve the quality of life of their citizens. However, it is difficult to achieve this objective. The main reason for this difficulty is that many factors must be taken into consideration at the same time in order to achieve economic development. Otherwise, countries will not be able to achieve this objective. In other words, it is important to clearly define the steps to be taken for the economic growth of the country and to formulate strategies accordingly.

Factors affecting economic growth are frequently discussed in the literature. In this context, different issues were emphasized, and recommendations were made according to the country groups examined. Especially in recent years, another issue that has been discussed about this issue is that the factors affecting economic growth will vary according to the structure of the country. In other words, while an issue affects the economic growth of a developing country, it may be secondary to a developed economy. Therefore, it would be more realistic for the analyzes to be conducted separately on the basis of country groups.

Among the factors affecting economic growth, the most discussed issue in the literature is the effectiveness of the financial system. The financial system is vital for a country's economy. This system, in its most general definition, brings together the parties that supply and request funds. This has significant advantages for both sides. First, thanks to an efficient financial system, fund offerers have the chance to earn interest income. On the other hand, individuals and institutions requesting funds can easily reach these objectives through this system. Therefore, it is accepted that there is a very important and positive relationship between the financial efficiency of a country and its economic growth.

In this book, analyzes related to financial issues have been made. In this context, assessments were made on 6 different important issues. In this way, it is aimed to identify the most important issues related to financial issues. In this process, both data science and fuzzy multi-criteria decision-making methods were considered. In this context, decision trees, artificial neural networks, text mining, methods such as AHP, ANP, DEMATEL, MOORA, TOPSIS, and VIKOR were used. The most important contribution of the study is the use of these methods, which are frequently preferred in the literature, in the same book.

In the study, firstly, the factors causing crises in developing and developed countries have been tried to be determined. In this framework, decision tree and fuzzy DEMATEL approaches are taken into consideration. The findings show that growth rate and capital adequacy of the banking industry are accepted as the leading indicators of the global crisis for developed economies. On the other hand, it is also concluded that inflation and industry development are accepted as the indicator of the financial crisis in addition to the economic growth and capital adequacy of the banks for developing economies.

Moreover, the second chapter is related to identifying the influencing factors of economic growth for both developing and developed economies. For this purpose, decision tree approach and fuzzy TOPSIS methodology are considered at the same time. The findings indicate that for developing economies, the most important determinants are foreign direct investment, interest rate, domestic credit, and research and development. On the other side, inflation, domestic credit, foreign direct investment, and unemployment play more significant role in the economic growth of developed economies.

Furthermore, the third chapter aims to estimate the factors affecting the profitability of the Turkish banking sector. For this purpose, 34 different variables were firstly determined by literature review. In the first stage of the analysis, decision trees method is applied to select the most important variables. After that, fuzzy ANP approach is used to weight these variables. It is concluded that the foreign exchange position is the most important variable for the profitability of the Turkish banking sector.

On the other side, the fourth chapter tries to understand the role of the politicians on the macroeconomic situation of the countries. For this purpose, the tweets of Donald Trump are taken into consideration. The text mining approach is used to evaluate these tweets and most used words are identified. After that, these keywords are ranked with the help of fuzzy VIKOR approach according to their impacts on macroeconomic performance. It is identified that political and economic factors are the most important items which affect macroeconomic situation of the country.

The fifth chapter aims to understand the main influence of the politicians' disclosure on the stock exchange index. In this context, a machine learning model is built in order to understand the hidden patterns behind the daily changes (rises and falls) of Dow Johns index. The findings show that when Mr. Trump uses the word witch at least once, it is certain that the index will rise. On the other side, when he uses both the word military and witch on the same day, the index gets a steep high. These results give an idea that when politicians use negative words, it increases the volatility in the stock market.

In the final chapter, it is aimed to determine the factors affecting the exchange rate risk of companies. In this context, firstly, articles in the ScienceDirect database that contain exchange rate risk in their titles, abstracts, and keywords are provided. Single, double, and triple words were identified in 152 different studies that were published after 2018, which met the relevant criteria. As a result of the analysis of these words, 4 different criteria that could affect the exchange rate risk were determined. The relevant criteria were then weighted with fuzzy AHP. The findings indicate that the macroeconomic performance of countries is the most important determinant of exchange rate risk. In addition, wrong risk management practices of companies play also an important role for this risk.

Appendix

Key Term and Definition

KNIME: Konstanz Information Miner

Index

G. Silahtaroğlu et al., *Data Science and Multiple Criteria Decision Making Approaches in Finance*, Multiple Criteria Decision Making,
https://doi.org/10.1007/978-3-030-74176-1